Puzzle Baron

BIG BOOK
OF
Puzzles

Stephen P. Ryder

A member of Penguin Random House LLC

Publisher: Mike Sanders
Associate Publisher: Billy Fields
Acquisitions Editor: Jan Lynn
Copy Editor: Christy Wagner
Cover/Book Designer: Kurt Owens
Compositor: Ayanna Lacey
Proofreader: Jamie Fields

First American Edition, 2017
Published in the United States by DK Publishing
6081 E. 82nd Street, Indianapolis, Indiana 46250

Published in the United States by Dorling Kindersley Limited.

ISBN: 9781465459121

Note: This publication contains the opinions and ideas of its author. It is intended to provide helpful and informative
material on the subject matter covered. It is sold with the understanding that the author and publisher are not
engaged in rendering professional services in the book. If the reader requires personal assistance or advice, a
competent professional should be consulted. The author and publisher specifically disclaim any responsibility for
any liability, loss, or risk, personal or otherwise, which is incurred as a consequence, directly or indirectly, of the use
and application of any of the contents of this book.

Trademarks: All terms mentioned in this book that are known to be or are suspected of being trademarks or service
marks have been appropriately capitalized. Alpha Books, DK, and Penguin Random House LLC cannot attest to the
accuracy of this information. Use of a term in this book should not be regarded as affecting the validity of any
trademark or service mark.

DK books are available at special discounts when purchased in bulk for sales promotions, premiums, fund-raising,
or educational use. For details, contact: DK Publishing Special Markets, 1745 Broadway, New York, New York 10019
or SpecialSales@dk.com.

Printed and bound in the United States of America

Contents

Introduction

Welcome to Puzzle Baron's Big Book of Puzzles! This book offers an assortment of 400 of our most popular puzzles, including word searches, acrostic puzzles, cryptograms, drop quotes, crossword puzzles, logic puzzles, sudoku, and many more. If you're not familiar with a particular puzzle type, don't worry! We include concise instructions at the start of each new section of puzzles that walk you through the basics of how that type of puzzle works. If you need more information, you can always check our online resources at PuzzleBaron. com.

In each section of the book, we ordered the puzzles by relative difficulty. The easiest puzzles are generally at the front of each section, and they get progressively more difficult as you move on down the line. Solutions are provided at the back of the book.

Want More Puzzles?

If you've finished all 400 puzzles in this book and want even more puzzle-solving fun, check out our website at PuzzleBaron.com, where hundreds of thousands of unique puzzles are just waiting to be solved. You can play for fun or compete with more than 200,000 other registered players to see how your solve times compare.

Acknowledgments

A big thank you goes out to Fred Bradshaw, Darlene Eckerman, Robert Gibson, Julie Gray, Melinda Jasani, Rima Kittner, Lisa Lapp, Cindy Mastrogiovanni, Laura Murphy, Katrina Virtsour, and the rest of our team of volunteer testers who ensured each puzzle in this book was solvable and error free. This book wouldn't have been possible without your help. Thank you!

Acrostics

Introduction

Acrostic puzzles are like a mix between cryptograms and traditional crossword puzzles, and you must solve the crossword clues to gradually fill in letters in the hidden quote. As the quote begins to emerge, it provides you with letter hints for the other clues you've not yet solved. Work the puzzle back and forth between the clues and the quote until you reveal the solution.

Remember: The first letter of every answer spells out the author and source of the hidden quote.

1 B	2 H	3 J		4 O	5 J	6 L	7 G	8 K	9 A	10 M	11 O	12 I		13 C	14 E	15 A	16 M	17 J		18 B
19 D	20 A	21 M	22 H		23 D	24 L	25 O	26 M	27 F	28 H	29 J		30 O	31 G	32 L	33 G	34 K	35 J		36 B
37 A		38 O	39 A	40 J	41 E		42 A	43 H	44 O	45 C		46 D	47 E		48 H	49 M	50 L	51 F		52 G
53 M	54 G	55 F	56 J	57 K	58 E		59 A	60 B	61 C	62 L		63 E	64 C	65 D		66 K	67 E	68 O	69 N	
70 I	71 M	72 C	73 J	74 F		75 B	76 I	77 E	78 B		79 K	80 C		81 C	82 A	83 L	84 N	85 M		86 L
87 D	88 M	89 K	90 B		91 J	92 C	93 F	94 G		95 A	96 B	97 E	98 J	99 M		100 L	101 D	102 H		103 M
104 I	105 F	106 L	107 O		108 C	109 M	110 G	111 L		112 L	113 I	114 H		115 J	116 B		117 N	118 F	119 I	120 N
121 C	122 J		123 B	124 J	125 N	126 L														

A

95 15 9 82 42 37 39 20 59

Laser entertainment (2)

B

18 123 90 60 96 1 75 36 78 116

Precisely then (3)

C

121 64 81 61 108 72 80 13 92 45

Deserving attention

D

23 101 19 65 46 87

Residential locale outside of the city

E

47 63 67 41 58 77 97 14

Upper canines

F

27 55 118 105 93 74 51

Innocence (var.)

G

52 31 110 54 94 7 33

"War is hell" speaker

H

102 2 48 114 28 43 22

Train of ___ (line of reasoning)

I

76 70 119 104 12 113

Must (2)

J

3 40 35 91 29 115 98 17 122 124 73 56 5

Spring children's event (3)

K

57 89 8 34 66 79

Wholeheartedly enthusiastic (2)

L

32 62 24 106 6 126 83 111 86 100 50 112

Without stopping

M

99 21 16 88 49 53 109 10 71 26 103 85

Financial crisis common in 1929 (4)

N

117 120 84 125 69

Ocean ___ (large ship)

O

11 30 68 25 38 44 107 4

Appetizers, to a Londoner

Puzzle #2

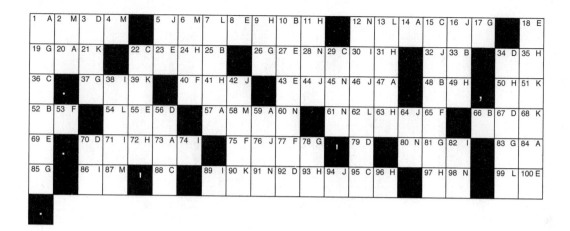

1 A	2 M	3 D	4 M		5 J	6 M	7 L	8 E	9 H	10 B	11 H		12 N	13 L	14 A	15 C	16 J	17 G		18 E
19 G	20 A	21 K		22 C	23 E	24 H	25 B		26 G	27 E	28 N	29 C	30 I	31 H		32 J	33 B		34 D	35 H
36 C		37 G	38 I	39 K		40 F	41 H	42 J		43 E	44 N	45 N	46 J	47 A		48 B	49 H		50 H	51 K
52 B	53 F		54 L	55 E	56 D		57 A	58 M	59 A	60 N		61 N	62 L	63 H	64 J	65 F		66 B	67 D	68 K
69 E		70 D	71 I	72 H	73 A	74 I		75 F	76 J	77 F	78 G		79 D		80 N	81 G	82 I		83 G	84 A
85 G		86 I	87 M		88 C		89 I	90 K	91 N	92 D	93 H	94 J	95 C	96 H		97 H	98 N		99 L	100 E

A __ __ __ __ __ __ __ __
73 84 57 20 1 47 59 14
Patisserie

B __ __ __ __ __ __
52 10 33 66 48 25
Didn't edit out (2)

C __ __ __ __ __ __
36 15 88 29 22 95
Good news (2)

D __ __ __ __ __ __ __
3 34 67 56 70 92 79
2005 Black Eyed Peas single (2)

E __ __ __ __ __ __ __ __
100 18 69 55 8 43 23 27
Alberta's capital

F __ __ __ __ __
65 77 40 75 53
Worn and shabby, as with clothes

G __ __ __ __ __ __ __ __
26 17 78 81 19 83 37 85
Obstructive (3)

H __ __ __ __ __ __ __ __ __ __ __ __ __
9 50 93 96 72 97 24 63 49 41 35 31 11
Self-righteous sort (3)

I __ __ __ __ __ __ __
74 71 89 82 30 86 38
Entered gently (2)

J __ __ __ __ __ __ __ __ __
44 16 46 32 64 5 76 42 94
Removes blemishes, as with a photograph

K __ __ __ __ __
68 51 39 90 21
"This ___" (shipping label) (2)

L __ __ __ __ __
54 13 62 99 7
___ dabba do

M __ __ __ __ __
4 87 6 58 2
Cultural group (prefix)

N __ __ __ __ __ __ __ __
28 98 45 80 12 91 61 60
2015 boxing film starring Jake Gyllenhaal

Puzzle #3

1 J	2 E	3 H	■	4 H	5 E	6 H	7 E	8 M	9 E	10 D	11 L	12 M	■	13 F	14 D	■	15 G	16 H	17 B	18 A
19 K	20 E	21 M	22 N	■	23 M	24 B	■	25 I	26 G	■	27 C	28 E	29 B	30 D	31 C	■	32 N	33 K	34 B	■
35 F	36 H	37 D	38 A	39 L	40 F	41 B	42 C	43 N	44 L	45 D	46 L	47 J	■	48 E	49 L	50 M	,	51 A	52 K	
53 G	54 L	55 C	56 H	57 L	■	58 I	59 G ,		60 E	61 I	■	62 N	63 L	64 F	65 K	■	66 J	■	67 B	68 H
69 K	70 D	71 C	72 J	73 D	■	74 H	75 J	76 L	■	77 L	78 A	79 H	80 F	81 G	■	82 E	83 L	84 J	85 I	■
86 E	87 A	88 G	89 C	90 E	■	91 N	92 K	■	93 F	94 K	95 E	96 A	97 M	■	98 I	99 K	100 C	■	101 N	102 E
103 H	■ .																			

A
‾51‾ ‾96‾ ‾87‾ ‾78‾ ‾18‾ ‾38‾
Get some air

B
‾24‾ ‾34‾ ‾17‾ ‾67‾ ‾29‾ ‾41‾
Go after a housefly, say (2)

C
‾42‾ ‾71‾ ‾100‾ ‾27‾ ‾55‾ ‾89‾ ‾31‾
Infamous spy, ___ Ames

D
‾70‾ ‾30‾ ‾45‾ ‾37‾ ‾10‾ ‾14‾ ‾73‾
Make less basic

E
‾102‾ ‾2‾ ‾7‾ ‾86‾ ‾95‾ ‾5‾ ‾20‾ ‾60‾ ‾90‾ ‾28‾ ‾82‾ ‾48‾ ‾9‾
Gabbing (3)

F
‾40‾ ‾35‾ ‾80‾ ‾93‾ ‾13‾ ‾64‾
One who woos

G
‾53‾ ‾26‾ ‾81‾ ‾88‾ ‾15‾ ‾59‾
Square-dance move (hyp.)

H
‾16‾ ‾74‾ ‾103‾ ‾3‾ ‾56‾ ‾6‾ ‾4‾ ‾68‾ ‾36‾ ‾79‾
Objective aims

I
‾98‾ ‾25‾ ‾61‾ ‾85‾ ‾58‾
Molecule's components

J
‾72‾ ‾75‾ ‾47‾ ‾66‾ ‾1‾ ‾84‾
Smooth and connected, musically

K
‾19‾ ‾52‾ ‾33‾ ‾65‾ ‾92‾ ‾99‾ ‾69‾ ‾94‾
Billing period, often (2)

L
‾57‾ ‾63‾ ‾39‾ ‾44‾ ‾54‾ ‾49‾ ‾77‾ ‾83‾ ‾11‾ ‾76‾ ‾46‾
Prime minister after Tony Blair (2)

M
‾21‾ ‾8‾ ‾97‾ ‾23‾ ‾12‾ ‾50‾
Not nice

N
‾22‾ ‾32‾ ‾62‾ ‾101‾ ‾43‾ ‾91‾
___ terrible (controversial person)

Puzzle #4

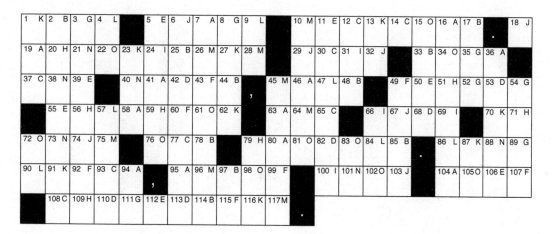

A ___ ___ ___ ___ ___ ___ ___ ___ ___ ___ ___ ___
104 19 58 94 7 63 41 36 16 46 80 95
Forearm tickers

B ___ ___ ___ ___ ___ ___ ___ ___ ___ ___
2 97 48 78 85 17 25 114 33 44
Like some commerce

C ___ ___ ___ ___ ___ ___ ___ ___
12 30 65 14 37 108 93 77
Condemned man's request (2)

D ___ ___ ___ ___ ___ ___
68 42 113 82 110 53
Young cat

E ___ ___ ___ ___ ___ ___ ___
39 5 50 55 112 106 11
Robert of Simpson's defense team

F ___ ___ ___ ___ ___ ___ ___
115 92 107 49 60 43 99
1960's hairdo

G ___ ___ ___ ___ ___ ___ ___
3 35 111 52 54 89 8
Avril ___ (singer)

H ___ ___ ___ ___ ___ ___ ___
56 59 51 71 79 20 109
Resident of Canada's capital

I ___ ___ ___ ___ ___
24 100 69 66 31
Division signs, formally

J ___ ___ ___ ___ ___ ___ ___
32 6 29 103 67 74 18
Suave

K ___ ___ ___ ___ ___ ___ ___ ___ ___
23 87 116 27 70 13 91 1 62
To some, they are mountains

L ___ ___ ___ ___ ___ ___ ___
47 9 84 86 90 57 4
Proficiently

M ___ ___ ___ ___ ___ ___ ___ ___
75 28 64 10 26 96 45 117
Black lead

N ___ ___ ___ ___ ___ ___
88 101 21 73 38 40
Sea east of Sicily

O ___ ___ ___ ___ ___ ___ ___ ___ ___ ___ ___
98 83 15 72 61 34 81 76 102 105 22
Made small talk

Puzzle #5

1 I	2 G	3 D	4 C		5 J	6 C	7 O	8 K	9 H		10 G		11 C	12 B	13 J		14 B	15 F		16 F
17 N	18 G		19 E	20 A	21 I	22 D		23 D	24 N	25 H	26 K	27 I		28 G	29 B		30 H	31 G		32 L
33 D	34 L	35 A	36 D		37 L	38 B	39 M	40 E	41 A	42 N		43 E	44 N	45 O	46 G		47 B	48 M	49 B	50 J
51 E	52 F	53 C		54 A	55 I	56 B		57 F	58 L	59 G	60 J		61 O	62 B	63 F		64 A	65 M	66 K	67 H
	68 K	69 M	70 K	71 L		72 K	73 I		74 E		75 L	76 D	77 N	78 C	79 B	80 M		81 O	82 E	
83 K	84 L	85 C	86 D		87 D	88 J	89 K	90 F	91 L	92 N	93 H		94 B	95 J	96 N		97 B	98 L	99 I	100 G
101 M	102 A		103 G	104 C	105 L	106 C														

A
__ __ __ __ __ __
20 35 64 41 102 54
___ Dumpty

B
__ __ __ __ __ __ __ __ __ __ __
29 38 97 56 79 47 12 14 62 49 94
Serving to exonerate, as with evidence

C
__ __ __ __ __ __ __ __
11 4 85 106 104 6 78 53
Spending a lot of time hitting the books

D
__ __ __ __ __ __ __ __
87 76 3 23 33 22 36 86
Ocean filler

E
__ __ __ __ __ __
40 74 43 82 51 19
What Jack Sprat couldn't do (2)

F
__ __ __ __ __ __
57 52 63 15 90 16
Like a haunted house

G
__ __ __ __ __ __ __ __ __
10 100 46 2 59 28 18 103 31
Sporting one's birthday suit (3)

H
__ __ __ __ __
9 30 25 93 67
Baker's mixture

I
__ __ __ __ __ __
27 21 1 73 55 99
Rosario or Richard

J
__ __ __ __ __ __
50 95 5 60 88 13
Game on ice

K
__ __ __ __ __ __ __ __
72 8 26 89 83 66 70 68
Urban stray (2)

L
__ __ __ __ __ __ __ __ __ __
75 37 32 58 34 98 71 91 84 105
Book of ___ (New Testament book)

M
__ __ __ __ __ __
80 101 65 39 69 48
Fencer's cry

N
__ __ __ __ __ __ __
44 24 96 77 42 17 92
Most populous city in Texas

O
__ __ __ __
45 7 61 81
Grand Theft ___ (video game series)

Puzzle #6

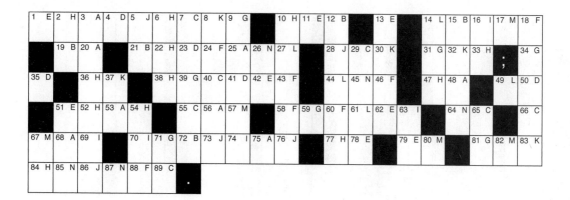

A ___ ___ ___ ___ ___ ___ ___ ___
  68 56 25 48 20 3 53 75
Salon offering

B ___ ___ ___ ___ ___
  72 12 19 15 21
___ of Ice and Fire (G. R. R. Martin series) (2)

C ___ ___ ___ ___ ___ ___ ___
  66 65 29 7 40 55 89
Gestures

D ___ ___ ___ ___ ___
  41 4 35 50 23
Emotionally shaken

E ___ ___ ___ ___ ___ ___ ___ ___
  1 42 79 78 11 51 13 62
Cut and run (2)

F ___ ___ ___ ___ ___ ___ ___
  24 60 46 58 18 88 43
Made some small changes to

G ___ ___ ___ ___ ___ ___ ___
  39 81 59 9 31 34 71
Jihad (2)

H ___ ___ ___ ___ ___ ___ ___ ___ ___ ___ ___ ___
  52 33 54 38 36 47 6 22 84 10 77 2
Cruise/Kidman film of 1999 (3)

I ___ ___ ___ ___ ___
  74 63 69 16 70
Skeptic's shout

J ___ ___ ___ ___ ___
  86 28 73 5 76
Fatty compound

K ___ ___ ___ ___ ___
  32 83 8 37 30
Cultural pursuits, in Spain

L ___ ___ ___ ___ ___
  27 61 49 14 44
Stares open-mouthed

M ___ ___ ___ ___ ___
  67 80 17 82 57
At the original length

N ___ ___ ___ ___ ___
  85 87 45 26 64
Odds opposite

Puzzle #7

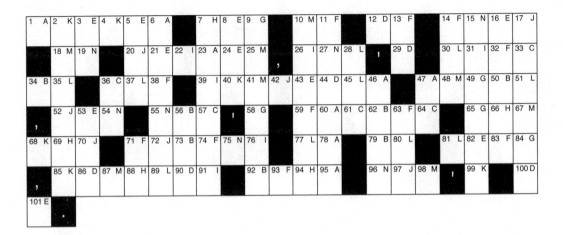

A __ __ __ __ __ __ __ __
   23 60 1 95 78 46 47 6
Championship games

B __ __ __ __ __ __ __
   73 92 50 62 79 56 34
Banner on a blue balloon? (3)

C __ __ __ __ __
   36 33 61 57 64
Low-powered chess pieces

D __ __ __ __ __ __
   86 12 100 44 29 90
Field formerly home to the Brooklyn Dodgers

E __ __ __ __ __ __ __ __ __ __
   8 16 53 3 101 82 43 24 21 5
Red-haired wizard of fiction (2)

F __ __ __ __ __ __ __ __ __ __ __
   14 11 38 83 74 71 93 13 32 59 63
Interfered (4)

G __ __ __ __ __
   84 65 58 49 9
Take another crack at

H __ __ __ __ __
   94 66 88 69 7
____ change only (toll booth sign)

I __ __ __ __ __ __
   39 22 26 91 31 76
Practices certain Alpine singing methods

J __ __ __ __ __ __ __
   72 52 42 17 70 97 20
Type of automobile roof

K __ __ __ __ __ __
   40 85 2 4 99 68
Sphere-shaped but flattened at the poles

L __ __ __ __ __ __ __ __ __ __
   89 28 51 30 35 77 80 81 37 45
Not conforming to aesthetic ideals (var.)

M __ __ __ __ __ __ __ __
   98 48 87 25 67 41 18 10
Golfer's compliment on the green (2)

N __ __ __ __ __ __ __
   54 15 75 96 27 19 55
State tree of Missouri and Virginia

Puzzle #8

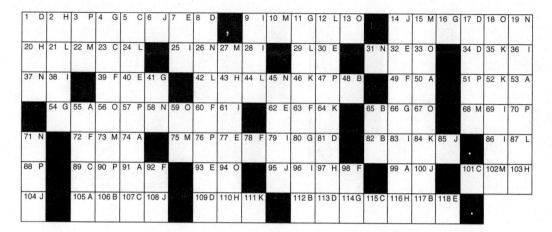

A
__ __ __ __ __ __ __
99 53 50 55 74 105 91
Lengths of service

B
__ __ __ __ __ __
106 65 48 117 112 82
Relaxed (2)

C
__ __ __ __ __ __
5 101 89 115 107 23
3,300, in Ancient Rome

D
__ __ __ __ __ __ __
113 1 109 34 17 81 8
Submit for acceptance

E
__ __ __ __ __ __ __ __
118 62 93 40 32 7 77 30
Puccini opera (2)

F
__ __ __ __ __ __ __ __
49 63 98 39 72 78 60 92
For practical purposes (2)

G
__ __ __ __ __ __ __ __
80 4 54 16 66 114 41 11
Close by (2)

H
__ __ __ __ __ __ __
20 43 110 116 103 2 97
"Honest Abe" or "Tricky Dick"

I
__ __ __ __ __ __ __ __ __ __ __
86 79 96 36 61 69 83 28 25 9 38
"That's baloney!" (3)

J
__ __ __ __ __ __ __
14 108 100 85 6 104 95
Belonging to Monica and Rachel's friend

K
__ __ __ __ __ __
52 111 84 35 46 64
"Theogony" poet

L
__ __ __ __ __ __ __
21 44 29 12 87 42 24
General ___ Burnside

M
__ __ __ __ __ __ __ __
22 73 10 15 27 68 102 75
Short tales

N
__ __ __ __ __ __ __
71 19 26 45 37 31 58
Northeastern Italian port city

O
__ __ __ __ __ __ __
18 59 33 67 13 94 56
Like two jacks in a deck (hyp.)

P
__ __ __ __ __ __ __ __
3 88 51 57 47 76 90 70
Ready to take over the ship, perhaps

Puzzle #9

1 B	2 K	3 J	4 M	5 B		6 N	7 L	8 O	9 F	10 B	11 H		12 M	13 G	14 H	15 N	16 E	17 F	18 I	19 F
20 E	21 H		22 M	23 L		24 J	25 A		26 K	27 A	28 E	29 C	30 O	31 I		32 I	33 B		34 M	35 G
36 O	37 B	38 C	39 E	40 J	41 M	42 N	43 F		44 N	45 F	46 G		47 N	48 J		49 M	50 A	51 K	52 D	,
53 L		54 G	55 O	56 H	57 N		58 N	59 K	60 C	61 O		62 N	63 B		64 I	65 H	66 N	67 I	68 N	69 J
	70 I	71 L	72 M	73 D	74 C	75 J		76 C		77 G	78 C	79 F	80 G		81 M	82 N	83 O	84 D		85 A
86 M	87 H	88 L		89 F	90 K	91 N	92 I	93 B		94 D	95 G	96 J	97 A	98 M	99 E		100 E	101 H		102 M
103 J	104 H	105 D	106 B	107 K	108 E															

A _ _ _ _ _
97 50 27 25 85
Praise excessively

B _ _ _ _ _ _ _ _
63 1 33 93 106 37 10 5
Less busy times (hyp.)

C _ _ _ _ _ _
74 76 60 78 38 29
Frasier's ex-wife on *Frasier*

D _ _ _ _ _
52 84 105 73 94
Works at a keyboard

E _ _ _ _ _ _ _
39 100 20 108 99 28 16
____ International (human rights organization)

F _ _ _ _ _ _ _
9 79 43 45 89 19 17
"You don't need to tell me!" (3)

G _ _ _ _ _ _ _
46 35 13 80 77 95 54
Merrymaker

H _ _ _ _ _ _ _ _
14 87 21 65 11 104 56 101
Cartilaginous winged fish (2)

I _ _ _ _ _ _ _
92 67 70 64 18 32 31
Moth repellent

J _ _ _ _ _ _ _ _
24 75 40 69 96 48 3 103
"Age before beauty!" (2)

K _ _ _ _ _ _
59 2 51 26 90 107
Nick and ____ Infinite Playlist (2008)

L _ _ _ _ _
7 53 23 88 71
____ Moore (stew brand)

M _ _ _ _ _ _ _ _ _ _ _
41 34 22 72 86 49 98 81 102 4 12
Dublin dwellers, for example (2)

N _ _ _ _ _ _ _ _ _ _ _ _
57 66 44 58 15 47 6 62 91 42 82 68
Acts of distortion via pressure

O _ _ _ _ _ _
55 8 36 83 30 61
Put to work

Puzzle #10

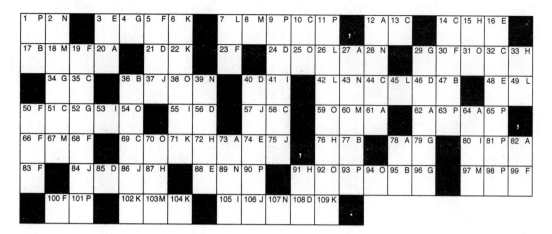

A $\overline{27}\ \overline{73}\ \overline{64}\ \overline{78}\ \overline{12}\ \overline{62}\ \overline{20}\ \overline{61}\ \overline{82}$
Circular sideways handspring

B $\overline{77}\ \overline{95}\ \overline{17}\ \overline{36}\ \overline{47}$
Nouveau ___ (those of new wealth)

C $\overline{44}\ \overline{69}\ \overline{13}\ \overline{32}\ \overline{58}\ \overline{14}\ \overline{51}\ \overline{35}\ \overline{10}$
Wolfed down too much

D $\overline{46}\ \overline{40}\ \overline{108}\ \overline{24}\ \overline{21}\ \overline{85}\ \overline{56}$
Second phase (2)

E $\overline{3}\ \overline{16}\ \overline{74}\ \overline{48}\ \overline{88}$
Guardian Angels founder Curtis

F $\overline{66}\ \overline{23}\ \overline{83}\ \overline{99}\ \overline{19}\ \overline{68}\ \overline{30}\ \overline{100}\ \overline{5}\ \overline{50}$
Angry date's request, perhaps (3)

G $\overline{52}\ \overline{79}\ \overline{29}\ \overline{96}\ \overline{4}\ \overline{34}$
"___ brown cow?" (2)

H $\overline{33}\ \overline{72}\ \overline{15}\ \overline{91}\ \overline{76}\ \overline{87}$
Crime writer James

I $\overline{105}\ \overline{55}\ \overline{41}\ \overline{80}\ \overline{53}$
Vermont ski resort

J $\overline{106}\ \overline{84}\ \overline{57}\ \overline{86}\ \overline{75}\ \overline{37}$
Cuban capital, in Spanish

K $\overline{6}\ \overline{104}\ \overline{71}\ \overline{109}\ \overline{22}\ \overline{102}$
Trap for certain elongated fish

L $\overline{7}\ \overline{45}\ \overline{26}\ \overline{42}\ \overline{49}$
Cook by simmering in liquid

M $\overline{60}\ \overline{18}\ \overline{67}\ \overline{97}\ \overline{103}\ \overline{8}$
Sounds from Kringle (3)

N $\overline{39}\ \overline{2}\ \overline{43}\ \overline{107}\ \overline{89}\ \overline{28}$
Anesthetic gas

O $\overline{54}\ \overline{31}\ \overline{25}\ \overline{94}\ \overline{59}\ \overline{70}\ \overline{38}\ \overline{92}$
Family tree entry

P $\overline{90}\ \overline{63}\ \overline{101}\ \overline{1}\ \overline{93}\ \overline{81}\ \overline{11}\ \overline{9}\ \overline{65}\ \overline{98}$
Action of damaging someone's reputation

Puzzle #11

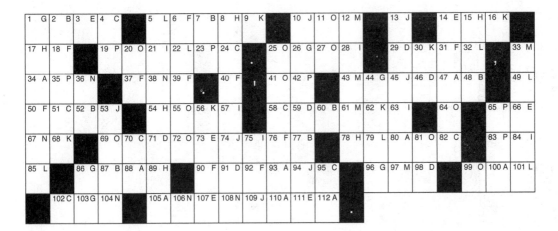

1 G	2 B	3 E	4 C		5 L	6 F	7 B	8 H	9 K		10 J	11 O	12 M		13 J		14 E	15 H	16 K	
17 H	18 F		19 P	20 O	21 I	22 L	23 P	24 C		25 O	26 G	27 O	28 I		29 D	30 K	31 F	32 L		33 M
34 A	35 P	36 N		37 F	38 N	39 F		40 F		41 O	42 P		43 M	44 G	45 J	46 D	47 A	48 B		49 L
50 F	51 C	52 B	53 J		54 H	55 O	56 K	57 I		58 C	59 D	60 B	61 M	62 K	63 I		64 O		65 P	66 E
67 N	68 K		69 O	70 C	71 D	72 O	73 E	74 J	75 I	76 F	77 B		78 H	79 L	80 A	81 O	82 C		83 P	84 I
85 L		86 G	87 B	88 A	89 H		90 F	91 D	92 F	93 A	94 J	95 C		96 G	97 M	98 D		99 O	100 A	101 L
	102 C	103 G	104 N		105 A	106 N	107 E	108 N	109 J	110 A	111 E	112 A								

A

___ ___ ___ ___ ___ ___ ___ ___ ___
110 47 93 100 112 105 34 88 80

Procedurally proper (3)

B

___ ___ ___ ___ ___ ___ ___
2 52 60 87 7 77 48

Conjures

C

___ ___ ___ ___ ___ ___ ___ ___
95 70 24 4 102 51 82 58

English garden resident, often (2)

D

___ ___ ___ ___ ___ ___
98 46 71 59 29 91

Inflict physical harm

E

___ ___ ___ ___ ___ ___
3 107 14 111 66 73

Like unsown crop land

F

___ ___ ___ ___ ___ ___ ___ ___ ___ ___
76 6 37 90 40 92 18 31 50 39

Salads and such, jocularly (2)

G

___ ___ ___ ___ ___ ___
26 86 1 96 44 103

Crazy Horse was one

H

___ ___ ___ ___ ___ ___
78 15 17 54 8 89

Put forward, as with a topic of discussion

I

___ ___ ___ ___ ___ ___
57 84 28 21 63 75

___ of Innocence (Wharton novel) (2)

J

___ ___ ___ ___ ___ ___ ___
74 94 13 53 45 109 10

Progress

K

___ ___ ___ ___ ___ ___
68 56 16 30 62 9

Actress Shirley and Olympian Ashton

L

___ ___ ___ ___ ___ ___ ___
49 79 22 85 5 101 32

Like some gems

M

___ ___ ___ ___ ___
61 97 12 33 43

"Made ___" (label line) (2)

N

___ ___ ___ ___ ___ ___
108 36 67 38 104 106

Created anew

O

___ ___ ___ ___ ___ ___ ___ ___ ___ ___ ___
69 99 72 64 27 25 55 11 41 81 20

Early 20th-century excavating machine (2)

P

___ ___ ___ ___ ___ ___
83 42 35 19 23 65

Fermented soy cake

Puzzle #12

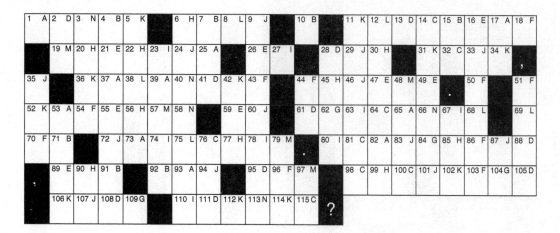

A
$\overline{53}$ $\overline{93}$ $\overline{17}$ $\overline{73}$ $\overline{25}$ $\overline{1}$ $\overline{37}$ $\overline{82}$ $\overline{39}$ $\overline{65}$
"This was their ___" (Churchill speech) (2)

B
$\overline{7}$ $\overline{71}$ $\overline{91}$ $\overline{10}$ $\overline{4}$ $\overline{92}$ $\overline{15}$
2008 Democratic primary candidate

C
$\overline{100}$ $\overline{76}$ $\overline{115}$ $\overline{32}$ $\overline{98}$ $\overline{14}$ $\overline{64}$ $\overline{81}$
They aren't good hitters (2)

D
$\overline{2}$ $\overline{105}$ $\overline{41}$ $\overline{61}$ $\overline{111}$ $\overline{95}$ $\overline{88}$ $\overline{108}$ $\overline{28}$ $\overline{13}$
Big boss (2)

E
$\overline{16}$ $\overline{55}$ $\overline{21}$ $\overline{89}$ $\overline{26}$ $\overline{49}$ $\overline{59}$ $\overline{47}$
Kansas town famous in railroad history

F
$\overline{96}$ $\overline{50}$ $\overline{86}$ $\overline{51}$ $\overline{54}$ $\overline{43}$ $\overline{18}$ $\overline{103}$ $\overline{44}$ $\overline{70}$
Settled (2)

G
$\overline{104}$ $\overline{84}$ $\overline{109}$ $\overline{62}$
Dolphinfish, when doubled

H
$\overline{56}$ $\overline{99}$ $\overline{90}$ $\overline{22}$ $\overline{77}$ $\overline{85}$ $\overline{45}$ $\overline{6}$ $\overline{20}$ $\overline{30}$
Enclave of impracticality (2)

I
$\overline{27}$ $\overline{78}$ $\overline{67}$ $\overline{74}$ $\overline{80}$ $\overline{23}$ $\overline{63}$ $\overline{110}$
Most spiteful

J
$\overline{94}$ $\overline{87}$ $\overline{46}$ $\overline{72}$ $\overline{83}$ $\overline{33}$ $\overline{60}$ $\overline{9}$ $\overline{35}$ $\overline{24}$ $\overline{107}$ $\overline{101}$ $\overline{29}$
Two movies for the price of one (2)

K
$\overline{114}$ $\overline{5}$ $\overline{42}$ $\overline{31}$ $\overline{11}$ $\overline{52}$ $\overline{102}$ $\overline{112}$ $\overline{106}$ $\overline{36}$ $\overline{34}$
Heredity scientists

L
$\overline{69}$ $\overline{8}$ $\overline{68}$ $\overline{12}$ $\overline{75}$ $\overline{38}$
Prefix meaning "of a joint"

M
$\overline{57}$ $\overline{97}$ $\overline{79}$ $\overline{48}$ $\overline{19}$
Mind ___ (Vulcan telepathic links)

N
$\overline{58}$ $\overline{113}$ $\overline{40}$ $\overline{66}$ $\overline{3}$
Follow

Puzzle #13

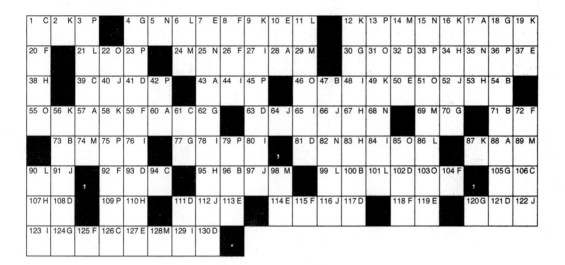

A
$\overline{60}$ $\overline{17}$ $\overline{28}$ $\overline{43}$ $\overline{88}$ $\overline{57}$
Single-celled alga

B
$\overline{96}$ $\overline{100}$ $\overline{71}$ $\overline{54}$ $\overline{47}$ $\overline{73}$
Random ____ kindness (good deeds) (2)

C
$\overline{106}$ $\overline{126}$ $\overline{39}$ $\overline{1}$ $\overline{61}$ $\overline{94}$
____ malt (type of blended scotch)

D
$\overline{102}$ $\overline{108}$ $\overline{63}$ $\overline{41}$ $\overline{93}$ $\overline{111}$ $\overline{32}$ $\overline{130}$ $\overline{81}$ $\overline{117}$ $\overline{121}$
Foot soldiers

E
$\overline{37}$ $\overline{10}$ $\overline{119}$ $\overline{114}$ $\overline{127}$ $\overline{113}$ $\overline{7}$ $\overline{50}$
Zany to the max

F
$\overline{20}$ $\overline{115}$ $\overline{104}$ $\overline{92}$ $\overline{26}$ $\overline{125}$ $\overline{118}$ $\overline{59}$ $\overline{8}$ $\overline{72}$
Alamo locale (2)

G
$\overline{18}$ $\overline{30}$ $\overline{77}$ $\overline{105}$ $\overline{124}$ $\overline{70}$ $\overline{62}$ $\overline{120}$ $\overline{4}$
Presented (2)

H
$\overline{83}$ $\overline{34}$ $\overline{110}$ $\overline{38}$ $\overline{95}$ $\overline{107}$ $\overline{67}$ $\overline{53}$
XIX

I
$\overline{27}$ $\overline{78}$ $\overline{65}$ $\overline{80}$ $\overline{76}$ $\overline{44}$ $\overline{84}$ $\overline{48}$ $\overline{129}$ $\overline{123}$
Western Indiana city (2)

J
$\overline{40}$ $\overline{52}$ $\overline{91}$ $\overline{122}$ $\overline{112}$ $\overline{116}$ $\overline{64}$ $\overline{66}$ $\overline{97}$
Rear Window director

K
$\overline{12}$ $\overline{19}$ $\overline{9}$ $\overline{2}$ $\overline{58}$ $\overline{49}$ $\overline{16}$ $\overline{56}$ $\overline{87}$
2007 Disney film starring Amy Adams

L
$\overline{11}$ $\overline{99}$ $\overline{6}$ $\overline{21}$ $\overline{90}$ $\overline{86}$ $\overline{101}$
Get into the action in Vegas (3)

M
$\overline{98}$ $\overline{24}$ $\overline{69}$ $\overline{74}$ $\overline{128}$ $\overline{89}$ $\overline{14}$ $\overline{29}$
Victor ____ II (19th-century Italian king)

N
$\overline{68}$ $\overline{25}$ $\overline{82}$ $\overline{15}$ $\overline{35}$ $\overline{5}$
Scarce supply

O
$\overline{85}$ $\overline{103}$ $\overline{31}$ $\overline{55}$ $\overline{46}$ $\overline{51}$ $\overline{22}$
Famous jazz player Benny

P
$\overline{45}$ $\overline{13}$ $\overline{79}$ $\overline{75}$ $\overline{33}$ $\overline{109}$ $\overline{42}$ $\overline{36}$ $\overline{23}$ $\overline{3}$
Precision

Puzzle #14

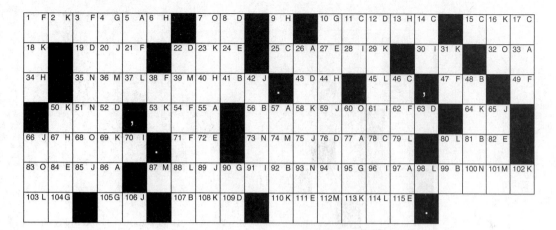

A
‎ ‎ ‎ ‎ ‎ ‎ ‎ ‎
97 33 5 86 57 77 55 26
Rougher, as seas

B
‎ ‎ ‎ ‎ ‎ ‎ ‎
107 92 81 99 41 56 48
Dean ___ (Truman's secretary of state)

C
‎ ‎ ‎ ‎ ‎ ‎ ‎
17 78 15 25 11 14 46
Does a second version

D
‎ ‎ ‎ ‎ ‎ ‎ ‎ ‎ ‎
76 43 19 12 8 22 52 109 63
Robin Leach's singular concern?

E
‎ ‎ ‎ ‎ ‎ ‎ ‎
115 82 84 72 111 24 27
Saw red

F
‎ ‎ ‎ ‎ ‎ ‎ ‎ ‎ ‎
49 21 1 54 47 38 71 3 62
Library employee, maybe

G
‎ ‎ ‎ ‎ ‎ ‎
10 95 105 4 90 104
Garden statues

H
‎ ‎ ‎ ‎ ‎ ‎ ‎
9 6 67 44 40 13 34
Wood source for bats (2)

I
‎ ‎ ‎ ‎ ‎ ‎ ‎
94 30 70 61 91 28 96
"___ Bob!" (emphatic denial) (2)

J
‎ ‎ ‎ ‎ ‎ ‎ ‎ ‎ ‎
66 59 106 65 85 42 75 20 89
Common kitchen item

K
‎ ‎ ‎ ‎ ‎ ‎ ‎ ‎ ‎ ‎ ‎ ‎ ‎ ‎ ‎
64 113 110 16 58 69 31 53 23 102 50 2 29 108 18
Euphoric (5)

L
‎ ‎ ‎ ‎ ‎ ‎ ‎ ‎
79 45 98 80 37 88 114 103
Portrait sessions

M
‎ ‎ ‎ ‎ ‎ ‎
74 87 36 101 112 39
Mickey's girlfriend

N
‎ ‎ ‎ ‎ ‎
93 35 73 100 51
A Dog of Flanders writer

O
‎ ‎ ‎ ‎ ‎
60 32 68 7 83
Composed

Puzzle #15

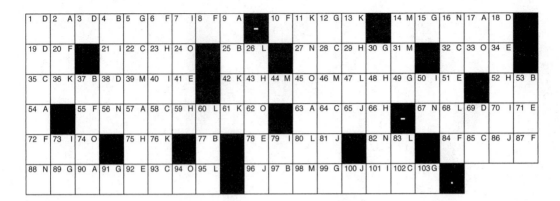

1 D	2 A	3 D	4 B	5 G	6 F	7 I	8 F	9 A	■	10 F	11 K	12 G	13 K	■	14 M	15 G	16 N	17 A	18 D
19 D	20 F	■	21 I	22 C	23 H	24 O		25 B	26 L		27 N	28 C	29 H	30 G	31 M	■	32 C	33 O	34 E
35 C	36 K	37 B	38 D	39 M	40 I	41 E		42 K	43 H	44 M	45 O	46 M	47 L	48 H	49 G	50 I	51 E	■	52 H	53 B
54 A	■	55 F	56 N	57 A	58 C	59 H	60 L	61 K	62 O		63 A	64 C	65 J	66 H	■	67 N	68 L	69 D	70 I	71 E
72 F	73 I	74 O	■	75 H	76 K		77 B		78 E	79 I	80 L	81 J		82 N	83 L		84 F	85 C	86 J	87 F
88 N	89 G	90 A	91 G	92 E	93 C	94 O	95 L		96 J	97 B	98 M	99 G	100 J	101 I	102 C	103 G	■			

A ___ ___ ___ ___ ___ ___ ___
   63 57 2   9   17 90 54
Bragged about one's achievements

B ___ ___ ___ ___ ___ ___
   77 4   37 53 25 97
In ___ (frenzied) (2)

C ___ ___ ___ ___ ___ ___ ___ ___ ___
   35 93 102 28 64 85 22 58 32
Element #44

D ___ ___ ___ ___ ___ ___
   69 19 1   18 38 3
"You're ___!" ("Thanks for nothing!") (2)

E ___ ___ ___ ___ ___ ___
   41 34 78 71 51 92
Join up

F ___ ___ ___ ___ ___ ___ ___ ___
   8   10 84 55 20 87 6   72
Gets tougher, as with competition

G ___ ___ ___ ___ ___ ___ ___ ___ ___
   12 91 30 89 99 49 5   15 103
Upward slope

H ___ ___ ___ ___ ___ ___ ___ ___
   59 52 29 48 66 43 75 23
Way too skinny (hyp.)

I ___ ___ ___ ___ ___ ___ ___ ___
   79 73 7   21 101 40 50 70
Lists, as with tax deductions

J ___ ___ ___ ___ ___
   65 86 96 100 81
Part of a keg

K ___ ___ ___ ___ ___ ___
   13 36 76 42 11 61
Tithers' amounts, usually

L ___ ___ ___ ___ ___ ___ ___
   68 83 80 95 60 26 47
Not on the internet

M ___ ___ ___ ___ ___ ___
   98 31 44 46 39 14
Grad student's work

N ___ ___ ___ ___ ___ ___
   56 82 27 67 16 88
Diet-worthy, for short (hyp.)

O ___ ___ ___ ___ ___ ___
   33 45 24 94 74 62
Long punctuation mark (2)

Puzzle #16

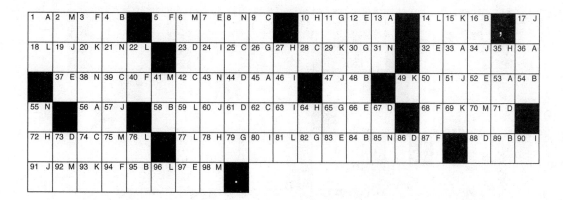

1 A	2 M	3 F	4 B		5 F	6 M	7 E	8 N	9 C		10 H	11 G	12 E	13 A		14 L	15 K	16 B		17 J
18 L	19 J	20 K	21 N	22 L		23 D	24 I	25 C	26 G	27 H	28 C	29 K	30 G	31 N		32 E	33 A	34 J	35 H	36 A
	37 E	38 N	39 C	40 F	41 M	42 C	43 N	44 D	45 A	46 I		47 J	48 B		49 K	50 I	51 J	52 E	53 A	54 B
55 N		56 A	57 J		58 B	59 L	60 J	61 D	62 C	63 I	64 H	65 G	66 E	67 D		68 F	69 K	70 M	71 D
72 H	73 D	74 C	75 M	76 L		77 L	78 H	79 G	80 I	81 L	82 G	83 E	84 B	85 N	86 D	87 F		88 D	89 B	90 I
91 J	92 M	93 K	94 F	95 B	96 L	97 E	98 M		.

A __ __ __ __ __ __ __
   1 53 13 56 36 45 33
King or queen

B __ __ __ __ __ __ __ __
  89 48 84 54 95 16 4 58
Nervously excited

C __ __ __ __ __ __ __
  74 9 42 39 28 62 25
Brief extract, as of an article

D __ __ __ __ __ __ __ __
  61 23 67 73 88 71 44 86
Connective tissue

E __ __ __ __ __ __ __ __
  83 52 66 97 32 12 7 37
Supply with references

F __ __ __ __ __ __
  94 5 3 40 87 68
Haim and Feldman

G __ __ __ __ __ __
  11 30 79 26 65 82
Legalese adverb

H __ __ __ __ __ __
  72 35 10 64 78 27
Resentful

I __ __ __ __ __ __
  50 24 63 90 46 80
Aunts' husbands

J __ __ __ __ __ __ __ __
  51 19 17 34 57 47 60 91
Runs a cord around, perhaps (2)

K __ __ __ __ __ __
  93 69 20 29 15 49
"Piece of cake!" (2)

L __ __ __ __ __ __ __ __
  81 14 18 77 96 59 76 22
Modest swimsuit (hyp.)

M __ __ __ __ __ __ __
  92 98 75 6 2 41 70
Identifying work outfit

N __ __ __ __ __ __ __
  31 43 38 55 85 21 8
Mill output

Puzzle #17

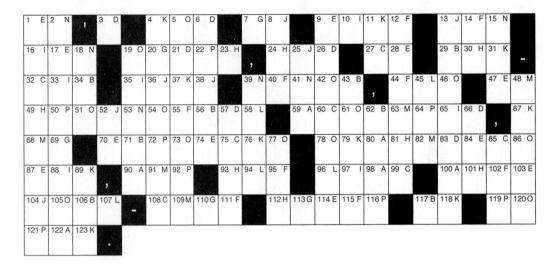

A $\overline{100}$ $\overline{90}$ $\overline{80}$ $\overline{98}$ $\overline{122}$ $\overline{59}$
Illinois city home to Ulysses S. Grant

B $\overline{62}$ $\overline{71}$ $\overline{29}$ $\overline{56}$ $\overline{117}$ $\overline{106}$ $\overline{43}$ $\overline{34}$
Most bonkers

C $\overline{85}$ $\overline{99}$ $\overline{60}$ $\overline{108}$ $\overline{32}$ $\overline{27}$ $\overline{75}$
Feature of some insects and old TVs

D $\overline{6}$ $\overline{83}$ $\overline{21}$ $\overline{3}$ $\overline{57}$ $\overline{26}$ $\overline{66}$
Gadgets, colloquially

E $\overline{74}$ $\overline{28}$ $\overline{87}$ $\overline{114}$ $\overline{9}$ $\overline{17}$ $\overline{84}$ $\overline{70}$ $\overline{1}$ $\overline{103}$ $\overline{47}$
Artisan's skill

F $\overline{12}$ $\overline{102}$ $\overline{95}$ $\overline{115}$ $\overline{111}$ $\overline{14}$ $\overline{44}$ $\overline{40}$ $\overline{55}$
___ an agreement (2)

G $\overline{20}$ $\overline{113}$ $\overline{7}$ $\overline{69}$ $\overline{110}$
Starbucks beverage offering

H $\overline{81}$ $\overline{23}$ $\overline{24}$ $\overline{93}$ $\overline{49}$ $\overline{30}$ $\overline{112}$ $\overline{101}$
Bill Withers classic song of 1972 (3)

I $\overline{33}$ $\overline{97}$ $\overline{88}$ $\overline{35}$ $\overline{10}$ $\overline{16}$ $\overline{65}$
Stupefy

J $\overline{104}$ $\overline{25}$ $\overline{13}$ $\overline{36}$ $\overline{8}$ $\overline{38}$ $\overline{52}$
Detaches, as a bra

K $\overline{118}$ $\overline{4}$ $\overline{79}$ $\overline{37}$ $\overline{11}$ $\overline{123}$ $\overline{67}$ $\overline{31}$ $\overline{76}$ $\overline{89}$
Viscosity increasers

L $\overline{58}$ $\overline{45}$ $\overline{94}$ $\overline{107}$ $\overline{96}$
Not tight

M $\overline{82}$ $\overline{91}$ $\overline{68}$ $\overline{109}$ $\overline{63}$ $\overline{48}$
"You're ___ your head!" (2)

N $\overline{2}$ $\overline{53}$ $\overline{15}$ $\overline{41}$ $\overline{18}$ $\overline{39}$
Exam answers in blue books

O $\overline{42}$ $\overline{77}$ $\overline{61}$ $\overline{19}$ $\overline{78}$ $\overline{54}$ $\overline{120}$ $\overline{86}$ $\overline{46}$ $\overline{5}$ $\overline{73}$ $\overline{51}$ $\overline{105}$
Restores to good health

P $\overline{116}$ $\overline{64}$ $\overline{119}$ $\overline{22}$ $\overline{92}$ $\overline{121}$ $\overline{50}$ $\overline{72}$
Social impasse

Puzzle #18

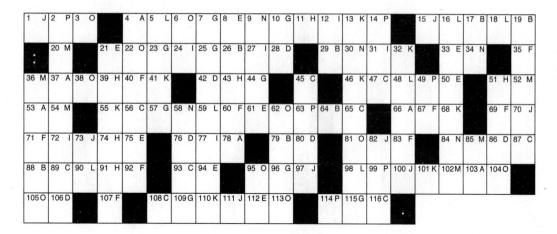

A $\overline{103}\ \overline{78}\ \overline{37}\ \overline{53}\ \overline{4}\ \overline{66}$
Designated limit point

B $\overline{19}\ \overline{26}\ \overline{88}\ \overline{29}\ \overline{64}\ \overline{17}\ \overline{79}$
Meeting place

C $\overline{45}\ \overline{93}\ \overline{89}\ \overline{56}\ \overline{47}\ \overline{65}\ \overline{87}\ \overline{116}\ \overline{108}$
Bar Association members

D $\overline{42}\ \overline{80}\ \overline{86}\ \overline{106}\ \overline{28}\ \overline{76}$
Insect with notoriously parasitic larvae

E $\overline{94}\ \overline{21}\ \overline{33}\ \overline{50}\ \overline{61}\ \overline{8}\ \overline{75}\ \overline{112}$
Newspaper announcement column, for short (2)

F $\overline{92}\ \overline{107}\ \overline{40}\ \overline{35}\ \overline{83}\ \overline{69}\ \overline{67}\ \overline{60}\ \overline{71}$
Certain farm female (2)

G $\overline{23}\ \overline{109}\ \overline{57}\ \overline{25}\ \overline{115}\ \overline{44}\ \overline{96}\ \overline{10}\ \overline{7}$
Got a tan

H $\overline{43}\ \overline{74}\ \overline{39}\ \overline{51}\ \overline{91}\ \overline{11}$
In ___ (together in pitch)

I $\overline{31}\ \overline{77}\ \overline{72}\ \overline{12}\ \overline{27}\ \overline{24}$
Uneven pattern of spots

J $\overline{111}\ \overline{70}\ \overline{100}\ \overline{73}\ \overline{15}\ \overline{82}\ \overline{1}\ \overline{97}$
Practice Zen

K $\overline{32}\ \overline{41}\ \overline{46}\ \overline{55}\ \overline{68}\ \overline{101}\ \overline{13}\ \overline{110}$
Soda shop drink with a misleading name

L $\overline{16}\ \overline{48}\ \overline{98}\ \overline{59}\ \overline{5}\ \overline{90}\ \overline{18}$
Newly enlisted person in the armed forces

M $\overline{52}\ \overline{20}\ \overline{54}\ \overline{85}\ \overline{36}\ \overline{102}$
OK city

N $\overline{30}\ \overline{9}\ \overline{84}\ \overline{34}\ \overline{58}$
Sailboat's must-have (2)

O $\overline{6}\ \overline{3}\ \overline{22}\ \overline{113}\ \overline{95}\ \overline{38}\ \overline{104}\ \overline{62}\ \overline{105}\ \overline{81}$
#2 on Billboard, say (3)

P $\overline{114}\ \overline{49}\ \overline{2}\ \overline{14}\ \overline{63}\ \overline{99}$
Showy bloomer

Puzzle #19

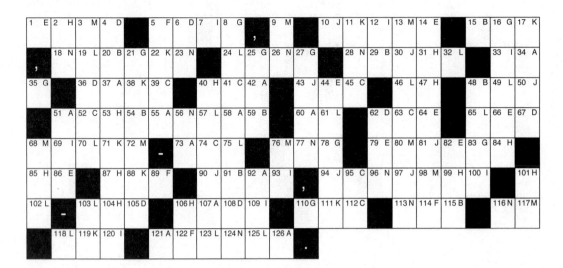

A
121 126 73 55 42 60 92 58 107 51 34 37
Skill of deciphering codes

B
29 115 15 20 91 54 48 59
Forecast figure

C
95 45 112 63 74 41 39 52
Feature of some off-grid homes

D
108 36 62 67 4 6 105
Followers

E
44 66 14 79 82 86 1 64
The English Patient author Michael

F
89 5 114 122
Word with lace or fly

G
21 35 8 78 110 16 27 25 83
Mind-reading

H
53 106 31 85 47 101 2 99 84 104 87 40
Association

I
69 7 93 100 12 109 33 120
Writers of poetic laments

J
10 30 81 90 50 97 94 43
Like some magazines

K
111 17 71 22 119 88 11 38
Perturb

L
118 102 24 49 57 123 32 46 19 61 65 103 75 70 125
Sometime soon (4)

M
80 72 68 98 9 117 3 76 13
Enormous Old Testament sea monster

N
124 56 77 96 28 26 18 116 113 23
Discardables

Puzzle #20

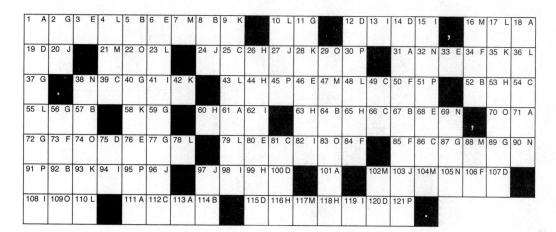

A
___ ___ ___ ___ ___ ___ ___ ___
61 71 31 113 111 101 1   18
Bottom of a diamond? (2)

B
___ ___ ___ ___ ___ ___ ___ ___
64 114 52   8 67   5 92 57
Has a zero in the loss column

C
___ ___ ___ ___ ___ ___ ___ ___
66 112 81 86 39 25 54 49
Attractive

D
___ ___ ___ ___ ___ ___ ___ ___
14 12 120 100 115 75 107 19
Arrow maker

E
___ ___ ___ ___ ___ ___ ___
3   46 33 68   6 76 80
3,103, to Nero

F
___ ___ ___ ___ ___ ___
85 84 106 50 73 34
Oscar-winning director of 2005 (2)

G
___ ___ ___ ___ ___ ___ ___ ___ ___ ___
77 89 59 37 72   2 87 40 11 56
Certain hotel room designation

H
___ ___ ___ ___ ___ ___ ___ ___ ___
60 116 99 26 44 65 63 53 118
Gets across

I
___ ___ ___ ___ ___ ___ ___ ___ ___
82 13 94 108 98 62 15 41 119
Certain women's footwear (2)

J
___ ___ ___ ___ ___ ___
103 20 24 27 97 96
Transplants

K
___ ___ ___ ___ ___ ___
58   9 28 42 35 93
Belgian seaport

L
___ ___ ___ ___ ___ ___ ___ ___ ___ ___ ___
79 23 10 78 17 36 55 48   4 110 43
State of being momentous

M
___ ___ ___ ___ ___ ___ ___ ___ ___
21   7 102 104 16 47 117 88
Drive to achieve

N
___ ___ ___ ___ ___
90 32 38 69 105
Impressed

O
___ ___ ___ ___ ___ ___
29 22 83 70 74 109
Record label owned by Sony

P
___ ___ ___ ___ ___ ___
51 95 91 30 45 121
Called out

Puzzle #21

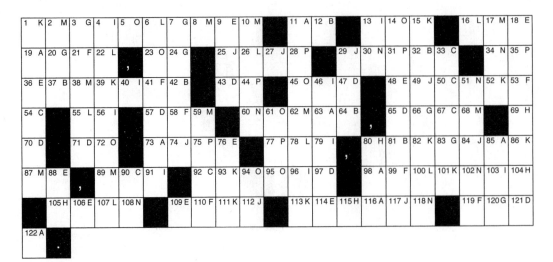

A ___ ___ ___ ___ ___ ___ ___ ___
   85 122 73 98 11 116 63 19
Securely stuck in one place

B ___ ___ ___ ___ ___ ___
   12 37 81 32 64 42
Start of a shoppe name at a Renaissance fair (2)

C ___ ___ ___ ___ ___ ___
   67 50 90 33 92 54
Some alcohols

D ___ ___ ___ ___ ___ ___ ___ ___
   97 121 57 71 65 47 43 70
Duplicates a post on a social network site

E ___ ___ ___ ___ ___ ___ ___ ___ ___
   88 106 114 109 36 9 18 76 48
Protected from the elements

F ___ ___ ___ ___ ___ ___ ___
   99 41 53 110 21 58 119
Electromagnetic radiation, briefly (2)

G ___ ___ ___ ___ ___ ___ ___
   3 20 7 83 66 24 120
Ancient Assyrian capital

H ___ ___ ___ ___ ___
   69 80 105 115 104
"___ crow flies" (2)

I ___ ___ ___ ___ ___ ___ ___ ___ ___
   4 40 56 79 96 91 103 13 46
Crystal anniversary

J ___ ___ ___ ___ ___ ___ ___ ___
   84 27 29 117 74 25 49 112
Ships' capacities

K ___ ___ ___ ___ ___ ___ ___ ___ ___ ___
   15 86 113 101 111 82 93 39 52 1
"___ of a larger problem ..."

L ___ ___ ___ ___ ___ ___ ___ ___
   26 107 22 6 78 100 55 16
Exhausted the supply (3)

M ___ ___ ___ ___ ___ ___ ___ ___ ___ ___
   10 2 68 17 89 87 38 8 59 62
Prohibitive sign text (3)

N ___ ___ ___ ___ ___ ___ ___
   34 60 51 102 108 30 118
Stood by

O ___ ___ ___ ___ ___ ___ ___ ___
   5 72 95 94 61 23 45 14
Rogaine goal, with hair

P ___ ___ ___ ___ ___ ___
   75 77 31 35 44 28
Be obsequious

Puzzle #22

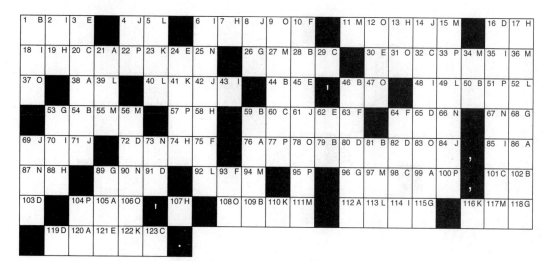

A ___ ___ ___ ___ ___ ___ ___ ___
76 112 120 38 86 105 21 99
Extreme excess

B ___ ___ ___ ___ ___ ___ ___ ___ ___ ___ ___
28 59 102 46 109 50 81 54 1 79 44
1988 Steven Seagal film (3)

C ___ ___ ___ ___ ___ ___ ___
98 60 32 29 20 123 101
12 times a year, say

D ___ ___ ___ ___ ___ ___ ___ ___
103 65 80 91 72 16 82 119
Removed police restraints from

E ___ ___ ___ ___ ___ ___
62 121 45 3 30 24
Bellyache

F ___ ___ ___ ___ ___
75 64 93 10 63
Shopping centers, for short

G ___ ___ ___ ___ ___ ___ ___
89 68 96 26 53 115 118
Taxus baccata, commonly (2)

H ___ ___ ___ ___ ___ ___ ___ ___
88 17 107 13 19 7 74 58
Marginal marking

I ___ ___ ___ ___ ___ ___ ___ ___ ___
35 6 43 2 18 85 48 70 114
Happy hour time, generally speaking (2)

J ___ ___ ___ ___ ___ ___ ___ ___
4 69 14 42 71 61 8 84
Bullfighters

K ___ ___ ___ ___ ___
110 122 23 41 116
Black ball in a pool hall

L ___ ___ ___ ___ ___ ___ ___
113 52 92 40 5 39 49
Absolutely floored by (3)

M ___ ___ ___ ___ ___ ___ ___ ___ ___ ___ ___
11 117 55 36 94 27 97 111 56 15 34
Owner of stock in a company

N ___ ___ ___ ___ ___ ___
73 87 66 67 90 25
___ Chili Peppers (rock band) (2)

O ___ ___ ___ ___ ___ ___ ___ ___ ___
78 37 47 9 108 83 31 106 12
At attention (2)

P ___ ___ ___ ___ ___ ___ ___ ___
104 95 22 100 33 57 51 77
More delicately pretty

1 M	2 M	3 O	4 I	5 E	6 D	7 A		8 J	9 P	10 J		11 N	12 F	13 M	14 I		15 F	16 E	17 O	
18 E		19 D	20 K	21 P	22 A	23 N	24 L		25 E	26 O	27 L	28 J		29 N	30 C	31 G		32 E	33 K	34 J
35 G		36 B	37 A		38 M	39 O	40 J		41 G	42 K	43 E	44 K	45 M		46 I	47 C		48 K	49 I	50 B
51 O	52 F	53 M		54 O	55 B	56 G	57 P		58 H	59 I	60 L	61 M		62 L	63 O	64 E		65 J	66 I	67 H
68 B	69 L	70 I	71 P	72 A		73 G	74 A	75 L	76 B		77 A	78 J	79 K	80 J	81 M	82 L	83 K	84 G	85 F	86 K
87 D	88 P		89 O	90 G	91 N		92 F	93 C	94 M		95 A	96 L	97 C	98 I	99 N	100 I	101 G		102 H	
103 O	104 P	105 D	106 J	107 K	108 M	109 D		110 D	111 N	112 B	113 M	114 E	115 I		116 M	117 D	118 H	119 B	120 K		121 P
122 A		123 F	124 K		125 H	126 B	127 J		128 E	129 K	130 A	131 C	132 F	133 G	134 A	135 P	136 D		137 D	138 H
	139 K	140 B	141 M	142 L	143 H		144 B	145 D	146 A	147 P		148 M	149 N	150 H	151 F		152 P	153 J	154 H	155 N
156 M		157 E	158 D	159 I	160 L	161 B	162 E	163 D		164 B	165 L		166 K	167 L	168 D	169 F	170 H	171 K	172 F	173 J
174 P	175 L																			

A

95 74 7 72 37 77 130 22 146 134 122

Unpopular company money-saving tactics (2)

B

68 112 126 76 164 119 55 161 144 36 50 140

Children's clothing brand since 1895 (2)

C

93 97 30 47 131

"On the ___ hand ..."

D

87 158 110 117 137 105 109 145 19 163 6 168 136

Pink flamingos, for some (2)

E

114 18 157 43 128 16 25 162 5 32 64

1980s sitcom set at a girls' school, with *The* (3)

F

132 123 92 52 172 12 15 169 85 151

Luther's ___ theses (hyp.)

G

84 133 73 31 101 41 35 56 90

Not on one side or the other (2)

H

170 150 102 67 118 138 143 58 154 125

Source of some breakfast juice

I

46 100 4 98 59 115 66 159 70 49 14

Deep-fried seafood side dishes (2)

J

106 8 127 28 173 10 153 65 34 80 78 40

Athenian politician and general

K

42 120 33 166 171 139 83 86 48 20 124 79 107 44 129

"Actually ..." (5)

L

175 27 24 142 165 167 82 160 62 96 60 75 69

Informational alerts

M

53 148 13 156 116 108 61 94 45 81 38 141 2 1 113

Occupy one's inner core? (4)

N

91 149 155 11 29 111 99 23

Editor's move

O

89 26 54 63 17 39 51 3 103

Like some elderly joints

P

88 174 152 147 21 9 71 104 135 121 57

Fiery Warner Bros. cartoon character (2)

Puzzle #24

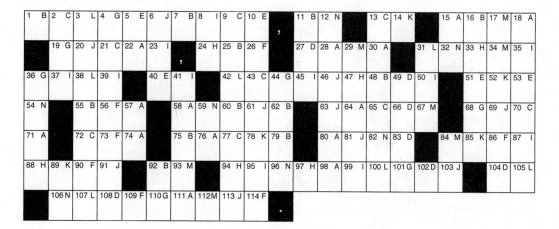

A
___ ___ ___ ___ ___ ___ ___ ___ ___ ___ ___ ___ ___
80 71 28 15 30 58 57 22 64 98 74 111 18 76
Report wrongdoing (3)

B
___ ___ ___ ___ ___ ___ ___ ___ ___ ___ ___ ___
25 16 1   60 55 79 11 48 62 7   92 75
Illegal alien's concern

C
___ ___ ___ ___ ___ ___ ___ ___ ___
65 72 13 21 43 70 77 9   2
Kentucky's northern border (2)

D
___ ___ ___ ___ ___ ___ ___
83 108 27 104 102 66 49
Most insensitive

E
___ ___ ___ ___ ___
40 53 51 5   10
Vegetarian staples

F
___ ___ ___ ___ ___ ___ ___
90 73 109 56 86 114 26
Every (2)

G
___ ___ ___ ___ ___ ___ ___
4   44 36 19 110 101 68
TV series with Johnny Knoxville and Steve-O

H
___ ___ ___ ___ ___ ___
24 94 33 88 47 97
Have an influence on

I
___ ___ ___ ___ ___ ___ ___ ___ ___ ___ ___
23 37 8   99 95 41 39 35 45 50 87
Basic structural units of DNA

J
___ ___ ___ ___ ___ ___ ___ ___ ___ ___
81 103 63 46 20 91 61 69 113 6
Dickensian title character (2)

K
___ ___ ___ ___ ___
78 89 14 85 52
Belgian painter James ____ (1860–1949)

L
___ ___ ___ ___ ___ ___ ___
105 100 3   38 107 42 31
Gave right of way to other traffic

M
___ ___ ___ ___ ___ ___ ___
93 67 34 112 17 84 29
They're free in some restaurants

N
___ ___ ___ ___ ___ ___ ___
82 96 106 54 32 12 59
Religious hermit

Puzzle #25

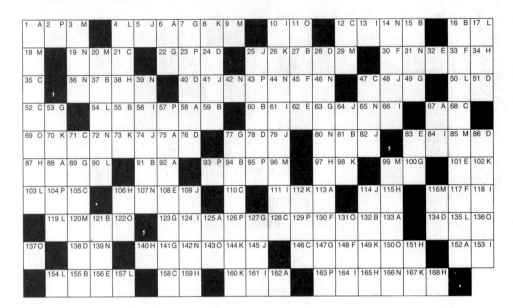

A ___ ___ ___ ___ ___ ___ ___ ___ ___ ___ ___
1 152 75 67 133 113 58 92 125 88 6 162
Slows a catastrophe (3)

B ___ ___ ___ ___ ___ ___ ___ ___ ___ ___ ___ ___ ___
16 155 27 59 15 55 81 121 132 60 37 94 91
Actress in *Bowfinger* and *The Hangover* (2)

C ___ ___ ___ ___ ___ ___ ___ ___ ___ ___ ___
35 52 12 71 158 146 47 110 68 21 128 105
Designer of one of the first U.S. automobiles (2)

D ___ ___ ___ ___ ___ ___ ___ ___ ___
86 138 76 24 40 51 78 28 134
Defunct data transfer device (2)

E ___ ___ ___ ___ ___ ___
83 156 32 62 108 101
Eastern European language

F ___ ___ ___ ___ ___ ___
130 45 148 30 117 33
"Master of the House" musical, for short (2)

G ___ ___ ___ ___ ___ ___ ___ ___ ___ ___ ___ ___
147 22 123 53 100 127 77 49 89 63 141 7
System used for disaster risk reduction (2)

H ___ ___ ___ ___ ___ ___ ___ ___ ___ ___ ___
168 38 34 106 97 165 87 159 140 115 151
Northwest Territories capital

I ___ ___ ___ ___ ___ ___ ___ ___ ___ ___ ___ ___
10 153 124 164 111 56 118 161 66 13 84 61
TV series starring Bruce Willis and Cybill Shepherd

J ___ ___ ___ ___ ___ ___ ___ ___ ___ ___ ___
114 145 79 64 5 82 25 48 41 109 74
Like every other consecutive digit (hyp.)

K ___ ___ ___ ___ ___ ___ ___ ___ ___ ___ ___
112 98 144 160 167 102 8 70 149 26 73
Chad Michael Murray TV series (3)

L ___ ___ ___ ___ ___ ___ ___ ___ ___ ___
157 17 54 50 135 4 90 154 103 119
Objectionably modern

M ___ ___ ___ ___ ___ ___ ___ ___ ___ ___
116 85 120 29 99 20 18 96 3 9
Saved a place in a novel

N ___ ___ ___ ___ ___ ___ ___ ___ ___ ___ ___ ___ ___ ___ ___
31 139 44 72 142 65 14 166 39 19 107 80 36 42 46
Not supported by evidence

O ___ ___ ___ ___ ___ ___ ___ ___
143 11 69 131 150 136 137 122
Troops on standby

P ___ ___ ___ ___ ___ ___ ___ ___ ___ ___
23 129 57 2 126 95 104 163 93 43
Places to dance until the early morning hours

Puzzle #26

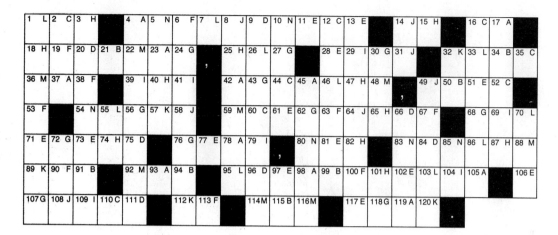

A
 $\overline{4}$ $\overline{17}$ $\overline{45}$ $\overline{42}$ $\overline{37}$ $\overline{23}$ $\overline{105}$ $\overline{78}$ $\overline{98}$ $\overline{93}$ $\overline{119}$
Competitors

B
 $\overline{115}$ $\overline{50}$ $\overline{94}$ $\overline{99}$ $\overline{34}$ $\overline{21}$ $\overline{91}$
Making a snake-like sound

C
 $\overline{44}$ $\overline{35}$ $\overline{2}$ $\overline{12}$ $\overline{60}$ $\overline{52}$ $\overline{16}$ $\overline{110}$
___ *Vice* (Paul Thomas Anderson film of 2014)

D
 $\overline{20}$ $\overline{9}$ $\overline{96}$ $\overline{75}$ $\overline{84}$ $\overline{66}$ $\overline{111}$
For the most part

E
 $\overline{13}$ $\overline{102}$ $\overline{71}$ $\overline{77}$ $\overline{73}$ $\overline{81}$ $\overline{28}$ $\overline{97}$ $\overline{106}$ $\overline{117}$ $\overline{61}$ $\overline{11}$ $\overline{51}$
Failing to remember something (3)

F
 $\overline{100}$ $\overline{63}$ $\overline{19}$ $\overline{6}$ $\overline{113}$ $\overline{90}$ $\overline{53}$ $\overline{38}$ $\overline{67}$
Lung-related

G
 $\overline{43}$ $\overline{107}$ $\overline{76}$ $\overline{62}$ $\overline{56}$ $\overline{68}$ $\overline{24}$ $\overline{72}$ $\overline{118}$ $\overline{27}$ $\overline{30}$
Government leader (3)

H
 $\overline{87}$ $\overline{40}$ $\overline{82}$ $\overline{3}$ $\overline{15}$ $\overline{18}$ $\overline{74}$ $\overline{101}$ $\overline{25}$ $\overline{65}$ $\overline{47}$
Impossible to describe precisely

I
 $\overline{69}$ $\overline{39}$ $\overline{109}$ $\overline{104}$ $\overline{41}$ $\overline{29}$ $\overline{79}$
Weekend chore, for some

J
 $\overline{14}$ $\overline{58}$ $\overline{31}$ $\overline{108}$ $\overline{8}$ $\overline{49}$ $\overline{64}$
Fruit juice company owned by Coca-Cola

K
 $\overline{112}$ $\overline{57}$ $\overline{32}$ $\overline{120}$ $\overline{89}$
___-frutti

L
 $\overline{33}$ $\overline{70}$ $\overline{26}$ $\overline{1}$ $\overline{103}$ $\overline{7}$ $\overline{55}$ $\overline{86}$ $\overline{46}$ $\overline{95}$
Indoor piece of greenery (2)

M
 $\overline{116}$ $\overline{36}$ $\overline{114}$ $\overline{22}$ $\overline{48}$ $\overline{92}$ $\overline{88}$ $\overline{59}$
Achieving ingress

N
 $\overline{80}$ $\overline{5}$ $\overline{83}$ $\overline{85}$ $\overline{10}$ $\overline{54}$
___ valve (heart part)

Puzzle #27

A
_ _ _ _ _
108 76 33 8 68
___ *and the Man* (1970's sitcom)

B
_ _ _ _ _ _ _
47 17 53 75 59 55 69
Chargers' group (2)

C
_ _ _ _ _ _ _
87 73 78 4 5 88 102
Make right

D
_ _ _ _ _
95 43 50 39 109
"___ go gentle into that good night ..." (2)

E
_ _ _ _ _ _
2 29 98 82 66 41
Sweethearts

F
_ _ _ _ _ _ _ _ _ _ _
56 30 44 34 106 105 99 16 9 52 90
Like Othello's and Desdemona's marriage

G
_ _ _ _ _ _ _ _ _ _
58 71 85 18 7 12 93 54 40 38
Caused enormous damage

H
_ _ _ _
45 65 104 1
Ship with a lateen sail

I
_ _ _ _ _ _ _
10 24 19 107 91 49 42
Be great at (2)

J
_ _ _ _ _
83 74 92 64 36
Boy band that featured Justin Timberlake

K
_ _ _ _ _ _
84 48 15 6 79 21
___ Otis (big name in elevators)

L
_ _ _ _ _ _ _
26 80 94 3 32 61 46
Restrain one's hands

M
_ _ _ _ _ _
67 89 51 96 13 22
North Atlantic sea bird

N
_ _ _ _ _ _
63 100 25 77 103 70
The Death of Ivan ___ (Tolstoy title)

O
_ _ _ _ _ _ _ _ _ _ _ _
81 60 97 35 14 23 28 37 31 57 62
Certain endangered ecosystems

P
_ _ _ _ _ _
86 101 20 27 11 72
Belonging to singer John

Puzzle #28

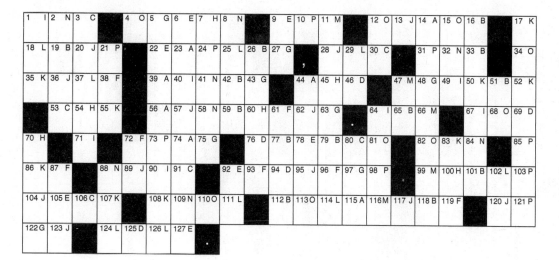

A ___ ___ ___ ___ ___ ___ ___
115 23 74 39 56 14 44
Register at the hotel (2)

B ___ ___ ___ ___ ___ ___ ___ ___ ___ ___ ___ ___ ___
79 101 26 77 33 19 51 42 59 118 16 112 65
For a long period of time (3)

C ___ ___ ___ ___ ___ ___
3 91 30 53 106 80
Like fiery pokers (2)

D ___ ___ ___ ___ ___
94 125 76 69 46
Unpaid factory worker

E ___ ___ ___ ___ ___ ___ ___
105 127 6 92 22 78 9
Worried or confused (3)

F ___ ___ ___ ___ ___ ___ ___
119 38 96 61 87 93 72
Rubbed it in

G ___ ___ ___ ___ ___ ___ ___ ___
5 27 75 48 97 63 122 43
Adopted

H ___ ___ ___ ___ ___ ___
7 45 60 70 54 100
Missile

I ___ ___ ___ ___ ___ ___ ___
64 71 67 49 1 90 40
Louis Armstrong's nickname

J ___ ___ ___ ___ ___ ___ ___ ___ ___ ___ ___ ___
89 62 104 36 123 117 20 28 120 95 13 57
Act of making something as efficient as possible

K ___ ___ ___ ___ ___ ___ ___ ___ ___
86 83 17 52 55 35 50 108 107
Questionable

L ___ ___ ___ ___ ___ ___ ___ ___ ___
37 114 25 124 111 126 29 102 18
Member of the gentry

M ___ ___ ___ ___ ___
47 99 116 66 11
Michigan and Ontario

N ___ ___ ___ ___ ___ ___ ___ ___
58 109 8 32 41 88 2 84
Showing lively interest

O ___ ___ ___ ___ ___ ___ ___ ___ ___
34 81 68 113 110 4 82 15 12
Stenographer's writing method

P ___ ___ ___ ___ ___ ___ ___ ___ ___
98 24 31 21 85 121 73 10 103
Endless, as with a task

Puzzle #29

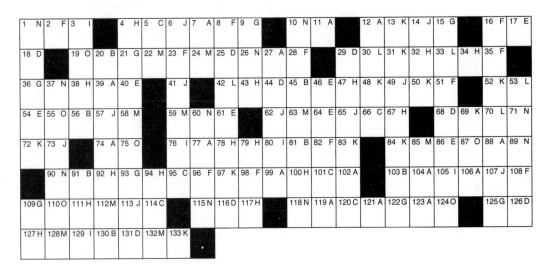

A

88 123 102 27 7 77 119 121 104 11 74 106 12 39 99
1984 Best Musical winner (4)

B

91 81 56 130 103 20 45
Disorder

C

5 101 114 66 95 120
Take a chance (2)

D

29 126 116 18 25 68 131 44
Of cheaper quality

E

54 61 40 64 86 46 17
Have food delivered (2)

F

82 16 98 28 23 96 51 108 8 35 2
Cosmetic lacquer, for a Londoner (2)

G

93 9 21 36 109 125 15 122
Part of it forms the flyleaf

H

78 111 47 92 4 94 79 43 38 67 34 32 117 127 100
Big name in lingerie (2)

I

129 105 3 76 80
Certain newspaper pages (2)

J

49 57 41 14 65 107 73 6 113 62
Like a koala or sloth (hyp.)

K

48 72 133 52 84 31 50 97 13 69 83
Hardly inviting

L

70 53 33 42 30
Lewinsky scandal figure

M

22 132 85 128 24 59 112 63 58
Wearing dress blues, e.g. (2)

N

60 26 1 10 115 90 37 118 71 89
Busted, in other words (3)

O

75 19 55 124 87 110
Bit of corn

Puzzle #30

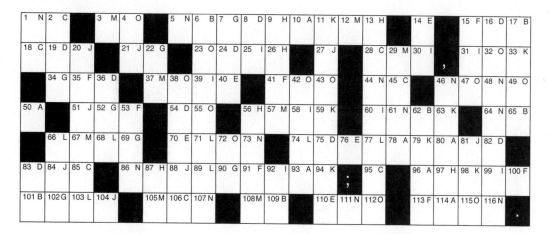

A
96 80 50 93 114 78 10
Caught, colloquially

B
101 6 62 65 17 109
18th-century artistic style

C
106 2 18 85 95 28 45
One way to stop? (3)

D
75 24 36 8 19 83 82 16 54
Not broken

E
110 70 14 76 40
Fleet of foot

F
113 35 15 100 91 41 53
Lhasa native

G
90 22 102 52 7 69 34
Scattered untidily

H
56 13 9 87 26 97
Physicist Heisenberg

I
31 99 60 92 39 30 25 58
Betroth

J
81 104 88 21 51 20 84 27
Capital of Chad

K
59 63 98 33 11 94 79
More indigent

L
74 89 77 66 71 68 103
Be adequate

M
37 67 108 12 57 3 29 105
Security guard

N
61 64 48 116 1 5 44 111 86 46 73 107
Chemistry mass figure (2)

O
4 112 43 42 55 49 38 23 47 32 115 72
Vespa simillima, commonly (2)

Clueless Crosswords

Introduction

These puzzles look like regular crossword puzzles, but as the name suggests, they contain no clues. Kind of like a mix between a cryptogram and a crossword puzzle, clueless crosswords require you to figure out letter distribution and word patterns just by looking at the three-letter combinations given at the start of the puzzle.

Remember: Every letter in the alphabet appears at least once in each puzzle.

Puzzle #1

Solution Grid and Checklist

1	2	3	4	5	6	7	8	9	10	11 D	12	13
14	15	16	17	18	19 W	20	21	22	23	24	25 P	26

A B C D̶ E F G H I J K L M

N O P̶ Q R S T U V W̶ X Y Z

Puzzle #2

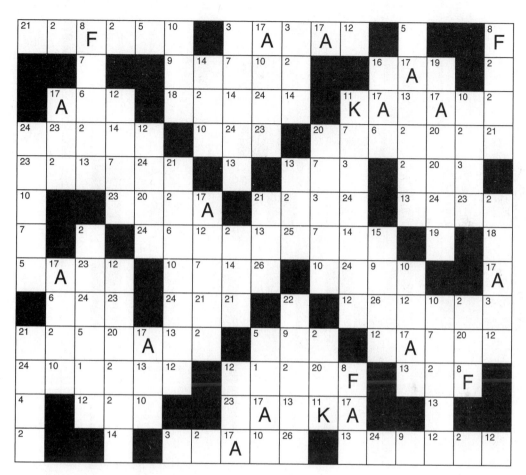

Solution Grid and Checklist

1	2	3	4	5	6	7	8 F	9	10	11 K	12	13
14	15	16	17 A	18	19	20	21	22	23	24	25	26

A̶ B C D E F̶ G H I J K̶ L M

N O P Q R S T U V W X Y Z

Puzzle #3

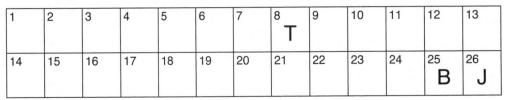

Solution Grid and Checklist

1	2	3	4	5	6	7	8 T	9	10	11	12	13
14	15	16	17	18	19	20	21	22	23	24	25 B	26 J

A B̶ C D E F G H I J̶ K L M

N O P Q R S T̶ U V W X Y Z

Puzzle #4

Solution Grid and Checklist

1	2	3	4	5	6	7	8	9	10	11	12	13
			E								D	
14	15	16	17	18	19	20	21	22	23	24	25	26
									P			

A B C ~~D~~ ~~E~~ F G H I J K L M

N O ~~P~~ Q R S T U V W X Y Z

Puzzle #5

9	1	13	23	18	■	23	14	8	18	23	■	13	24	11	21	7
■	23	15	13	25	14	10 W	■	1	16	26 Q	8	14	7	■		
12	14	11	14	7	■	4	21	10 W	21	7	■	17	7	13	2	14
8	4	15	14	14	3 K	■	25	13	25	■	26 Q	8	21	8	21	25
20	21	12	■	1	16	25	■	5	■	14	8	7	■	12	13	25
■	23	13	2	21	25	■	19	■	16	4	15	13	1	21		
23	■	13	■	4	14	10 W	17	16	17	■	16				7	
11	16	18	11	14	21	■	22	■	17	13	23	16	1	■		
21	7	13	■	17	19	21	14	■	21	1	24	■	4	16	17	
12	14	7	13	23	23	■	6	14	17	■	21	7	13	23	21	7
23	4	13	3 K	21	■	17	8	23	21	23	■	13	7	21	4	13
■	25	16	23	9	14	23	■	21	21	7	16	21	7	■		
1	16	21	4	23	■	13	11	14	4	21	■	25	13	11	21	25

Solution Grid and Checklist

1	2	3 K	4	5	6	7	8	9	10 W	11	12	13
14	15	16	17	18	19	20	21	22	23	24	25	26 Q

A   B   C   D   E   F   G   H   I   J   K̶   L   M

N   O   P   Q̶   R   S   T   U   V   W̶   X   Y   Z

Puzzle #6

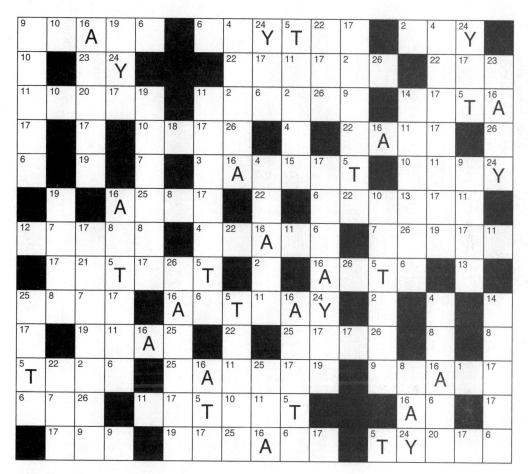

Solution Grid and Checklist

1	2	3	4	5	6	7	8	9	10	11	12	13
				T								

14	15	16	17	18	19	20	21	22	23	24	25	26
		A								Y		

A̶ B C D E F G H I J K L M

N O P Q R S T̶ U V W X Y̶ Z

Puzzle #7

	23	19	8	26	16	15 U	7		20	2	2	8	26	7	11	
22 C		7		11	15 U	14	24	5		7	3	20		13		11
23		22 C	1	7	7	5	7		25	20	26	11		22 C	20	3
25		24	23	20	8	20		3	26	18 T	10	9		26	3	7
12	8	23	21		8	26	17	7	3		7	8	26	18 T	7	5
9		14		20		11	7	8	20	9		26	22 C	7		5
		4	15 U	6		18 T	26	22 C		5	24	9			
23		6	23	18 T		6	23	20	8	5		7		5		1
12	23	3	6	23	18 T		26	14	7	2	18 T		26	22 C	24	9
12	8	15 U	22 C	23	15 U	14	18 T		26	3	23	14	9			7
20	11	11		3	15 U	14	6		18 T	3	15 U	20	14	18 T		14
8		6		20	22 C	18 T		16	15 U	20	22 C	24		1		20
	25	7	14	18 T	1	23	8		19	8	7	5	5	7	5	

Solution Grid and Checklist

1	2	3	4	5	6	7	8	9	10	11	12	13

14	15 U	16	17	18 T	19	20	21	22 C	23	24	25	26

A ~~B~~ C D E F G H I J K L M

N O P Q R S ~~T~~ ~~U~~ V W X Y Z

Puzzle #8

The crossword grid (numbers represent letters; known letters shown):

Row 1: 7, ■, 18, 26, 26, 16, ■, 3, 15, 7, 17, 16, ■, 10, 13, 16, 16
Row 2: 18, ■, ■, 11(R), 6, 13, 16, 18, ■, 13, 15, 24, ■, 15, ■, ■, ■
Row 3: 13, ■, 1, 4, 11(R), 16, 18, 16, ■, 20, 7, 18, 18, 21, 18, 11(R), 16
Row 4: 22, 11(R), 15, 13, 24, ■, 6, ■, 9, ■, ■, 18, ■, 18, ■, ■, 13
Row 5: 25(H), 15, 19, 16, ■, ■, 5(F), 18, 4, 10, ■, 21, 15, 24, 13, 24, 22
Row 6: ■, 6, ■, 18, 1, 25(H), 15, ■, 18, ■, 14, 18, 24, ■, 24, ■, 24
Row 7: 19, 11(R), 4, 10, 18, ■, 15, 19, 18, 11(R), 6, ■, 17, 13, 12, 18, 16
Row 8: 18, ■, 14, ■, 17, 13, 10, ■, 24, ■, 23, 15, 3, 16, ■, 2, ■
Row 9: 18, 8, 19, 18, 17, 16, ■, 6, 17, 16, 15, ■, ■, 17, 6, 13, 10
Row 10: 11(R), ■, ■, 2, ■, 16, ■, 3, ■, 11(R), ■, 5(F), 6, 26, 17, 18
Row 11: 16, 15, 17, 13, 20, 4, 10, 18, ■, 17, 18, 6, 11(R), 24, 16, ■, 2
Row 12: ■, ■, 17, ■, 18, 3, 18, ■, 6, 10, 10, 18, 10, ■, ■, ■, 13
Row 13: 25(H), 13, 20, 16, ■, 10, 18, 17, 6, 3, ■, 10, 18, 16, 12, ■, 17

Solution Grid and Checklist

1	2	3	4	5	6	7	8	9	10	11	12	13
				F						R		

14	15	16	17	18	19	20	21	22	23	24	25	26
											H	

A B C D E ~~F~~ G ~~H~~ I J K L M

N O P Q ~~R~~ S T U V W X Y Z

Puzzle #9

24	10	19		10	25	17	4	5	17	8	3	11		25	17	12
17	15	10	26			9	15	17	25	17			25	10	8	7 U
18	3	12	17	12		4	17	8	10	15		24	3	15	4	26
	26	4	15	3	9		25		22 G		9	3	4	5	17	
3		4	15	7 U	25	9		3	12	3	4	10	19		19
25		13		16 F	15	17		17		3	15	4		5		5
12	17	17	18		26	7 U	12	24	3	6	26		23	3	2	2
11		8		17	7 U	15		8		17	8	10		8		2
10		16 F	5	1	5	8	22 G		14	7 U	5	9	26			6
	12	5	19	10	4		17		7 U		9	5	11	11	26	
11	3	19	10	8		3	8	8	3	11		13	17	17	11	26
3	15	10	3			15	10	7 U	26	10			4	15	10	10
12	10	19		17	21	10	15	8	5	22 G	20	4		10	24	10

Solution Grid and Checklist

1	2	3	4	5	6	7 U	8	9	10	11	12	13
14	15	16 F	17	18	19	20	21	22 G	23	24	25	26

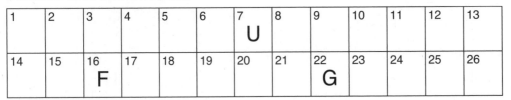

A B C D E F̶ G̶ H I J K L M

N O P Q R S T U̶ V W X Y Z

Puzzle #10

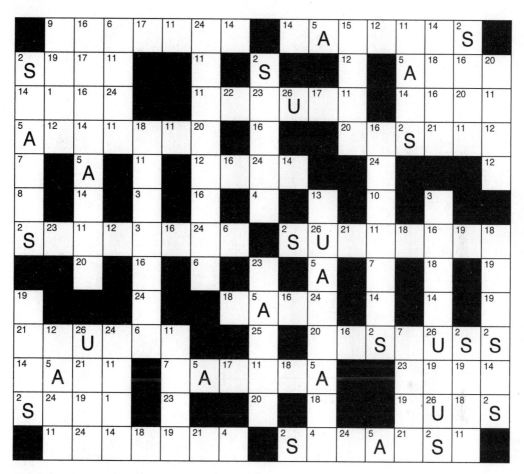

Solution Grid and Checklist

1	2	3	4	5	6	7	8	9	10	11	12	13
	S			A								
14	15	16	17	18	19	20	21	22	23	24	25	26
												U

~~A~~ B C D E F G H I J K L M

N O P Q R ~~S~~ T ~~U~~ V W X Y Z

Puzzle #11

	23	12 P	4	15	14	23		22	21	7	7	5	7	
	23	24	15	21	3			6	20	18	1		4	21	7
	24	7	21	22	23		22	20	14	10	7		9	18	11	7
13	4	14	18	23		26	21	18	22	23		26	15	23	13
14	7	17 F	3		16	4	4	23			25	7	9	20	7
20			7			3	16	15	23	3		18	10	21	7	7
9		4		12 P	15	7	23		13	24	7	17 F		7		8
10	18	11	11	18		26	7	13	4	21			18			20
	20	9	15	3	7			20	12 P	4	9		22	4	9	26
	26	15	23	24		23	13	21	7	16		3	24	21	7	7
19	15	22	7		13	18	14	14	23		12 P	21	4	22	7
	4	20	21		4	2 K	18	1			14	20	21	15	26
	23	1	23	3	7	11		16	21	1	7	23	3	

Solution Grid and Checklist

1	2 K	3	4	5	6	7	8	9	10	11	12 P	13
14	15	16	17 F	18	19	20	21	22	23	24	25	26

A B C D E ~~F~~ G H I J ~~K~~ L M

N O ~~P~~ Q R S T U V W X Y Z

Puzzle #12

Solution Grid and Checklist

1	2	3	4	5	6	7	8	9	10	11	12	13
U	B		C									
14	15	16	17	18	19	20	21	22	23	24	25	26

A ~~B~~ ~~C~~ D E F G H I J K L M

N O P Q R S T ~~U~~ V W X Y Z

Puzzle #13

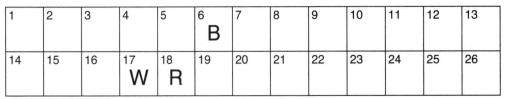

Solution Grid and Checklist

1	2	3	4	5	6	7	8	9	10	11	12	13
					B							

14	15	16	17	18	19	20	21	22	23	24	25	26
			W	R								

A B̶ C D E F G H I J K L M

N O P Q R̶ S T U V W̶ X Y Z

Puzzle #14

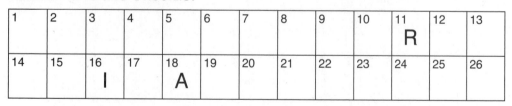

Solution Grid and Checklist

1	2	3	4	5	6	7	8	9	10	11	12	13
										R		

14	15	16	17	18	19	20	21	22	23	24	25	26
		I		A								

~~A~~ B C D E F G H ~~I~~ J K L M

N O P Q ~~R~~ S T U V W X Y Z

Puzzle #15

18		24	12	23	13		24	21	25	13	18		23	15	24	6
11			26	15	24	23	19		15	24	2		13			
23		11	24	18	2	13	19		2	23	9 U	22	22	25	13	18
1	2	24	25	17 Y		22		18			19		13			11
10	9 U	20	7			9 U	20	1	2		1	18	23	24	13	25
	18		13	24	18	2		14		19	15	2		23		1
18	7	1	19	18		13	3	24	19	13		24	19	13	11	2
13		25		7	1	19		16 B		18	24	23	1		23	
13	20	25	1	18	2		16 B	25	1	11			18	25	1	11
11			6		12			13		24		2	13	24	6	18
18	4	9 U	24	18	26	13	19		5	1	10	18	24	8		24
			10		13	23	24		24	23	13	24	18			25
18	15	23	13		19	23	17 Y	13	23		2	23	13	7		6

Solution Grid and Checklist

1	2	3	4	5	6	7	8	9 U	10	11	12	13
14	15	16 B	17 Y	18	19	20	21	22	23	24	25	26

A ~~B~~ C D E F G H I J K L M

N O P Q R S T ~~U~~ V W X ~~Y~~ Z

Puzzle #16

Solution Grid and Checklist

1	2	3	4	5	6	7	8 P	9	10	11	12	13
14	15	16 L	17	18	19	20	21 G	22	23	24	25	26

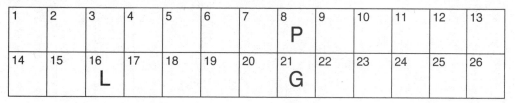

A B C D E F ~~G~~ H I J K ~~L~~ M

N O ~~P~~ Q R S T U V W X Y Z

Puzzle #17

The grid (numbers with filled-in letters shown):

3	16	18	18	23 E	6	■	16	6	5	2	1	■	22	■	■	18
■		10	■	2	25	19 F	23 E	10	■		19 F	4	23 E	■	16
■	26	23 E	16	11	14	19 F	19 F	22		13	23 E	25	25	23 E	7
7	23 E	16	22	21	■	25	2	1	■	12	2	24	16	10	6	22
14	25	1	2	23 E	22	■	20	■	22	16	6	■	1	16	18	■
25	■		16	5	11	22	■	16	13	2	25	■	16	18	23 E	22
16	■	13	■	11	23 E	25	13	25	2	9	23 E	22	■	23 E	■	1
10	14	25	22	7	16	2	6	■	23 E	26	23 E	22	■	■	23 E
■	11	4	11	7	2	6	■	8	■	22	16	1	2	10	23 E
15	4	7	4	25	23 E	7	■	15	14	23 E	■	1	2	6	16	7
14	25	7	4	16	6	■	15	7	2	25	18	■	10	2	18	■
10	■	22	13	26	■	4	14	1	6	4	■		4	■	■
17 B	■	22	■	18	7	4	17 B	22	■	17 B	4	1	1	7	23 E

Solution Grid and Checklist

1	2	3	4	5	6	7	8	9	10	11	12	13

14	15	16	17 B	18	19 F	20	21	22	23 E	24	25	26

A B̶ C D E̶ F̶ G H I J K L M

N O P Q R S T U V W X Y Z

Puzzle #18

Solution Grid and Checklist

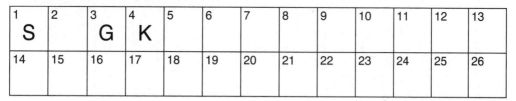

1	2	3	4	5	6	7	8	9	10	11	12	13
S		G	K									
14	15	16	17	18	19	20	21	22	23	24	25	26

A B C D E F G̶ H I J K̶ L M

N O P Q R S̶ T U V W X Y Z

Puzzle #19

	4	5	9	25	3	17		7		25	7	15	23	17	5	
		8	3	8			13	15	7			17	3	3		
	25	8	4	11		11	5	1	26	7		8	5	7	26	
1	5	24	17		22	18	7		5	13	18		7	26	6	25
15	1	11		22	6	25	7		9	3	8	18		25	18	5
7			22	3	10					15	24	24			16 **D**
15	9	21	3	2	15	9	23		16 **D**	18	7	5	15	24	18	16 **D**
14 **Z**		23	18	24							5	7	18			24
18	24	19 **F**		4	18	16 **D**	3		1	5	8	18		23	18	18
9	5	15	24		18	3	9		5	25	26		5	24	5	25
	16 **D**	4	6	23		1	24	18	4	2		18	20	15	7	
		18	23	3			11	18	7			2	15	9		
	5	25	25	3	4	7		24		12	6	18	25	7	25	

Solution Grid and Checklist

1	2	3	4	5	6	7	8	9	10	11	12	13

14	15	16	17	18	19	20	21	22	23	24	25	26
Z		**D**			**F**							

A B C ~~D~~ E ~~F~~ G H I J K L M

N O P Q R S T U V W X Y ~~Z~~

Puzzle #20

Solution Grid and Checklist

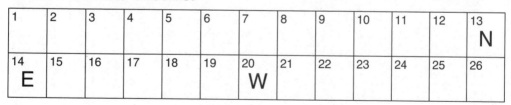

1	2	3	4	5	6	7	8	9	10	11	12	13
												N

14	15	16	17	18	19	20	21	22	23	24	25	26
E						W						

A B C D E̶ F G H I J K L M

N̶ O P Q R S T U V W̶ X Y Z

Puzzle #21

Solution Grid and Checklist

A B C D E F G H̶ I J K L M̶

N O P Q R S T U V W X Y̶ Z

Puzzle #22

Solution Grid and Checklist

1	2	3	4 Y	5	6	7	8	9	10	11	12	13 R
14	15	16	17	18	19	20	21	22	23	24 O	25	26

A B C D E F G H I J K L M

N O̶ P Q R̶ S T U V W X Y̶ Z

Puzzle #23

A codeword puzzle grid with numbered cells. Selected cells contain given letters:

- Cell value 4 = **G**
- Cell value 2 = **F**
- Cell value 19 = **H**

(Given letters shown in the grid: G at the 4s, G at the 4s, G at the 4, F at the 2, G at the 4s, G at the 4, H at the 19, F at the 2, H at the 19, H at the 19, F at the 2, F at the 2)

Solution Grid and Checklist

1	2	3	4	5	6	7	8	9	10	11	12	13
	F		G									

14	15	16	17	18	19	20	21	22	23	24	25	26
					H							

A B C D E ~~F~~ ~~G~~ ~~H~~ I J K L M

N O P Q R S T U V W X Y Z

Puzzle #24

Solution Grid and Checklist

1	2	3	4	5	6	7	8	9	10	11	12	13
				K		I				P		
14	15	16	17	18	19	20	21	22	23	24	25	26

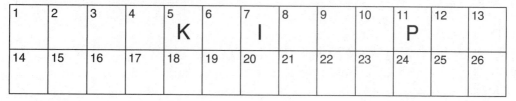

A B C D E F G H ~~I~~ J ~~K~~ L M

N O ~~P~~ Q R S T U V W X Y Z

Puzzle #25

Solution Grid and Checklist

1	2	3	4	5	6	7	8	9	10	11	12	13
E	M											

14	15	16	17	18	19	20	21	22	23	24	25	26
									C			

A ~~B~~ C ~~D~~ ~~E~~ F G H I J K L ~~M~~

N O P Q R S T U V W X Y Z

Puzzle #26

Solution Grid and Checklist

1	2	3	4	5	6	7 H	8	9	10	11	12	13
14	15	16	17	18	19	20	21 L	22	23	24	25	26 G

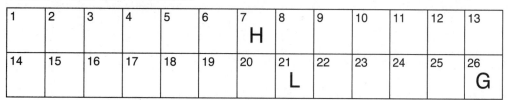

A B C D E F G̶ H̶ I J K L̶ M

N O P Q R S T U V W X Y Z

Puzzle #27

6	■	22 S	26	16	10	■	20 A	19	20 A	1	15	■	2	20 A	22 S	15
20 A	■	20 A	1	12	20 A	22 S	■	10	21	5 Y	■	20 A	■	■	■	■
9	■	24	1	18	7	2	6	■	18	26	19	16	1	12	21	26
16	26	12	15	22 S	■	2	■	22 S	■	12	■	18	■	■	■	20 A
2	16	19	5 Y	■	18	25	8	22 S	■	7	16	24	24	18	24	
■	16	■	1	16	20 A	24	■	18	■	18	10	10	■	12	■	25
2	1	21	22 S	6	■	18	26	19	15	5 Y	■	1	21	24	24	5 Y
1	■	22 S	■	26	1	22 S	■	15	■	18	4	18	22 S	■	18	■
20 A	9	18	1	22 S	18	■	25	12	26	17	■	21	22 S	18	24	
13	■	18	■	25	■	2	■	1	■	6	20 A	19	19	5 Y		
18	11	21	20 A	25	12	15	5 Y	■	22 S	16	1	18	25	5 Y	■	12
■	■	24	■	18	23	18	■	15	23	12	1	25	■	7		
3	12	10	22 S	■	14	16	20 A	26	5 Y	■	17	16	5 Y	22 S	■	10

Solution Grid and Checklist

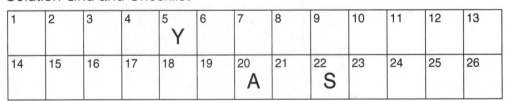

1	2	3	4	5	6	7	8	9	10	11	12	13
				Y								

14	15	16	17	18	19	20	21	22	23	24	25	26
						A		S				

~~A~~ B C D E F G H I J K L M

N O P Q R ~~S~~ T U V W X ~~Y~~ Z

Puzzle #28

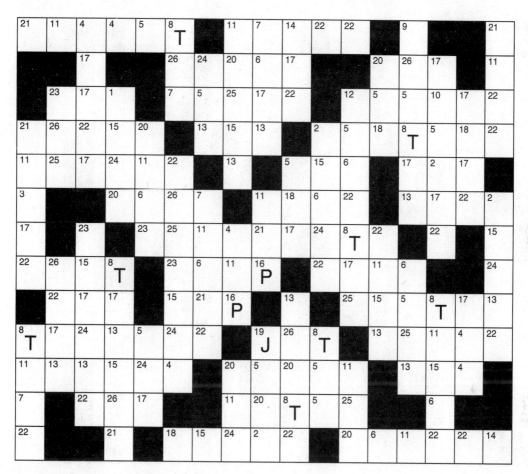

Solution Grid and Checklist

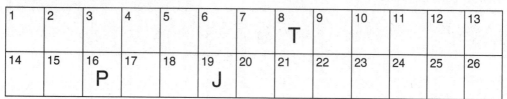

1	2	3	4	5	6	7	8	9	10	11	12	13
							T					

14	15	16	17	18	19	20	21	22	23	24	25	26
		P			J							

A B C D E F G H I J̶ K L M

N O P̶ Q R S T̶ U V W X Y Z

Puzzle #29

	20	12	4	4	15	20		25	14	22	4	2	6		
	15	12	4	5	2			11	4	23	14		9	7	8 **M**
	5	4	18	13	14		3	4	5	14	20		15	9	18	15
20	18	2	2	22		25	7 **I**	23	14	6		6	7 **I**	5	15
12	14	14	6		15	7 **I**	2	14		8 **M**	4	10	7 **I**	14	
9		20		6	7 **I**	20	26 **C**	20		5	14	14	6	20
12		20	21	7 **I**	14	20		9	15	4	8 **M**		20		7 **I**
20	15	4	5	14		15	12	14	20	14			3		17
	4	8 **M**	14	13	9		16	18	9	6		21	9	20	15
	1	14	15	20		18	20	18	9	21		20	4	18	15	12
21	9	6	22		9	2	2	9	21		9	4	5	15	9
	19	9	1		7 **I**	6	4	21		1	5	7 **I**	4	5
	22	14	21	21	4	24		25	21	14	14	6	20		

Solution Grid and Checklist

1	2	3	4	5	6	7 **I**	8 **M**	9	10	11	12	13
14	15	16	17	18	19	20	21	22	23	24	25	26 **C**

A B C̶ D E F G H I̶ J K L M̶

N O P Q R S T U V W X Y Z

Puzzle #30

Solution Grid and Checklist

1	2	3	4	5	6	7	8	9	10	11	12	13
												E
14	15	16	17	18	19	20	21	22	23	24	25	26
							J		H			

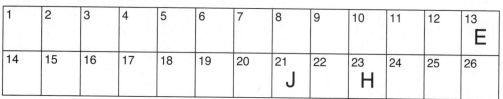

A B C D E̶ F G H̶ I J̶ K L M

N O P Q R S T U V W X Y Z

Crosswords

Introduction

The granddaddy of all puzzles, crosswords need no introduction! Our 15×15 puzzles will put your crossword-solving skills to the ultimate test with clues spanning all manner of knowledge, including history, science, literature, music and film, and much, much more!

Puzzle #1

Across

1. Not good, not bad
5. Give some lip
9. Process flour
13. ___ bargain (court deal)
14. Bonjour opposite
16. Assert
17. Certain angled joints
18. Silty soils
19. Word after black or pie
20. Beach Boys hit song from 1965
23. "Any day now"
24. Chasm
25. High school grp.
28. Not yet stored on a disk, say
32. Heart or kidney
34. Chocolate or black dog, briefly
35. Autumnal stone
39. Beach Boys hit song from 1966
43. Dance bit
44. Shock and ___
45. Classification
46. AA helper
49. "Yikes!"
50. Opera voice
54. Common fertilizer ingredient
56. Beach Boys Christmas song of 1963
63. On a boat, old-style
64. Loud, in musical direction
65. Elmer's product
66. Hefty slice
67. Lars von ___ (Danish film director)
68. "Your excellency"
69. Bill & ___ Excellent Adventure
70. Certain swirl
71. Type of tale

Down

1. Built on ___
2. Spanish ceramic soup jar
3. Hawk, as wares
4. Camel's watering spot
5. Bar of the Old West
6. Decorates
7. Capital of Shaanxi province (var.)
8. Big truck
9. Hindi "master"
10. Ebony and ___
11. Cuts down, as a tree
12. Bit of hair
15. "Born in the ___"
21. Came upon
22. Rove, with "about"
25. Certain captives, briefly
26. Easy gait
27. Fever fit
29. ___ and Sedition Acts
30. Big vessel
31. ___ and flow
33. Mont Blanc, for one
35. Individual
36. Ache (for)
37. Farm measure
38. Onionlike vegetable
40. Afternoon snooze
41. Couple
42. White water bird
46. Cusco coin
47. Befitted
48. Bad tempered
50. Explosion
51. "___ or window?"
52. Word with home or farm
53. Pierces with a knife
55. Apprehensive feeling
57. Young newt
58. Achy
59. Dry as a bone
60. Hip bones
61. Crimped lock
62. ___ over (fall down)

Puzzle #2

Across

1. Breakfast chain, briefly
5. ___ *Dreams* (1994 film)
9. Actress Lamarr
13. Henry VIII's last wife, Catherine ___
14. Belly button type
16. "I cannot tell ___"
17. "If you prick ___ we not bleed?"
18. Chinese "Hello"
19. "In-A-Gadda-Da-___" (Iron Butterfly song)
20. #3 in a series
23. Dept. of Labor branch
24. Certain tropical hardwoods
25. Asner and Harris
28. Haydn's homeland
32. Soviet labor camp system
34. Over there, once
35. Prefix with -logue or -gram
39. #22 and #24 in a series
43. Aromatic herb
44. Ending with block or lemon
45. DEA agent, for short
46. Kind of underwear
49. Prefix meaning three times
50. "For ___ waves of grain ..."
54. Forensic concerns
56. #25 in a series
63. ___ vera
64. City in Marion County, Florida
65. "___ happy to!"
66. Croat or Serb
67. Bottom point
68. Farm equipment
69. Successful songs
70. Russian river
71. Govt. IDs

Down

1. "___ a Spell on You" (1956 song)
2. Corned beef concoction
3. Novus ___ seclorum
4. Advertising ploy, for short
5. Island of Japan
6. Boards from beyond
7. "Top ___ mornin' to you"
8. "La Vie en Rose" singer Edith
9. Le ___ (French port)
10. *Aeneid* queen
11. Got a B, say
12. Has a kid, in a way
15. Computer prog. abbr.
21. "There lived ___ in days ..." (Thackeray)
22. Abbr. on an itinerary
25. Baker's supply
26. ___ mater (brain cover)
27. Move through the mire
29. #10 in a series
30. ___ v. *Wade*
31. Itemized bill (abbr.)
33. ___ Maria
35. Dock workers' org.
36. Objet ___
37. Ending with differ or prefer
38. Unpleasant smell
40. Fan cry
41. AB followers
42. Chou ___ (Chinese politician)
46. Prefix meaning three
47. 1,654, in Ancient Rome
48. Turkish capital
50. Filled (with)
51. ___ Vanilli
52. Become swollen
53. Mountain stats, for short
55. Cuts with scissors
57. "I got an ___ it!" (student's exclamation)
58. Thom ___ (footwear brand)
59. "___ in China"
60. "Bad" cholesterol figs.
61. Black, in verse
62. Certain conifers

Puzzle #3

Across

1. Brouhahas
5. Carry with effort
9. *Tea with Mussolini* star
13. Bathe
14. Starts a pot
16. Hoisted, nautically
17. *Man ___ Mancha*
18. Cedar Rapids native
19. "Same ___ ever was"
20. Painter of *The Last Supper* (1498)
23. Earth, in Berlin
24. Compose a letter
25. Compass pt.
28. Dishes the dirt
32. Big name in hi-fis
34. Weekly literary review pub.
35. Al ___ (former VP)
39. Painter of *Liberty Leading the People* (1830)
43. Cholesterol varieties
44. "... or ___ thought"
45. "I get ___ five"
46. 1981 Supreme Court appointee
49. Swedish carrier
50. The Eocene, for one
54. Bad grades
56. Painter of *At the Moulin Rouge* (1890)
63. Former Yugoslavian leader
64. Light, brushing sound
65. "Hear ye"
66. Have ___ to pick
67. Chief port of Italy
68. First-class window seat, maybe
69. Holy women in Fr.
70. Bumper boo-boo
71. Bambi, for one

Down

1. Off base, say
2. Auto-___ (ceremonial burning)
3. Capital NNW of Copenhagen
4. 1953 Alan Ladd Western
5. Beehive, for one
6. Battery poles
7. Bono's band, spelled out
8. Pb, in chemistry
9. Committee head, briefly
10. ___ Mubarak
11. Throw out, as a tenant
12. Fix shoelaces
15. John Wayne Airport code
21. A noble gas
22. Beetles and Golfs, briefly
25. Donkey, in Dusseldorf
26. Arabian royal house
27. Australia's lang.
29. Ale vessel
30. Ailing
31. Noncommercial TV spot, for short
33. "Owner of a Lonely Heart" band
35. He's between RMN and JEC
36. Punch in the gut responses
37. Antipiracy org.
38. Part of many tel. numbers
40. Computer keyboard key
41. "Yabba Dabba ___!"
42. Greek vacation isle
46. "Well, well, well!"
47. Victor at Trafalgar in 1805
48. At the drop ___
50. Belonging to singer James
51. "At this ___ in time ..."
52. Belly button type
53. Coagulates, as cream
55. Got up from a chair
57. Eighteenth president's monogram
58. Neighbor of Nor.
59. "___ kleine Nachtmusik"
60. Baseball's Sandberg
61. Extra wide, for a shoe
62. Russian leader

Puzzle #4

Across

1. Skeletor's foe
6. End of a play, maybe
10. Big oafs
14. Cornhusker state's most populous city
15. Surfer's request?
16. Will-___-wisp
17. Hostage crisis hero
19. Road reversals, slangily
20. Bluegrass state
21. Deceits
23. Mrs., in Madrid
24. Arikara tribe name
25. Army units, for short
26. ___ gratia artis
27. Lacking significance
31. Annual golf tournament
35. Opus ___
36. Singer Guthrie
37. Short shot onto the green
38. Marie de la Ramée's pseudonym
40. Alternative to ja
41. Give for free
42. State section (abbr.)
43. Cooks in the oven
44. ___ Lately (talk show)
46. Basketball Hall-of-Famer Hank
48. In the Valley of ___ (2007 film)
49. "No way"
50. "___ Could Turn Back Time" (1989 song)
53. Beaver state
56. Natural state
58. ___-kiri
59. In an atypical manner
61. "I'm only ___ for the money"
62. Arm part
63. Remove pencil marks
64. Ile-de-France river
65. Readied a golf ball
66. 2015 World Series player, for short

Down

1. Beeps
2. Arabian ruler
3. Carta lead-in
4. Cat on ___ Tin Roof
5. The ___ (1984 sports film)
6. Comes to
7. Word with hall or slicker
8. Mitford middle
9. Old Dominion state
10. Pelican state
11. Monopoly prop. type
12. Clarified butter
13. Meeting (abbr.)
18. Bakery job
22. Certain rays, for short
25. Bit the dust
28. Nursery school abbr.
29. "Would ___ to You?" (1985 song)
30. Oxford profs
31. 800, in Ancient Rome
32. Cry of anticipation
33. "___ of the Ancient Mariner"
34. Married... with Children actress Christina
35. Home improvement abbr.
38. Undersea explorer
39. Beehive state
43. "Who Let the Dogs Out" group
45. ___-mo
46. Advance
47. Abu ___ (7th c. caliph)
50. Faith of 47 down
51. Type of prophet
52. "The best ___ to come ..."
53. Buckeye state
54. Indian princess
55. Ares's twin sister
56. Rice or Hathaway
57. Not, in dialect
60. Ending with no and capa

Puzzle #5

Across

1. Tulsa sch. founded by televangelist
4. "Hold ___ your hat!"
8. Cease-fire
13. "___ blimey!"
14. Gardener, sometimes
15. Agatha Christie detective
16. African desert
18. ___ State Building
19. 2001 World Series winners
21. Forbidden option
24. Mauna ___ (volcano in Hawaii)
25. Years, in Cuba
26. Kind of pliers
33. "Gloria in Excelsis ___" (Latin hymn)
34. 1975–76 World Series winners
35. *Goldfinger* actress Shirley
36. 2009 World Series winners
38. 2003 World Series winners
40. Early name in video games
41. Shakespearean schemer
42. United Nations, in Sp.
43. Alamo locale
46. "Ah!"
47. Mobile phone company
48. 1986 World Series winners
49. Born out of wedlock
57. *SNL* alumnus Kevin
58. 1924 World Series winners
62. 1984 World Series winners
63. Granola ingredients, often
64. Bite the dust
65. "Hypothetically ..."
66. GPS output (abbr.)
67. Donkey Kong, for one

Down

1. Doc ___ (Spiderman foe)
2. Kiwi bid
3. Web address, briefly
4. Casual greeting
5. Hurricane watch grp.
6. Time in office
7. 1983 World Series winners
8. Burial chamber
9. Gifford replacement
10. ____ acid
11. Bottle stopper
12. Summers, in France
15. "Put the ____ to the metal"
17. Kerfuffles
20. Land east of Eden
21. Vladimir Lenin's wife, *et al.*
22. ___ time (individually)
23. Political writer Peggy
26. Genealogy word
27. Newspaper employees, for short
28. Architect Saarinen
29. Ending with inter or pater
30. Futile
31. Poem type
32. Follows
34. Bit attachment
37. Isthmus in Thailand
38. ___ tai
39. "Fourscore and seven years ___ ..."
41. Front tooth
44. Makes less dense
45. Baseball great Mel
46. *How ___ Your Mother* (TV show)
49. Mate lead-in?
50. Eric the Red's son
51. Doesn't keep up
52. Home of Parmenides
53. Bloody
54. ___ and potatoes
55. Initial poker stake
56. One-time Soviet news agcy.
59. ___ Mae Brown (*Ghost* role)
60. ___ Van Winkle
61. "Oh say can you ___ ..."

Puzzle #6

Across

1. Karaoke equipment
5. Detox place
10. Batter's hope
13. 1,154, in Ancient Rome
15. ___ Cologne
16. Lemon or lime finisher?
17. Plan a performance
19. Educational org.
20. Portuguese explorer (1480–1521)
21. 1957 Ford flop
23. Mil. ranks
24. Movie FX tech.
25. ___ Eddy (guitar legend)
27. English explorer (1540–1596)
31. Take care of, as duties
34. "No ifs, ___, or buts!"
35. How-___ (guides)
36. 1980s rock group
37. ___ Peron (famous first lady)
39. Water-___ (dental devices)
40. Name on a Chinese menu
41. Hebrew month
42. Cold weather drink
43. Spanish conquistador (1485–1547)
47. Unconscious states
48. Moray or conger
49. Coastal inlet
52. ___ con carne
54. Rousing receptions
56. Cries of dismay
57. Icelandic explorer (970–1020)
60. Pick, with "for"
61. Bottom point
62. Michael ___ (*Alfie* actor)
63. Fight finishers
64. Crumble, as support
65. ___-do-well

Down

1. 13 Across + MDCCXCVI
2. Defunct Apple messaging prg.
3. Plumber's issues
4. "Your excellency"
5. Win back
6. ___ a living
7. Mao's successor
8. Payroll company
9. Decapitates
10. ___ League (commercial confederation)
11. ___ fixe (obsession)
12. Blue-green shade
14. Fabric fastener
18. Soviet gymnast Korbut
22. Patient request (abbr.)
25. By ___ of (due to)
26. Beef-rating org.
27. Bragg and Sumter (abbr.)
28. Capital of Egypt
29. Sign language gorilla
30. She, in Italian
31. *Revenge of the ___* (2005 film)
32. Massachusetts motto start
33. Demon removers
37. ___ Krabappel (Bart's teacher)
38. Dyson prods.
39. Opposite of neg.
41. *Winnie the Pooh* writer
42. Larry Bird, once
44. Lon ___ (Cambodian leader)
45. Revolutionary rider
46. Drop from the eye
49. Robot maid on *The Jetsons*
50. "___ ear and out the ..."
51. Actor Ed
52. British explorer (1728–1779)
53. Prefix with glycemic or allergenic
54. *The Wizard ___* (comic)
55. "___ See for Miles" (The Who song)
58. Cochlea site
59. Vow phrase

Puzzle #7

Across

1. Tolkien tree creatures
5. Cream ___ crop
10. Fed. support org.
13. Belonging to Mr. Vidal
15. Chick ___ (jazz pianist)
16. "It ___ to Be You"
17. Spice rack staple
19. Grand ___ Opry
20. Concentrates, in a way
21. Mooed
23. Yiddish "yuck"
24. ___ Harbor, Fla.
25. Baggy
27. Conifer-derived spice
31. Black tea type
34. Actress Hathaway
35. 104, in old Rome
36. Domino of "Blueberry Hill"
37. Terre ___, IN
39. Spice made from nutmeg
40. Food store chain
41. Pickling herb
42. Backs of the neck
43. John Steinbeck novel
47. Major artery
48. Comparative suffix
49. TV brand name
52. From that moment on
54. Lawmakers, often
56. Jackie's husband #2
57. Spicy spice rack resident
60. Noble ___
61. Toothpaste dispensers
62. Seven in Spain
63. Extra-wide shoe size
64. Climbing plant
65. ___ the line

Down

1. Musical scale letters
2. "Honest!"
3. Discard
4. Religious branch
5. Eyespots
6. Dandies
7. Boy Scout div.
8. ___ haw
9. Piercing spot
10. Hair protector
11. Store event
12. Carded, as at a club
14. Slopes enthusiast, colloquially
18. Scheme
22. Suffix for sugars
25. Pre-Easter fasting time
26. Normandy river
27. Yeses, in Berlin
28. Abdul or Zahn
29. Sushi ingredient
30. ___ Saint Laurent
31. Pitch ___ (get angry)
32. Kind of tropical palm
33. Spice popular in Asia
37. Dagger handle
38. "... and to ___ good night!"
39. Small rug
41. Dish Network rival
42. 2015 Netflix crime series
44. Book part (abbr.)
45. Complete
46. Ballerina's move
49. Cowboy event
50. Minotaur's island
51. Start of a lobster comparison?
52. Aromatic herb
53. "Dies ___" (hymn)
54. Util. bill abbr.
55. Idiot
58. Color property
59. Teamster org.

Puzzle #8

Across

1. Ocean spray prefix
5. Homer's dad, in *The Simpsons*
8. ___ Bien Phu
12. Car
13. Aberdeen native
14. One official language in India
15. Dance bit
16. *Cat on ___ Tin Roof*
17. "... and God I know ___" (1964 lyric)
18. Consequently
20. ___ Lipinski (Olympian)
21. Black-and-white cookies
22. Baseballer Maris, to friends
23. Official language in Egypt
26. Official language in Dhaka
30. Cinch ___ (garbage bag brand)
31. Official language in Busan
34. "Tune ___ eleven"
35. Aids and ___
37. Casual greetings
38. "I'm ___ Be (500 Miles)" (1993 song)
39. XY type
40. One official language in Afghanistan
42. "___ in Adam"
43. Official language of San Marino
45. ___ Earhart
47. Mil. ranks
48. Official language of Cambodia
50. Lugosi or Bartok
52. Enlivened
56. One official language in Sri Lanka
57. Bryn ___, PA
58. Apple heart
59. One-time majority leader Dick
60. Turner and Eisenhower
61. Arrogance, colloquially
62. Flying formations
63. Man, in Latin
64. Twirled

Down

1. List of actors
2. "The Babe"
3. Suit to ___
4. "Can do!"
5. Sneeze sound
6. Unmannerly sorts
7. Ending for cigar or launder
8. "Joltin' Joe"
9. "Are you ___ out?"
10. ___ Ferber (novelist)
11. Never, in German
13. Auto insurance company
14. Make a pass at
19. Estrada *et al.*
22. Stimpy's partner
23. "Me, too"
24. Capital of Morocco
25. Kipling's wolf
26. Slam
27. Year's record
28. Hawaiian porch
29. "Take ___ compliment!"
32. *Saving Private ___* (film)
33. Canon model
36. Fib
38. Pyle of TV
40. ___ de deux
41. Lion handlers
44. Boot-shaped country
46. Raises, as a building
48. Pants material
49. Lumberjack
50. Undressed
51. 1990's model with palindromic name
52. 904, in Ancient Rome
53. Make pretty
54. One official language of Pakistan
55. Part of a hammer head
56. 23rd Hebrew letter

Puzzle #9

Across

1. Actress Gershon
5. Office fill-in
9. Separates out
14. "No man ___ island"
15. Ron Howard role
16. "He's ___ nowhere man ..."
17. *Octopussy* actress Adams
18. Cairo's river
19. Machine shop tool
20. 2007 Best Actress Oscar winner
23. Former French coin
24. These, to the French
25. Distress letters
26. Cabinet Dept.
27. Northern CA school
29. Govt. assistance program
32. Orange ___ tea
35. "___ Brute?"
36. Actor McGregor
37. 1968 Best Actress Oscar winner
40. Buck___ Banzai
41. Scottish native
42. Soda brand
43. Beehive St. capital
44. Dino ending?
45. ___ Wei (restaurant chain)
46. Christian denom.
47. ___mart (retail chain)
48. Evil deed
51. 1983 Best Actress Oscar winner
57. Hang around for
58. Former soldier
59. Pell follower
60. Bit part
61. Stratford-upon-___
62. ___ Office
63. Detect a scent
64. Serenade

65. The Florida ___ (island chain)

Down

1. Very short putt, often
2. Author Asimov
3. Pacific island country
4. *The King ___* (Broadway title)
5. British weights
6. Expansive stories
7. *The Adventures of ___ and Otis*
8. Actress Amanda
9. ___ *Duty* (video game series)
10. Russian border mountains
11. "___ smile be your umbrella ..."
12. Cowardly Lion actor
13. Snow transport
21. Orangish yellow
22. Topic for discussion
26. Tramp
27. Say out loud
28. Keyboard key
29. ___ Lake
30. Film director Gus Van ___
31. *Ali G ___house* (2002 film)
32. Cops' orgs.
33. ___ Grey tea
34. Ray of McDonald's
35. Biblical twin
36. Morales of *La Bamba*
38. Amazed
39. "If ___" (Beatles song)
44. The ___ the Earth
45. Story tempo
46. Legal summary
47. Word with chuck or station
48. Kitchen utensil
49. Mosaic work
50. Gwyn and Carter
51. Cul-de-___ (dead ends)
52. Old Korean currency
53. "___ Said" (Neil Diamond song)
54. Affirmations
55. 1,016, in Ancient Rome
56. Run ___ (go wild)

Puzzle #10

Across

1. Cable sports channel
5. Actress in *Psycho* (1998)
10. "Come on, be ___!"
14. Biblical pronoun
15. "Don't shed ___"
16. Caramel-filled candy
17. Candy with white and yellow filling
20. Calls for quiet
21. Nincompoop
22. Take back, as with words
23. Beauty mark
24. Mae or Adam
26. ___ Joy (coconut-filled candy)
29. Peppermint Pattie maker
30. Uncle ___
33. Suffix meannig "lizard"
34. "___ Macabre" (Saint-Saëns piece)
35. Neighbor of Penn.
36. Candy bar with a fluffy filling
40. McDonald's magnate's monogram
41. City near Dayton
42. Six, in Spain
43. Ending with transit or audit
44. Difference between bared and barred
45. ___ Crunch (crisped rice candy bar)
47. A/C units
48. Angel's ring
49. Part of a play, often
52. Poetic evenings
53. Email symbols, for short
56. Candy bar with a nebulous name
60. ___ and learn
61. Island in *Jaws*
62. Wine descriptor
63. *Je ne ___ quoi*
64. Certain lepidopterans
65. Candy bar sold in pairs

Down

1. List-ending abbrs.
2. Former Iranian leader
3. Street sign abbr. for walkers
4. Kan. neighbor
5. ___ *and Maude* (film)
6. Jaguar model
7. Singer Peniston
8. Part of a laugh?
9. "... ___ I saw Elba"
10. "Well, ___ you clever!"
11. Edgar Allan, and family
12. Tiny photosynthetic organism
13. Lethargic
18. Japanese noodle
19. Revolutionary War weapon
23. "The ___ the merrier"
24. Willy ___ (chocolate factory owner)
25. Language of Ireland
26. George Jetson's dog
27. Volcanic mudflow
28. Cloudy, as water
29. ___ Arafat
30. Candylike
31. Pop singer Lavigne
32. En ___ (as a group)
34. Sand drifts
37. Strikingly foreign
38. Restaurant handout
39. Exxon, once
45. Reagan and Pelosi
46. *Frozen* queen
47. Takes the bait
48. ___ bar (toffee and chocolate candy)
49. Hole-punching tools
50. ___ Pet
51. Rikki-Tikki-___
52. Radiate
53. ___ unto himself
54. Torch type
55. Mythological river
57. Type of radio
58. "I love," in Latin
59. Parcel of land

Puzzle #11

Across

1. *Stand* ___ (1986 film)
5. Carter or Gwyn
9. "... Paul I know, but who ___?" (Acts 19:15)
14. Sinn ___ (Irish party)
15. Tony-winner Judith
16. Queen of ___ (biblical figure)
17. Start of a J. R. Lowell quote
20. Bay area airport letters
21. "99 Red Balloons" singer
22. Thespians
23. Meat loaf ingredient
24. Future doctor's exam
25. With hands on hips
28. "___ giorno!"
29. Neighbor of Alg.
32. Mundane
33. Polite rural reply
34. Jet-speed word
35. Middle of the quote
38. Swedish furniture chain
39. Eliza's 'iggins
40. UV part
41. Type of Gibbon
42. Rock guitarist Ford
43. Singer Redding, and namesakes
44. Cartoon explorer
45. Mecca pilgrim
46. Journalist Charles
49. "___ Jail" (Monopoly space)
50. Animated film unit
53. End of the quote
56. Israeli port city
57. "What's ___ pleasure?"
58. Pantyhose problem
59. Make embarrassed
60. Belief systems, in brief
61. Carry a tune

Down

1. #1 buddies, for short
2. "Oh, ___ little faith"
3. Spanish artist Joan
4. Ending for differ or depend
5. "___ Five" (Dolly Parton song)
6. ___ the score (gets revenge)
7. Luke's sister
8. River in France
9. Early 20th-century art movement
10. *Gone with the Wind* hero
11. Architect Saarinen
12. ___ City (Tampa area)
13. St. Louis bridge designer
18. Lacking the skill
19. Toyota truck
23. Mutual of ___ (insurance company)
24. Like some colognes
25. Bubbling on the stove
26. *The Metamorphosis* author
27. Prefix with change or woven
28. ___ resemblance
29. Damon and Lauer
30. Earth tone
31. Ostrich cousins
33. Gossipy sort
34. 1,552, in Ancient Rome
36. Kook
37. Synonym for 36 Down, maybe
42. Natural sponge
43. Old West films
44. Removes, as with a hat
45. Boring
46. Govt. workplace safety org.
47. ___ in the dark
48. Earth goddess
49. Classic muscle cars
50. "___ help you?"
51. One-time Indiana governor Bayh
52. ___ Mason (financial company)
54. "Just so you know ..."
55. Online feed format

Puzzle #12

Across

1. Pequod captain
5. Quite some way away
9. Broccoli ___
13. Salt, chemically
14. Lyme disease vector
15. Disturbingly weird
16. Start of a quote by Charles de Secondat
19. Heb. teacher
20. Parental threat
21. French author Zola
22. ___ for Ricochet (Grafton novel)
23. Leave quickly
24. Some Muslims
27. Mamma ___! (Abba musical)
28. "The Banana Boat Song" starter
32. ___ for Murder (1954 film)
33. Sends out a fishing line
35. Spanish hero, with El
36. Middle of the quote
39. Guitar virtuoso Steve
40. Like a dirty chimney
41. Barely beat, with "out"
42. River islands (Br.)
44. Army cops
45. Where you might find 44 Across
46. Tax experts, briefly
48. Janitor's tool
49. WWII German vessel
51. Sea ___ (manatees)
52. Apple's mobile platform
55. End of the quote
58. Convenes
59. Gratify completely, as with an appetite
60. You've Got Mail director Ephron
61. Certain D.C. VIPs
62. Tavern in The Simpsons
63. King Kong actress

Down

1. Largest U.S. wildlife refuge (abbr.)
2. Chuckle
3. Hail ___
4. Certain sandwich, for short
5. For three, in French
6. Italian cars
7. Play part
8. Rival of MGM
9. Counted (on)
10. Sea near the Caspian
11. 2005 American Idol singer Bo
12. Cartoon cry
15. Name in a Salinger title
17. Interstate entrances
18. Tell, as with a story
23. Suspicious
24. Biblical mount
25. Seen enough
26. ___ de la Cité (in Paris)
27. Belonging to actor Damon
29. Make ___ for (justify)
30. "Egad!"
31. Took too many meds
32. Prima donna
33. Cuts, as with wood
34. Nerve connection
37. Ketchup ingredient
38. Apr. and Aug.
43. Scurries
45. Camilla Parker ___
47. Picks up the tab
48. The Count of ___ Cristo
49. Fencer's sword
50. Bingo call
51. See you, in Sorrento
52. Fictional humpbacked assistant
53. Other, in Spain
54. Kind of carriage
55. Hesitant sounds
56. Sch. in Hattiesburg
57. Compass dir.

Puzzle #13

Across

1. ___ Davis (*Grumpy Old Men* actor)
6. Tennis great Arthur
10. Biblical water-into-wine town
14. Regional weather
15. Rise to great heights
16. Kind of frost
17. Start of the quote
20. Bodily apertures
21. Coffee shop request
22. Battle of the ___ (1918)
23. Churchillian gesture
25. Yesses at sea (var.)
26. Quick raid
30. Extremely dry
31. Newspaper piece, for short
32. Like some fingerprints
34. One hundred yrs.
37. Middle of the quote
40. French possessive
41. Free from care
42. Biblical wise men
43. Object
44. Virginia ___ (author of the quote)
45. Diplomatic figure (abbr.)
48. Break, as a balloon
49. Indians, on a scoreboard
51. Frontiersman Daniel
53. Board member
58. End of the quote
61. ___ vera
62. Lyrical poems
63. "___ looking at you, kid"
64. Makes illegal
65. Not harmful
66. Secret romance

Down

1. Eight, in Spain
2. Disparaging remark
3. ___ Valley (Los Angeles suburb)
4. "___ the opinion ..."
5. In a spooky manner
6. Horse relatives
7. Drunkards
8. Skeptical laugh
9. "___ I saw Elba"
10. Pet popular in the 1980s
11. Major artery
12. Mean-spirited
13. Cultural pursuits, in Spain
18. Like a slick road
19. Armadas
23. Changes course suddenly
24. Kovacs or Banks
26. Cloudy mists
27. ___ and Anthony (radio duo)
28. Field figures
29. Home security co.
30. Type of sauna
32. Game of chance, for short
33. "Not ___ out of you!"
34. Arrivederci
35. Neighbor of Scot.
36. Innocent one
38. Taiwan's capital
39. Med. care group
44. Scale reading
45. BBC sitcom, briefly
46. Money, slangily
47. Atomic number 5
49. Wild goose ___
50. PC hookup
52. Maiden name indicators
53. Bass or treble
54. Sorry sort
55. ___Tyler Moore
56. Gets older
57. Bird's home
59. Get-___ (beginnings)
60. Legal doc. to protect company secrets

Puzzle #14

Across

1. Ending for myth or log
5. Internet greeting, of a sort
10. Rep.'s opponents
14. Baseball's Sandberg
15. ___ Lama
16. "Time ___ My Side" (Rolling Stones song)
17. ___ and crafts
18. Percussion instruments
19. General ___'s chicken
20. Start of a quote by Mark Twain
23. Orbital outpost, briefly
24. Itsy-bitsy
25. Santa ___ winds
26. Fleur-de-___
27. Small islands
29. Here, to Henri
32. *Network* director Sidney
35. Suffix meaning "eater"
36. ___ Nordegren (Tiger Woods's ex-wife)
37. Middle of the quote
40. Old English letters
41. You are, in the Yucatan
42. Saint with an alphabet named after him
43. One-time Mideast org.
44. USAF rank
45. "Let It Ride" (1974) band initials
46. Feline sound
47. ___ krob (Thai noodle dish)
48. Notice
51. End of the quote
57. Alpine goat
58. Paddled watercraft
59. Shed, as skin
60. Big name in jeans

61. "If ___ possible ..."
62. To ___ (precisely)
63. *Jurassic Park* antagonist, briefly
64. Kathmandu's country
65. Mother, in French

Down

1. Ramadi native
2. Singer Miley
3. Those against
4. "___ we forget ..."
5. Vedder and Bauer
6. Chili con ___
7. Chug-___
8. Male sheep
9. Aghast
10. One-time Bears coach
11. They, in Italy
12. Bewail
13. Kiss, to a Brit

21. Blockheads
22. Carry-___ (luggage)
26. Grazing spots
27. Envy
28. Mars, to the Greeks
29. Robert ___ (A. J. Soprano actor)
30. 103, in Ancient Rome
31. Like a transatlantic flight, briefly
32. "In ___ of flowers ..."
33. Beef-rating org.
34. More, in Munich
35. It borders Mary.
36. Companion of 28 Down
38. 2008 campaign slogan
39. Eight-person group
44. Spanish 101 verb
45. Happened to
46. 1,519, to Tacitus

47. Bread
48. Beat down, biblically
49. Certain fisherman
50. ___ Lauder (cosmetics brand)
51. Dagger handle
52. "Deutschland ___ Alles"
53. Actress Campbell
54. Desert fruit
55. Ginger cookie
56. Islamic religious leader

Puzzle #15

Across

1. Self-assured declaration
5. Big burden
9. "___ expert, but ..."
13. Jazz great Fitzgerald
14. Frasier's brother
16. Hans ___ (UN inspector)
17. Paper measure
18. Film critic Roger
19. Former soldier
20. Start of a Kelvin Throop quote
23. Dust Bowl figure
24. Novelist Zola
25. Nonprofit org. for public broadcasting
28. One-time Acura model
32. Sketched
34. Affirmative vote
35. Puzzle's center?
39. Middle of the quote
43. Marvel mutants
44. Life story, in brief
45. Like some Andean ruins
46. *Where the ___ Grows* (Rawls novel)
49. Aliens, for short
50. Assertive person, maybe
54. Queen Anne's ___
56. End of the quote
63. Belted out
64. Plant seeds again
65. Cajun vegetable
66. "___ upon a time ..."
67. Princess's headwear
68. Met or Cub, in brief
69. Highest degrees
70. "This is not ___!" (parental scolding)
71. Quaker product

Down

1. Yesterday, in Italian
2. Musical sign
3. "Take ___!" (coach's punishment)
4. "... and Bingo was his ___"
5. Bowler's target, often
6. Bit of corn
7. 1997 title role for Peter Fonda
8. Croat neighbor
9. Skyscraper support
10. Battle of Hastings year, in Roman numerals
11. ___ Farage (UKIP politician)
12. Iron ___ (rust)
15. Sault ___ Marie, MI
21. Giving approval
22. "Isn't ___ bit like you and me?" (Beatles lyric)
25. 10 Across minus DCVI
26. ___ and proper
27. Make a cake
29. ___ the storm
30. Fra. neighbor
31. Operated
33. ___ Jiabao (Chinese premier, 2003–2013)
35. Buddhist discipline
36. Ending for confer or differ
37. Coup d'___
38. 9-digit IDs
40. Award for a knight (abbr.)
41. YouTube item, briefly
42. Chop finely
46. Car in reverse?
47. Matador's foe
48. Neighbor of Newark
50. Iron Mike
51. Robin of baseball
52. Boxer's hit
53. Slight advantages
55. ___ Lodge (hotel chain)
57. ___ deco
58. Carrie Fisher role
59. Exam for future attys.
60. Ark. neighbor
61. ___-a-porter (ready-to-wear)
62. Health scare of 2002–2003

Puzzle #16

Across

1. "___ load of this guy!"
5. Roasting skewer
9. Miami's county
13. Sleep like ___
14. Buff
16. Spanish rivers
17. Attorney General Janet
18. Pre-Halloween prankster, maybe
19. Burden
20. Start of a quote by Norman Vincent Peale
23. Modern *carpe diem* acronym
24. Borscht ingredients
25. Compass dir.
28. Aden natives
32. Metronome measurement
34. Obi-___ Kenobi
35. Certain tide
39. Middle of the quote
43. Vet's concern, briefly
44. Defunct country music channel
45. Artistic theme
46. Jailbird's pic
49. Map abbrs.
50. "You ___ Beautiful" (Joe Cocker song)
54. Vow phrases
56. End of the quote
63. ___ *vincit omnia*
64. Knife brand sold on TV
65. Bruins' sch.
66. Bueno's opposite
67. Thread holder
68. Actor Julia of *The Addams Family*
69. Clothes fastener
70. Holds title to
71. Skedaddle

Down

1. Clothing
2. Robert ___ (Civil War general)
3. Braxton or Morrison
4. "The ___ of defeat"
5. *Remington ___* (Pierce Brosnan role)
6. Organized persecution of a minority group
7. *Picnic* playwright William
8. Golfer's gadgets
9. Pilotless aircraft
10. Danny ___ (1980's Celtics star)
11. Meryl Streep film of 2008
12. Mississippi has four
15. ___ *& the Women* (Altman film)
21. "Happy birthday ___!"
22. GI ailment
25. Stair part
26. Conveyed
27. Paramedics, briefly
29. Belonging to actor McGregor
30. "___ in Nancy ..."
31. Savings acct. abbr.
33. Advanced deg.
35. Mil. rank category
36. Has a meal
37. Have ___ to pick
38. Adobe files, briefly
40. Disco ___ (*The Simpsons* character)
41. Gerund's ending
42. "___ Sexy" (1990's song)
46. Bon ___ (witty remark)
47. Flirts with
48. Nonalcoholic beer brand
50. Second U.S. president
51. Type of numeral
52. ___ *Gay* (WWII bomber)
53. Sharpening belt
55. Blue cartoon character
57. Dept. of Justice heads
58. Cosmetic surgery, briefly
59. ___-it-all
60. Golden Bears's sch.
61. You're reading one now
62. Revolutionary Nathan

Puzzle #17

Across
1. Common dog name
5. "Love ___" (Beatles song)
9. High-level bus. degs.
13. Self-help website
14. ___ the Terrible
15. *The Wonder ___* (TV show)
16. Start of a quote by Elbert Hubbard
19. Appropriate
20. Ambiance
21. Light neutral shades
22. Japanese telecom co.
23. Elliptical
24. "... baker's man, bake me ___ as fast ..."
27. Barely get by, with "out"
28. Deep desires
32. Not aflame
33. Listened to
35. *The ___ of Pooh* (1982 book)
36. Middle of the quote
39. Ending with humor or riot
40. *Inglorious Basterds* bad guys, generally
41. Extreme sports camera brand
42. British submachine gun
44. R&B singer Des'___
45. Again and again
46. ___ one's loins
48. 1501, to Tacitus
49. John Philip ___ (composer)
51. Brings legal action against
52. How to get noticed by Google? (abbr.)
55. End of the quote
58. "This isn't my first ___!"
59. Figure skater Katarina
60. Thaw
61. "No Doubt" singer Stefani
62. Eye ailment
63. Like two ___ in a pod

Down
1. Disaster org.
2. Breakfast chain, briefly
3. Warning word
4. Be beholden
5. 60 seconds
6. 1970's tennis champ Chris
7. *Galileo's Daughter* author Sobel
8. Unified
9. At a high cost
10. Singer Erykah
11. War god
12. Fed. retirement org.
15. 1978 Village People hit
17. City in South Dakota
18. Audio issue on stage
23. Gives a thumbs up
24. Have ___ (be able to escape)
25. Almost but not quite
26. Be sick
27. ___, meenie, miney ...
29. Jaguar classic
30. Scottish seaside resort
31. ___ speak (as it were)
32. Roswell visitors, briefly
33. Initiated in an unpleasant manner
34. Shark type
37. Actress Fawcett
38. It's in i and j, but not k
43. Common Vietnamese surname
45. *Swan Lake* princess
47. Immature retort
48. Moldy-smelling
49. Winter precipitation
50. Ye follower, at Renaissance fairs
51. Emmy winner Loretta
52. Captain Hook's sidekick
53. ___ Varner (Faulkner character)
54. Picks
55. End of some domains
56. Cries of discomfort
57. Weaponized radiation burst, for short

Puzzle #18

Across

1. ___ Pop (punk star)
5. Indian cuisine ingredient
9. Air ___ (airline)
13. One "Desperate Housewife"
14. Track event
15. Mike of *Austin Powers*
16. Start of a quote by Pliny the Elder
19. Word pt.
20. And others, for short
21. Incursions
22. Starter with cue or toon
23. Burton and Curry
24. Run ___ of the law
27. 8-bit console of note
28. Ski lift type
32. "All ___ the Watchtower" (1968 song)
33. Milk, in Madrid
35. Angst-filled and dark, scene-wise
36. Middle of the quote
39. ___Pen (anaphylaxis treater)
40. Strains, as with flour
41. Great ape, briefly
42. Arab boat
44. Certain roads, for short
45. Purveyors of mendacities
46. Guffaw sounds
48. Ending for men or den
49. Queen's term
51. Miss ___ (actor's worry)
52. Thee, now
55. End of the quote
58. Corn covers
59. Queue
60. Arm part
61. ___ out (declines)
62. ___ Zatopek (Czech runner)
63. Lift, as with spirits

Down

1. Belonging to Big Blue
2. Jennifer of *Dirty Dancing*
3. High rank in mil.
4. Affirmative vote
5. Grimm girl
6. Gaza group
7. Environmental sci.
8. Suffix with employ or pay
9. Keyboard user
10. AARP part, in brief
11. Word with martial or graphic
12. D.C.-based music group initials
15. "Just the facts, ___"
17. Sanctuaries
18. Country singer Yearwood
23. Computer support experts
24. First Hebrew letter
25. Shakespeare collection
26. Ending for pepper or macar
27. Certain salamanders
29. Joy of *The View*
30. Prayer enders
31. ___ Biv
32. Still asleep
33. Some turns
34. Stars, in Paris
37. Four-armed Hindu deity
38. "___ la la ..."
43. Kitchen implements
45. Hardy partner
47. FBI employees, for short
48. Ancient Celtic tribe
49. Enlist again
50. New York City river
51. Take ___ view of
52. China–North Korea river
53. ___ account (absolutely not)
54. Saddam's son
55. JFK's killer
56. Phillies' div.
57. Movie popcorn holder

Puzzle #19

Across

1. Donkey noise
5. Everyone, in German
9. That, in German
13. Tabula ___ (clean slate)
14. Word with bag or kidney
15. Some English nobles
16. Start of a quote by Charles F. Kettering
19. Former telecom giant
20. Like some losers
21. Small ones
22. Baseball stat.
23. Ivy League school
24. Actress Moorehead
27. *Days of ___ Lives* (TV soap)
28. Columnist Maureen
32. Love, in French
33. Kournikova and Paquin
35. Pi follower
36. Middle of the quote
39. Diet prod. banned in 2011
40. Synthetic fabric
41. "Rope-___" (boxing style)
42. Biblical verb
44. *The ___ in the Hat* (children's book)
45. North Pole name
46. Belonging to author Umberto
48. Indian lentil dish (var.)
49. Toothbrush brand
51. Prefix for wine
52. They come in six-packs, for some?
55. End of the quote
58. "___ as a hatter"
59. "What did I ever ___ you?"
60. Med school subj.
61. Ship pole
62. "Billie ___" (Michael Jackson song)

63. Architect I.M., *et al.*

Down

1. Military jail
2. Huck's transport
3. "___ sow, so shall ..."
4. Basketball's ___ Ming
5. Loathes
6. Some jets
7. Wash, old-style
8. Compass dir.
9. "and then it ___ on me ..."
10. Smell ___ (detect an informer)
11. Stallone, and others
12. Mil. draft org.
15. Last Hebrew month
17. Herald, as with an era
18. Turkish mountain

23. Chinese province (var.)
24. Gas company bought by BP
25. Large percussion instruments
26. Naked, in French
27. Walk ___ coals
29. "Will it be me ___?"
30. Defeats by a large margin
31. Shower affection
32. Adderall target, briefly
33. Mythical strongman
34. Take, as a pill
37. Baseball great
38. Dentist's org.
43. Try to rip open
45. Bryce ___ National Park
47. Clump of earth

48. Actress Burke
49. Mount near Olympus
50. Dashboard numbers, briefly
51. Woodwind instrument
52. Primo
53. ___ B'rith
54. Superiors of cpls.
55. End of a Descartes quote
56. Noun modifier (abbr.)
57. Beat the ___ (avoid a guilty verdict)

Puzzle #20

Across

1. Nadirs
5. Helps
9. Web page code
13. Wyatt of the Wild West
14. German automaker
15. Eagle's home
16. Start of a quote by Abbie Hoffman
19. Our nearest star
20. Negative responses
21. Gymnist Comaneci
22. Long Island or Puget (abbr.)
23. ___ double take (looked twice)
24. Honks
27. ___ for Burglar (Grafton novel)
28. Belgian river
32. Charon's vessel
33. Sinful city
35. Much ___ About Nothing
36. Middle of the quote
39. French friend
40. Belonging to Brockovich
41. Gets corroded
42. Russia, once
44. Line part (abbr.)
45. Brewing brand
46. Popular laptop brand
48. Sashimi choice
49. Celebrate
51. Tehran's place
52. Anguish
55. End of the quote
58. Computer symbols
59. Wheel and ___
60. Newsman Lester
61. Soup containers
62. ___-serif
63. Divine Secrets of the ___ Sisterhood (2002 film)

Down

1. Allows
2. Hawaiian island
3. Small songbird
4. Lotion abbr.
5. Burr and Copland
6. "Somebody that ___ to Know" (2012 song)
7. Banned insecticides
8. Caesar or Vicious
9. Golden period
10. Star Trek: TNG counselor Deanna
11. "do, re, ___, sol ..."
12. Actress Thompson
15. Little bit
17. Fashionable
18. In ___ (together)
23. Belinging to an ancient Carthaginian queen
24. Overflows (with)
25. Sporting goods company
26. Gold, in Guatemala
27. Spring sound
29. Permission
30. Archie Bunker's wife
31. ___ Perot (presidential candidate)
32. German Mrs.
33. Hogs' homes
34. James Bond cocktail
37. Author Le Guin
38. 1921 play by Karel Capek
43. Baltimore team
45. Shoulder warmers
47. Hardens
48. Nordic type
49. Portuguese cape
50. Ghostbusters role
51. UN watchdog org.
52. Cowboy's command
53. Unctuous
54. Jazz singer James
55. ___-tac-toe
56. Dictionary entries (abbr.)
57. Your, once

Cryptograms

Introduction

Cryptograms are simple-substitution ciphers in which every letter of the alphabet has been switched to another. Your task when solving these types of puzzles is to use pattern recognition and your grammar and vocabulary skills to decipher the hidden quote.

Hint: Start with the one-, two-, and three-letter words, and remember that the most common letters in the English language are E, T, A, I, O, and N, in roughly that order.

Puzzle #1

SEVHV BJ LVBSEVH ECMMBLVJJ LAH

XLECMMBLVJJ BL SEBJ UAHDK; SEVHV

BJ ALDZ SEV OAFMCHBJAL AG ALV

JSCSV UBSE CLASEVH.

—Alexandre Dumas

Puzzle #2

NKL SFCCLALPTL ZLNHLLP NKL

FBEQIIFZXL UPS NKL EQIIFZXL XFLI FP

SLNLABFPUNFQP.

—Tommy Lasorda

Puzzle #3

JK JH JYTFHHJWIQ KF KMVBQI OVHKQM

KGVE KGQ HTQQZ FO IJRGK, VEZ

XQMKVJEID EFK ZQHJMVWIQ, VH FEQ'H

GVK SQQTH WIFAJER FOO.

—Woody Allen

Puzzle 4

MWQGQ BGQ MTH ZOECFME OH WCSBO

JQZOU TZFF QOACGQ —MWBM WQ WBE

OH EQOEQ HD WCSHG, BOA MWBM WQ

WBE OQLQG ROHTO MGHCJFQ.

—Sinclair Lewis

Puzzle #5

HEB VLBJHBWH VFOH J IJLBKH RJK

VFZB J REFQM FW AKRDKMFHFDKJQ

QDZB. HEBLB'W KDHEFKV ULDKV UFHE

HDAVE QDZB, JW QDKV JW HEB QDZB

FW AKRDKMFHFDKJQ.

—George Herbert Walker Bush

Puzzle #6

BXIEI ZL DJ EJNY BJJ HJDK BJ BXI

RND SXJ NYPNDUIL YIHZCIENBIHM

NDY SZBXJGB GDYGI XNLBI.

—Jean de LaBruyère

Puzzle #7

CYCBE AUE JI JNB PSYCR OC UBC JV

KDC YCBMC JI ZUQSVM KDJRC RPSMDK

WDUVMCR KDUK OJNPA ZUQC UPP

KDC ASIICBCVWC.

—Mignon McLaughlin

Puzzle #8

UTX IECO BEUXJXWUBEK GEWHXJW

GJX UTIWX HTBPT QXWUJIO UTX

NSXWUBIEW.

—Susan Sontag

Puzzle #9

LK MNO SEYD UZZY NY NHLEQ EP QLYZ

KMNK KMZ SLKKSZ KMLYDO NBZ

LYPLYLKZST KMZ QEOK LQGEBKNYK.

—Sir Arthur Conan Doyle

Puzzle #10

D SZJDZGZ MQNM DM DO SZMMZP MC
MZJJ MQZ MPTMQ MQNF N JDZ. D
SZJDZGZ DM DO SZMMZP MC SZ IPZZ
MQNF MC SZ N OJNGZ. NFX D SZJDZGZ
DM DO SZMMZP MC BFCR MQNF MC SZ
DEFCPNFM.

—H.L. Mencken

Puzzle #11

BLI SEWB JSREHBZPB BLJPK JP
NESSOPJNZBJEP JW BE LIZH FLZB
JWP'B XIJPK WZJA.

—Peter Drucker

Puzzle #12

UP UM STF SO PRF VWFMMUTJM SO
SWX OAUFTXM PRHP BSN EHT HOOSAX
PS VF MPNZUX DUPR PRFI.

—Ralph Waldo Emerson

Puzzle #13

XSK SMOPKCX CXOZAARK YV MRR LC

XY NK CYBKXSLHA PLVVKOKHX VOYB

QSMX XSK MIKOMAK BMH LC.

—Charles Schwab

Puzzle #14

VLVXB CUI NJRTFP JULV U YRFFVZV

VPTYUESRI SI RXPVX ER NJRQ JSC JRQ

FSEEFV EJV EJSIZ SN XVUFFB QRXEJ.

—Elbert Hubbard

Puzzle #15

CYMFM KFM CTN CYOJER TYOUY TOQQ

KQTKZR LM DMFZ SOXXOUAQC XNF K

SMWNUFKCOU JKCONJ: CN RCKFC K

TKF KJS CN MJS OC.

—Alexis de Tocqueville

Puzzle #16

OTD XDHO OTWQJ LXKPO JWIWQJ KG

KPMHDEIDH WH OTLO BTLO BD JDO WH

LEBLRH XDOODM OTLQ BTLO BD JWID.

OTD MDLZOWKQ WH JMDLODM OTLQ

OTD LZOWKQ.

—Orison Swett Marden

Puzzle #17

B DSWSN EDLI IXJQ B QXBDE JOLKQ

ULPSQXBDH KDQBT B NSJC IXJQ B'WS

INBQQSD LD BQ.

—William Faulkner

Puzzle #18

JYN JWDTSHN EZJY NXJZGU ZJXHZXG

BDDC ZR JYXJ BZPN DW RZM CXIR

HXJNW IDT'WN YTGUWI XUXZG.

—George Miller

Puzzle #19

KVFXF QP ROLREP UWXF UQPFXE

RUWTS KVF OWLFX GORPPFP KVRT

KVFXF QP VJURTQKE QT KVF VQSVFX.

—Victor Hugo

Puzzle #20

NIPCP ZCP NGW AXMQU WS HPWHTP,

NIWUP GIW SXMXUI GIZN NIPD UNZCN

ZMQ UW WM.

—Robert Byrne

Puzzle #21

MC MO FDQDOOWVR CU EMOCMFYTMOX

GDCKDDF CXD JMVCTD WFE CXD JMQD

US UGDEMDFQD.

—Lemuel K. Washburn

Puzzle #22

YUG YUEPAK ZG USYG SNQWY

QWTKGDLGK STGP'Y HQTG TGSD YUSP

YUEPAK ZG DEFG SNQWY QWTKGDLGK.

—Ellen Goodman

Puzzle #23

Q GPO'E LOSWDFEPOS KMI P HWDFYO

KQBB EPCW P IWPD EY KDQEW P OYTWB

KMWO MW GPO WPFQBI JLI YOW ZYD P

ZWK SYBBPDF.

—Fred Allen

Puzzle #24

RZGTG FC JXRZFJW PGRRGT NXT RZG

CDFTFR XT RZG PXHU RZKJ K EXMG

KNNKFT. FR GEGMKRGC RZG RZXSWZRC

KJH NEKRRGJC RZG CRXOKIZC.

—Barbara Howar

Puzzle #25

FBGJTPV BG JFO PORTPM TD EU

OURTNUJOP AOJCOOU RFEPERJOP EUM

RBPRNIGJEUROG.

—Donald Creighton

Puzzle #26

CRUHU FHU CYA YFPX AD UWUHCZJB:

AJU'X XCHUJBCR AJU ZX ILXRZJB NAYJ,

CRU ACRUH ZX ILVVZJB LI.

—Booker T. Washington

Puzzle #27

NUSDS BA MJNUBMK NUWN RBOO XBOO

W PWM AJ AJJM WA UWCBMK MJYJHZ NJ

VBMH VWION RBNU YIN UBPASOV.

—George Eliot

Puzzle #28

SCIYI WYI SZL SCJDVK SCWS LDI UPKS

VIS PKIF SL LY LDI ZJHH RJDF HJRI

PDIDFPYWGHI: SCI FWUWVIK LR SJUI

WDF JDTPKSJOIK LR UID.

—Nicolas Chamfort

Puzzle #29

GJ GZ RIJJIP JV PGZI XPVW OGXI KZ

XPVW K RKFMHIJ—FIGJNIP JNGPZJQ

FVP SPHFBIF.

—Aristotle

Puzzle #30

QXC KYOS WCIBKY BKFC MCKMOC LCQ

OKBQ VY QXKELXQ VB RCPIEBC VQ'B

EYTIFVOVIW QCWWVQKWS.

—Paul Fix

Puzzle #31

JU HGW GRFNQ IBNJQ MWBW EL

EJFATW HGNH MW PLRTC RQCWBEHNQC

JH, MW MLRTC IW EL EJFATW HGNH MW

PLRTCQ'H

—Emerson M. Pugh

Puzzle #32

CIKXQCR YWYV RYKE LCFZXYVY. KXY

YLVKX SYYNE KDVCQCR VIDCH LCH

VIDCH LCH RYKE CIZXYVY. KXY

PIPYCK QE KXY ICUF KXQCR KXLK

OIDCKE.

—Jean Cocteau

Puzzle #33

YWD MDJY PIBZND DOSJYJ RWDH XIA

HDQDB WDZB YWD RIBC PDHYSIHDC.

RWDH XIA WDZB Z NIY IL YZNE ZMIAY

SY, SY'J AJAZNNX NIAJX.

—Dwight D. Eisenhower

Puzzle #34

RIKRYI OIWKZI JQQJWVIU QK QVISC

OXCUIDP PKZIQSZIP ZKCI QVJD QVI

OXCUIDP JCI JQQJWVIU QK QVIZ.

—George Bernard Shaw

Puzzle #35

NKFYF JO ST QJSC TP CJOKTSFONZ

JSNT LKJRK TNKFYLJOF DTTC HFTHVF

XTYF FUOJVZ USC PYFWEFSNVZ PUVV

NKUS NKUN TP CFPYUECJSD NKF

DTMFYSXFSN.

—Benjamin Franklin

Puzzle #36

ZJPTP'O VB TPLOBV ZB IP ZJP TUDJPOZ

ALV UV ZJP DPAPZPTN. NBF DLV'Z EB

LVN IFOUVPOO YTBA ZJPTP.

—Colonel Sanders

Puzzle #37

BXMTM UDQ RYBXERH UTYRH UEBX

QYCBXMTR WDPEVYTRED BXDB D TEQM

ER BXM YWMDR PMSMP UYCPIR'B WCTM.

—Ross MacDonald

Puzzle #38

CGM'K ZP BJTBOC KG KBNV KG

HGQTUPNJ. OK'U KXP GMNH YBH

HGQ EBM ZP UQTP UGDPZGCH'U

NOUKPMOMS.

—Franklin P. Jones

Puzzle #39

ADR BFIIRGRZWR NRAPRRZ Y SUN YZB

Y WYGRRG FT ADR BFIIRGRZWR

NRAPRRZ IUGAO YZB TFVAO DULGT

Y PRRJ.

—Robert Frost

Puzzle #40

PBL PT RZL VILNRLJR ALHCJUPBJ UB

RZL DPIHA UJ RZL ZPSL RZNR RZL

LQUHJ UB RZUJ DPIHA NIL RP EL FCILA

EK HLVUJHNRUPB.

—Thomas B. Reed

Puzzle #41

AGBFB'L H OYUB DYUB TBARBBU

OYLGYUW HUN EKLA LAHUNYUW SU

AGB LGSFB DYVB HU YNYSA.

—Steven Wright

Puzzle #42

NPK YKRN XQEUKGRWNAQER FANP

TQNPKGR WHFWVR NWMK CHWXK AE

RAHKEXK, FPKE QEHV NPK PKWGN

RCKWMR.

—Carrie Latet

Puzzle #43

BZA BP OSA SUHJACO OSQZKC QZ XQPA

QC SURQZK NBHJC QZ EBMH SAUHO

OSUO EBM VUZ'O MOOAH.

—James Earl Jones

Puzzle #44

QIOQ RS POZ PDNJKSISZM QIS WTQQWS

RS AZDR OWKSOMU TF NTZM-EDYYWTZY

TZ TQFSWC.

—Tom Gates

Puzzle #45

OQ ON ZDFKTMPWN QP HT MOKYQ OF

VDQQTMN PF UYOJY QYT TNQDHBONYTZ

DWQYPMOQOTN DMT UMPFK.

—Voltaire

Puzzle #46

VGY DKMUI GLW VGY GLJEV KP SLXEAH

MKKS PKM VGY SLA DGKWY LFVEKAW

WGKD VGLV GY XAKDW DGYMY GY EW

HKEAH.

—Napoleon Hill

Puzzle #47

IDTUDWJ SHKPWMCLWST TLLC M

YDSSYL YDBL FYMXDWJ SLWWDT GDSU

YDZDWJ EMYYT.

—Jim Harrison

Puzzle #48

AYO WYOCYOGQ VSEVMW AGFOW AH

COGWKVQO AYO WYOOC AYVA AYOFG

FLAOGOWAW VLQ YFW HEL VGO

AYO WVTO.

—Stendhal

Puzzle #49

IZXA PGLOC FJ W TLMZ FJIIJE PGEOC

XD TGEJ TWEEXJC MGLUOJA PJEJ WA

CJJUOK XB OGHJ WA IZJK WEJ XB CJFI.

—Earl Wilson

Puzzle #50

GJGBF ILF X ZGM AH LKI YWWQ

MNBWAZN MNG EWBRGO YXOM WE MNG

BXPNGOM HGWHYG XK LCGBXPL. XE X'C

KWM MNGBG, X ZW MW DWBQ.

—Robert Orben

Puzzle #51

IFCHC DHC ECHFDEB QX TDMB XU XGH

YFAJTFXXT ZC JARCT BX UGJJM DB

IFXBC ZC BECQI ZAIF D UDRXHAIC

OXXW.

—Marcel Proust

Puzzle #52

KBAANKK GK DYN INANKKRWP

CGKHQWDBIN QH FGHN, EBD GD GK

QIFP DQ DYN XNWP BIHQWDBIRDN

DYRD GD AQCNK NRWFP.

—Anthony Trollope

Puzzle #53

NBNLQIDFGU MGN FGBNGIT FT ILRN,

QMR ZXQ HN ONLKNVIJQ TRLN MK IDXI.

OMNILQ FT XT OLNVFTN XT UNMZNILQ.

—Gustave Flaubert

Puzzle #54

R JEXXDJU RA RJ GESN GDIU

SDGPDIAHTMU AD TU GHK HLK BLDO RA

ANHL AD TU JHLU HLK NHZU DLU'J

KDETAJ.

—G. B. Burgin

Puzzle #55

YLYAJNSY FOK POEYSP. QFOP VK AOAY

VK PFY ZNGAOCY PN RNEENQ PFY

POEYSP PN PFY IOAX HEOZY QFYAY VP

EYOIK.

—Erica Jong

Puzzle #56

BLRM-QSUD SB ZCV IZVBU LELGD, HEW

SM IL DSLRW UZ SU, IL OHE ELJLV WZ

HEDUPSEA AZZW SE UPL IZVRW.

—Helen Keller

Puzzle #57

XIZSTYCTN TSEOROPO SH TLSSOREQ

NSMY XRTPCPSYO CHPIY PLIN'AI PSKX

NSM BLCP RP RO NSM BCEP PS LICY.

—Alan Coren

Puzzle #58

TI AXCCVJ AVCJWVG JKI IDOG JVCYBIE

VR VJKIWE NBJ X YVVS GORI ICXNGIE

BE JV SOEWIYXWS JKIH.

—Cato the Elder

Puzzle #59

MQ CBT RGHV VB EGDI AILVGMH G NBP

XIVZ WBHI, XMFI MV VB ZBEIPBWC RUB

MZ LIGSSC PTZC. VUIC'SS UGFI VUIML

ZIALIVGLC WB MV.

—Joe Moore

Puzzle #60

NJT IWD DVZ VMTEQVHT OJDGTOO PO

NV XTQVHT OV IEWKKTC ZK PG

OVHTNJPGF NJWN DVZ UVEFTN NV XT

WUEWPC.

—Lady Bird Johnson

Puzzle #61

YVSYVK XC OW ODDOAAXWS TOCKV QE

VWVYSU; UQB ZOW'K IBXAR QW XK;

XK'C QWAU SQQR EQY TOAAQTXWS XW.

—Katherine Mansfield

Puzzle #62

DQINUPMN PE OUX EXMEQOPCM CT

TXXDPMN NCCH QDD CWXB QMH

EUCKPMN PO GBPMJPGQDDF PM

CMX EGCO.

—Josh Billings

Puzzle #63

ILCT GQO CTKQOTHCS DCCENTPBG

PQQJ VJRNKC HLVH KQTHSVJNKHD

QHLCS DCCENTPBG PQQJ VJRNKC,

NPTQSC HLCE XQHL.

—Al Franken

Puzzle #64

HYI ZBVI WUKF YUW IWNULIF OVBZ HYI

YBMVXEUWW BO BMV EROI, HYI

NEIUVIV TI WYBMEF WII HYVBMXY RH.

—Jean Paul

Puzzle #65

SGP TEPRSPE HUQQUZMWSN, SGP

IBEP TWBEN UA LMEIBMASUAT US.

LFUWWQMW DUWBSL TRUA SGPUE

EPDMSRSUBA QEBI LSBEIL RAH

SPIDPLSL.

—Epicurus

Puzzle #66

N ESMBFS B AGGZ WNVMXSK CXSR N

LVGWWSZ VKPNRA VG FBYS VXSF FNLL

VXS EBOO BRZ LVBKVSZ VKPNRA VG

FBYS VXSF XNV NV.

—Sandy Koufax

Puzzle #67

NCE IACEKF XMLMO ABLM NCEO VMIZ

ZOCEIMOI CX GAMX NCE ZEOX CEZ ZC

DQHAZ DCO DOMMFCY BXF ZOEZA.

—Henrik Ibsen

Puzzle #68

VNMQDKY QMUI RXNR XZYRUKC ZY

ZMSGNRZUMNKC NMT RXNR JUMDC ZY

RXD GNYR RXZMW N IZYD JNM IZGG

XUNKT.

—Will Durant

Puzzle #69

ATQHP NE ETRHBJNVO TU QJNXJ N DR

XTVWNVXHL BJHPH NE VT NVVTXHVXH

BJNE ENLH TU BJH QTRY.

—Nadine Gordimer

Puzzle #70

HQ PQA OYYQD NSQNYS AQ HFG VQLC

KUFPS XSWOLKS AUSV OCS XYFPHSH.

ASYY AUSG AQ NLA QP KQGS

KLPEYOKKSK.

—Lady Gaga

Puzzle #71

KEV PAFXK KELJH RWACK VCFATV LX

KERK IAC QRJ'K HA ACK LJ KEV

GLOOYV AZ KEV JLHEK RJO HVK

R XYCFTVV.

—Tellis Frank

Puzzle #72

NXHR NT IB FC MTCC RXHZ H ISBU FZ

RXT BGTHZ. OPR FD FR NTST LFCCFZY,

RXT BGTHZ NBPMI MHGV CBLTRXFZY.

—Mother Teresa

Puzzle #73

COPSIF LTXF JBPSFXCIBS, COPSIF SEI

CXPJY, OBQ SEIB MTFWIS OAA SEOS

YFOU OBQ RXPS UAOL.

—Charlie Parker

Puzzle #74

FPM FO RGM JFUR BWZMPRXSFXU

RGLPVU HMOR XU LU RF VF RF TMW.

OFS PF FPM KBP HBN B GBPW FP FXS

WSMBJU.

—Edward Verrall Lucas

Puzzle #75

WGSSROW TICCRGF RJ I HQS HRYG

WGSSROW ROSQ I SDU QE PQS XISGC.

IESGC ZQD WGS DJGF SQ RS, RS IRO'S

JQ PQS.

—Minnie Pearl

Puzzle #76

SWM PWHRM WLESHGU HD KWUELXE

KGHJME SWNS N QMP BLEXHJMGU LE

VALSM RLZMRU RAGZLQF NS SWM QMYS

BMXLCNR KRNXM.

—F.K. Richtmyer

Puzzle #77

ZY BPU OZQPB ZI SHNL OZYU PJK

EPJIQUC BH SUOOHV, Z LUEHAAUIC

SHN YOHHL ZB. ZB'K KJYUL BPJI BPU

JOBULIJBZFU.

—Jeb Dickerson

Puzzle #78

RPSPL YJBRG YJQY EQL, RU KQYYPL

JUE RPDPHHQLW, RUL JUE NAHYBXBPV,

BH RUY Q DLBKP.

—Ernest Hemingway

Puzzle #79

WQVXQB SQOQB VQDDIYE YNWF PAQ,

PSL P EFPBX WISAJQ NE WFQ ISDK

QLAQL WIID WFPW ABIYE UQQSQB

YNWF HISEWPSW JEQ.

—Washington Irving

Puzzle #80

IC RODDXK CHROQC ECOJ. IC ROD XDUZ

KJODHEXJN GK GDKX O RXNQODGXD

KVOK ORRXNQODGCH LH XD OUU XLJ

CFRGKGDY OWMCDKLJCH.

—Susan Jeffers

Puzzle #81

GZHOHNHF UZHFH VM R QJOPWVQU

DHUGHHO ZYSRO FVKZUM ROL

XFJXHFUA FVKZUM, ZYSRO FVKZUM

SYMU XFHNRVW.

—Abraham Lincoln

Puzzle #82

O EQTL PQW IWOXHIHQG VOC GLTLW
ULODLGLX O GOIHQG, HGXLLX HI VOC
CIWLGRIVLGLX GOIHQGC HG IVLHW
VQJW QP ZLWHE.

—Winston Churchill

Puzzle #83

OEJZ EBZQIISBHNN ZQN JGOH SBDG
DZH UGFKY RHJQENH GC
RHUSKYHFOHBD QBY DZSBMN KHCD
EBNQSY.

—Fyodor Dostoyevsky

Puzzle #84

HVRD VE HVLLHD PYQD LMGB G HYGB
EMGQU: VL DKGWLE G ZDQC MVOM
QGLD YR VBLDQDEL RYQ LMD RDT
XHDGEAQDE VL WYBWDFDE.

—Luigi Pirandello

Puzzle #85

UYY ICLYAGAICLTG, LE MAF KLST BCTJ

CAJT, UKT QAQGTQGT, RFB GAJT UKT

PKTUBTK QAQGTQGT BCUQ ABCTKG.

—Samuel Butler

Puzzle #86

JGHNOJGHZAD ZD GD JPAN GM GDXOAH

YK APTHPSO GD ZH ZD G AYTTOAHZYM

YK GTEYSZHNJD.

—Carl Boyer

Puzzle #87

BV OAUUGPQ DHHO JU BG DAOG

DAUUDG JPMGDQ, JPZ JDTJVQ JXUGI

ZHAPM QHBGUKAPM GQFGWAJDDV

ZGLADAQK.

—Jamie Ann Hunt

Puzzle #88

R ILJVG RW DGL NGZEQV FRLLJRKG

VEGN QEW PGRL R OGJS. NDG PRQWN

WE NGG PDRW NDG JN KGWWJQK.

—Helen Rowland

Puzzle #89

NM UND JMMJ ZNM ZAXZN, CMZ NKF

TADLCYKF KZ, UKZNDXZ YJRKWQ UND

KJ HDA KZ DA UND KJ YQYKWJZ KZ.

—Henry George

Puzzle #90

XMMNGIXFNWLO XGV YNPV

AGVODGNAFNWLO MWG DVGFXNL

XOAVDFO WM EWJGOVYM EWJ UXLF

FW DBXLHV.

—Jerry Fankhauser

Puzzle #91

XRJALI UM FGMA AQJ JEUBJVDJ RH

WUHJ. UH IRGL WUHJ UM TGLVUVN,

CJWW, XRJALI UM FGMA AQJ ZMQ.

—Leonard Cohen

Puzzle #92

HTL FBHIVN QL KIFS MF GMALZIV JT

GBHHFJTD HTL'F XVLMFIALF MF JT

MOHJNJTD GMVMWJSJLF.

—Chinese Proverb

Puzzle #93

VC KHNWU YGXWMVHN BGNG TVKRUJ

CHUUHBVQD NLUGT, BG FHLUE

RNHDNWK W FHKRLPGN PH YG KHNWU.

—Samuel P. Ginder

Puzzle #94

MAHX MYNHX PTH WHQTHLLHW, DAHU

HVDAHT HPD YT KY LAYQQVXK. NHX

VXJPWH PXYDAHT OYRXDTU.

—Elayne Boosler

Puzzle #95

QPFHU CGA INFKU. UF LFDN FKE

CGHEXHEO HEUAVAEUAECRL. TA CGA

IGAYY VRQLAN, EFC CGA IGAYY VHAIA.

—Ralph Charell

Puzzle #96

PNU TUPPD UBZYZJWUF ZX PNU GWBN

RGU MLFP RF RJRSWYE RF PNU FWOOD

UVPGRARERYBUF ZX PNU TZZG.

—William Feather

Puzzle #97

EVDWA UACKQBU KQFRFX VCA XWEAO,

DIW VQWFR CV LCSMJDQBU EMMWEAO

DC PW AWELIQBU QDO QBVEBLX.

—John Pierce

Puzzle #98

GCM CWSIMJG OXK NDIJ TWFM GXIWR

DJ VMWSLDLP PXXI ZWLLMSJ BDGCXQG

JMMDLP WLR.

—Fred Astaire

Puzzle #99

XPUT RGHTT WKHHTWR SZTBBTB

WKABTWZRJOTFI PAN IKZ MJFF

TBRPDFJBG P HTCZRPRJKA PB PA

TVCTHR.

—Laurence J. Peter

Puzzle #100

OP XFBELOQYJ EHX LHEOYJ
LAHXEMOYR LAX VEYMJZENX QP
YBGIXHJ, LAXY YQ LHEOY JLQNJ EL NO.

—Richard Preston

Puzzle #101

BZ EOCJZB TIJ OFOC NZBZCOM HZC
TNIS NO COXOPFOM. NZBZC NIJ DOOB
SNO COTICM HZC TNIS NO WIFO.

—Calvin Coolidge

Puzzle #102

IQCFC OL OFCXOKCHOBK VOFOHPI GD
VBXOA. FCHTPFCHOAL OL VBXOA
VOFOHPI GD OFCXOKCHOBK.

—Nathan Campbell

Puzzle #103

FNABOENW VK CUOY ABFNF UO
FVRAUBNS; KVA NWUF ZBBMF SVIA
ABHFVO IOJTVIYBY RS MHFFUVO.

—Pythagoras

Puzzle #104

BYZX SLMHYHIH MLI YM ULBGYMQ QLLG
SDWGH RCI YM KBDVYMQ IULHX VLC
ULBG PXBB.

—Josh Billings

Puzzle #105

NS DJOLOSNV HJOGBJ OC SDG DSB HYD
OWOGNGBC SDMDXQ, MKG DSB HYDW
SDMDXQ ZNS OWOGNGB.

—Chateaubriand

Puzzle #106

IQKQTX UV GQBS QB ACELQTX NHH VDJ

RIQHH UTZ PCQIZQTX FNCG YQTXB NT

VDJ YUF ZNYT.

—Ray Bradbury

Puzzle #107

MBWSVJX HVIU JBIHAFP BTBOGIVEBD

VD SVPB ZBVJX JVZZSBM IA MBWIU

ZC MGOPD.

—Eric Sevareid

Puzzle #108

WLCJKBZNB MI NQMLBZ XE KBQDLMLN;

YDPIY XE ZCPXY; IWMKK XE

TDQRYMRB; KCFB XE KCFB.

—Thomas Szasz

Puzzle #109

XPQ QCHMP ICH IHZXG INBQP CPNHBD

YHPUM UWAP QCPBN XBLP W CPNHBD

YHPU.

—John Milton

Puzzle #110

XIHGITL GFYAJ B EIG IO NBGYZAGL BTZ

HDTZX CFI FBWZ LYRNEV UDYG YA

XYLPDLG.

—Don Herold

Puzzle #111

KCXLQVXQTY QT VJXOE CE CLSQXLCLI

AOEOLCXQVE VJ LOCW OTXCXO CSVAO

KLQEBQKWOT.

—George Jean Nathan

Puzzle #112

THURZCS GJU RNP NJSU PW MOIUGZCD

IU — QS OHWIUZCD PIO NZUGHU JCT

QS WIVWZVVZCD RGHK.

—Henri Frederic Amiel

Puzzle #113

BOGWAG LH HNAOTOWX XSKLBSXT MW

UKLG DMWI, QKG HNAOTOWX XSKLBSXT

DOYA HNAOTOWX NMPAT.

—John Wilkins

Puzzle #114

ESG FQZV RGQ VFO YHQL FQ ESG EFKN

FY DFOQEXHQN HN ESG RGQ VFO

JBHQW OK ESGBG.

—Robert M. Pirsig

Puzzle #115

GK WKSQ KS WCRFT WCG QSCN XK

AKSWLRFP, KS RLGQ XK ACXJ, CX FKUT

WCG QK NLJI C XLGZFT JISTCQ.

—Robert Burton

Drop Quotes

Introduction

Your goal with drop quote puzzles is to uncover the hidden quote. The black-and-white crossword-style grid is set up for each quote, with a group of letters "hovering" above each column. Your task is to "drop" each of those letters into the appropriate square in the column below until the entire quote is revealed.

Note: All punctuation marks—commas, periods, dashes, etc.—have been removed from the quotes.

Puzzle #1

George Bernard Shaw

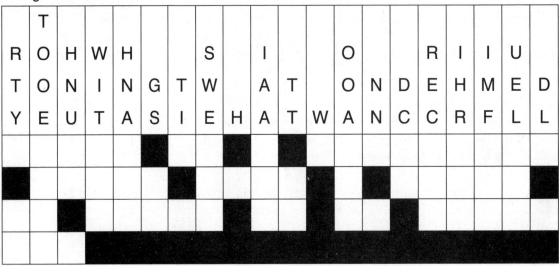

Puzzle #2

Will Rogers

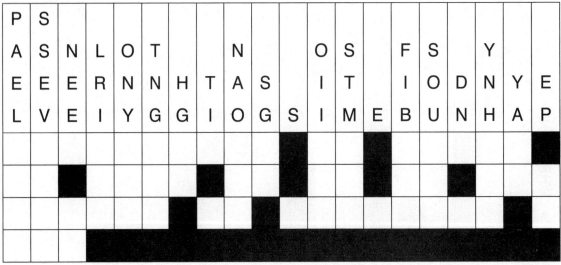

Puzzle #3

Eric Hoffer

Puzzle #4

Lily Tomlin

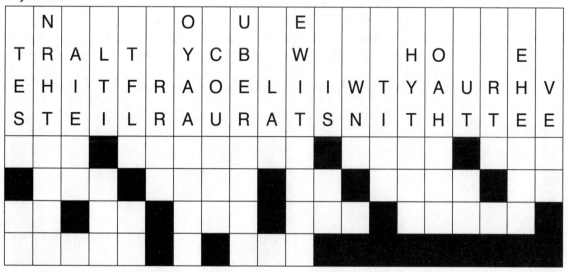

Puzzle #5

Simone Weil

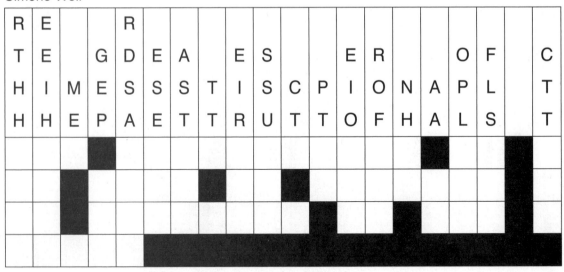

Puzzle #6

Percy Bysshe Shelley

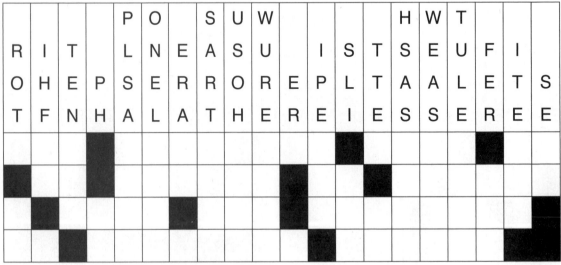

Puzzle #7

Eleanor Roosevelt

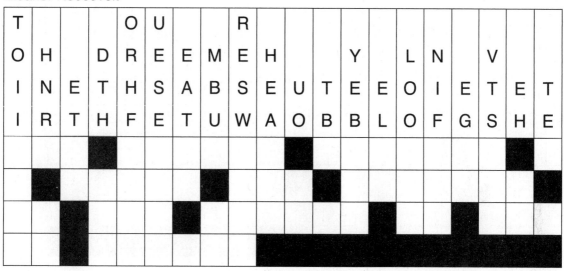

Puzzle #8

Charles Baudelaire

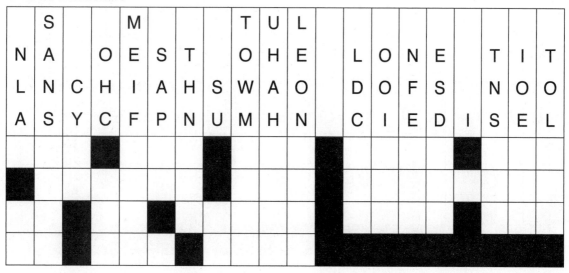

Puzzle #9

Adrian Mitchell

M	O	S		O	O	P	R	E											M
O	S	T		P	P	E	T	P	Y		I	N	A	O	S	S			M
O	S	T		P	O	E	T	L	Y		I	G	G	O	U	R	E		M
O	S	T	T	P	E	E	O	R	L	E	B	E	C	N	R	E	E		M
			■									■					■	■	■
		■									■					■	■	■	■
		■									■	■	■	■	■	■	■	■	■
		■									■	■	■	■	■	■			

Puzzle #10

Arnold Palmer

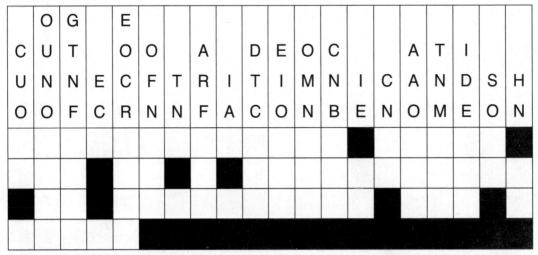

	O	G		E												A			
C	U	T		O	O		A		D	E	O	C			A	T	I		
U	N	N	E	C	F	T	R	I	T	I	M	N	I	C	A	N	D	S	H
O	O	F	C	R	N	N	F	A	C	O	N	B	E	N	O	M	E	O	N
												■						■	
		■				■		■											
■		■										■					■		
			■	■	■	■	■	■	■	■	■	■	■	■	■	■			

Puzzle #11

Mark Twain

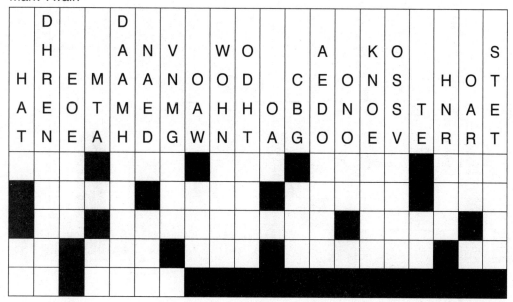

Puzzle #12

Gertrude Stein

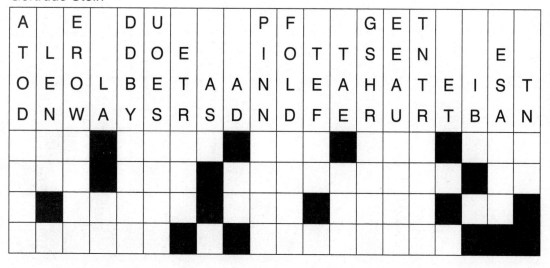

Puzzle #13

Elbert Hubbard

Puzzle #14

Knute Rockne

Puzzle #15

André Maurois

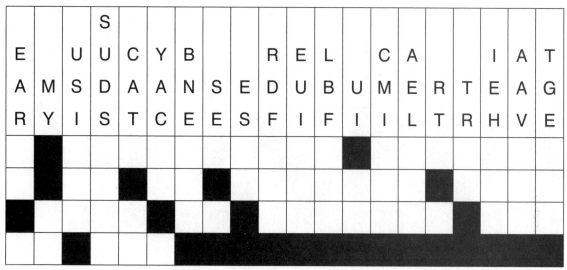

Puzzle #16

Douglas MacArthur

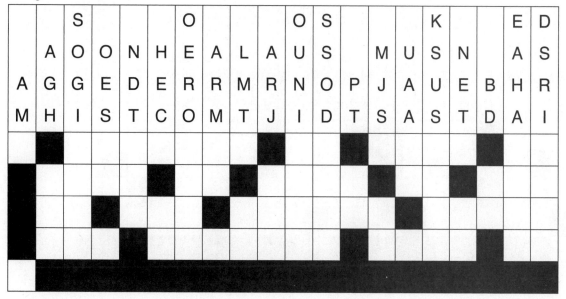

Puzzle #17

William M. Thackeray

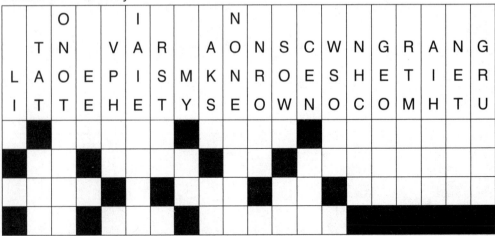

Puzzle #18

Woodrow Wilson

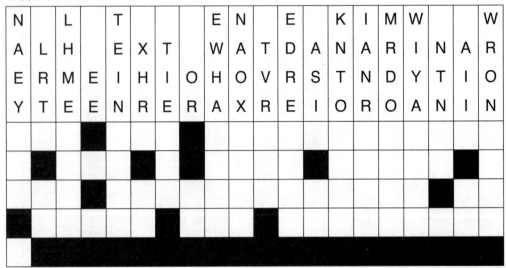

Puzzle #19

Arthur C. Clarke

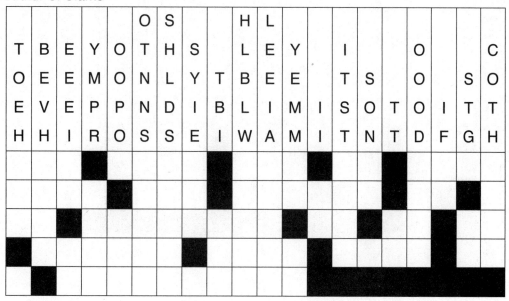

Puzzle #20

Adam Smith

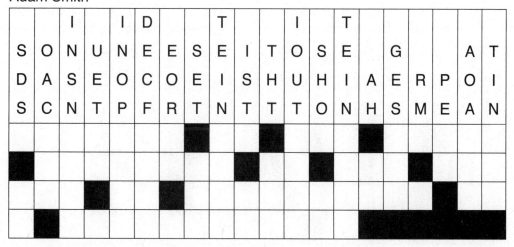

Puzzle #21

Wendell Phillips

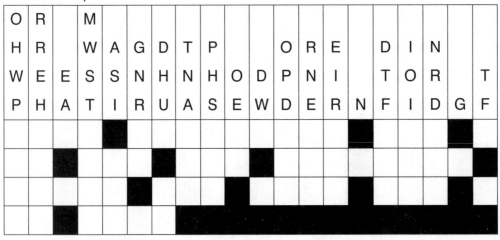

Puzzle #22

G. K. Chesterton

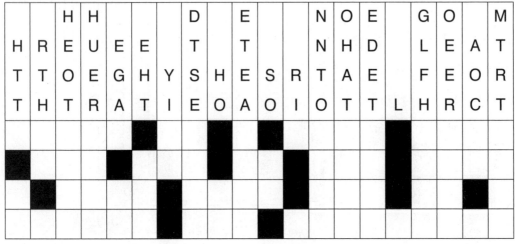

Puzzle #23

Aeschylus

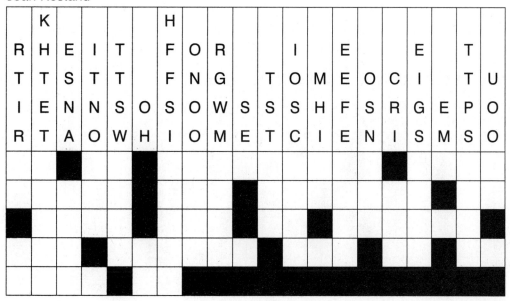

Puzzle #24

Jean Rostand

Puzzle #25

Henry Ward Beecher

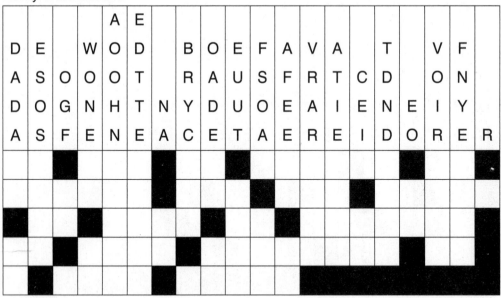

Puzzle #26

Thomas Carlyle

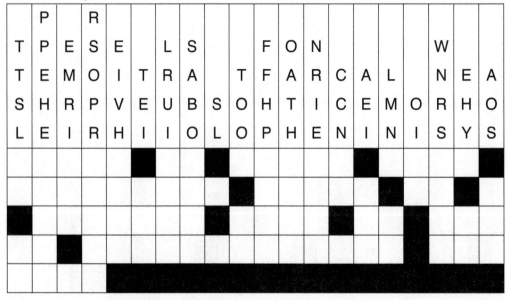

Puzzle #27

Dwight D. Eisenhower

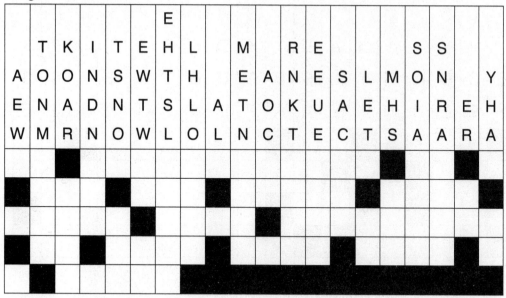

Puzzle #28

Albert von Szent-Györgyi

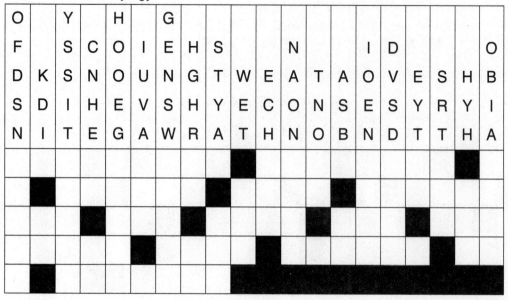

Puzzle #29

Voltaire

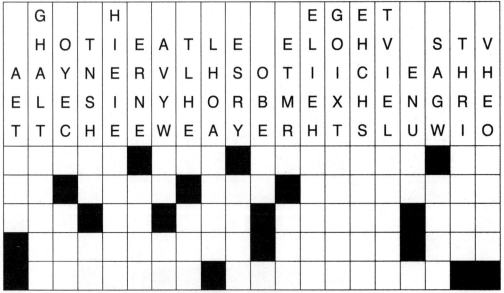

Puzzle #30

Aldous Huxley

Puzzle #31

Bill Watterson

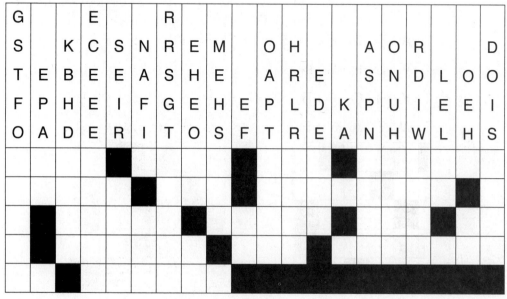

Puzzle #32

Jean-Jacques Rousseau

Puzzle #33

E. B. White

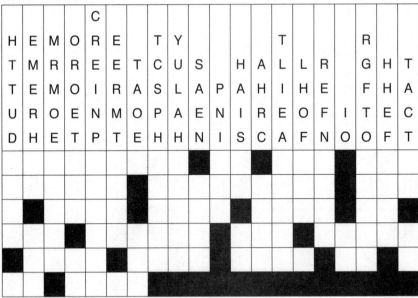

Puzzle #34

Albert Camus

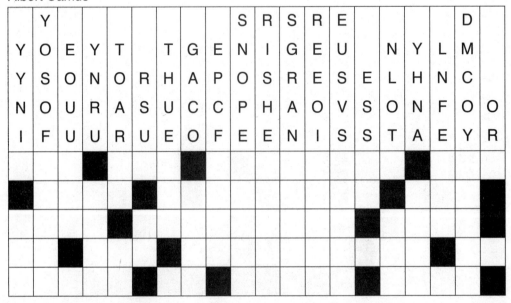

Puzzle #35

Winston Churchill

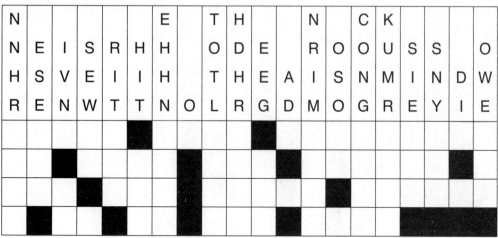

Puzzle #36

George Orwell

Puzzle #37

Blaise Pascal

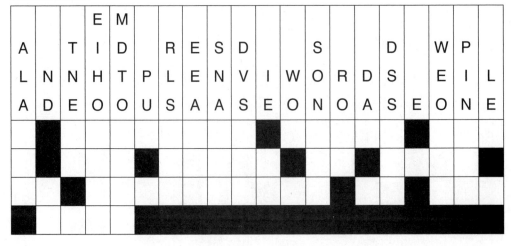

Puzzle #38

Henrik Ibsen

Puzzle #39

Josh Billings

M	E			L			S		I	E					N				
T	A	L	E	W	N	R		C	R		A	A	T			N			
G	N	N	E	I	A	S		A	I	L	C	H	E	D		T	E	O	
A	T	T	E	V	S	O	W	N	E	T	T	S	N	E	E	L	E	W	
E	R	G	T	L	E	G	A	E	D	N	H	T	A	L	B	A	H	L	I

Puzzle #40

A. A. Milne

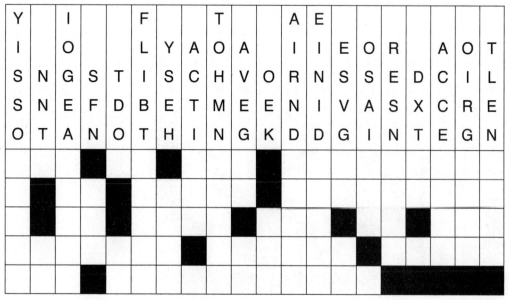

Y		I			F			T			A	E							
I		O			L	Y	A	O	A		I	I	E	O	R		A	O	T
S	N	G	S	T	I	S	C	H	V	O	R	N	S	S	D	A	C	I	L
S	N	E	F	D	B	E	T	M	E	E	N	I	S	A	E	X	C	R	E
O	T	A	N	O	T	H	I	N	G	K	D	D	G	I	N	T	E	G	N

Puzzle #41

George S. Patton

I																			
N	H	Y	O			T		L			I				S				
O	U	E	M		W	H		T		T	P	R	S	P	T	E	E	L	
W	H	T	Y		D	I	E	T	H	E	U	R	O	O	I	G	E	D	O
T	E	V	E	I	T	H	L	L	H	S	O	G	D	I	N	A	N	N	Y
T	T	E	W	R	W	O	A	T	L	I	N	E	P	R	L	E	L	H	U

Puzzle #42

Oliver Wendell Holmes Sr.

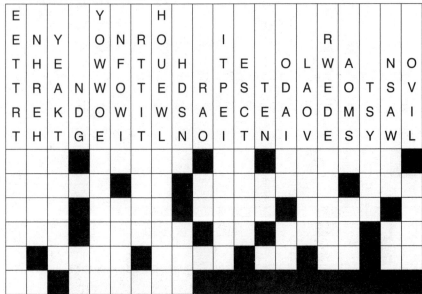

E			Y			H													
E	N	Y	O	N	R	O			I				R						
T	H	E	W	F	T	U	H		I	T	E		O	L	W	A		N	O
T	R	A	N	W	O	T	E	D	R	P	S	T	D	A	E	O	T	S	V
R	E	K	D	O	W	I	W	S	A	E	C	A	O	D	M	S	A	I	
T	H	T	G	E	I	T	L	N	O	I	T	N	I	V	E	S	Y	W	L

Puzzle #43

Benjamin Disraeli

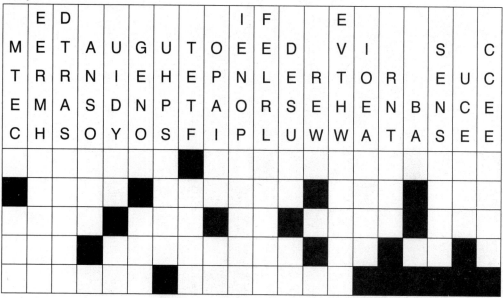

Puzzle #44

Samuel Butler

Puzzle #45

Henry Miller

	B			T	H				A	I	E								
I	F			O	M		B		T	H	E	Y		O		L	E		O
E	V	E	C	T	Y	A	C	E	O	S	L	L		S	O	D	E		I
H	E	N	D	A	H	E	Y	E	W	R	M	E		G	I	R	S	L	T
N	E	E	M	E	N	E	T	W	C	O	M	S	T	W	U	B	L	L	Y
		■				■						■			■				
			■					■					■					■	
		■				■							■					■	
			■					■					■						
■							■						■	■	■	■	■	■	■

Puzzle #46

Anatole France

I																			
T		G		A	T	R				A			L		T			A	
R		T		T	N	D			S	E	A	U	F		N			O	V
F	H	G	O	F	E	U	E	F	M	T	F	B	O	O	O		M	L	I
I	E	E	H	M	R	K	T	Y	V	E	E	U	G	R	T	O	H	E	O
E	N	P	I	V	A	S	E	U	A	T	L	U	E	H	R	F	P	T	H
	■						■					■				■			
			■					■			■					■			
	■								■							■			■
			■					■						■			■		
	■						■							■			■		
		■	■	■	■	■	■	■	■	■	■	■	■	■	■	■	■	■	■

Puzzle #47

Helen Keller

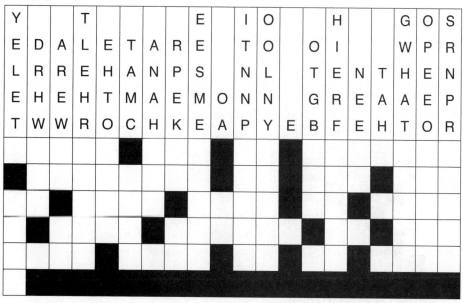

Puzzle #48

Seneca

Puzzle #49

Agnes Repplier

			S							I	I									
E	I	R	U	A		T				M	H				L	E		S	Y	
L	T	T	I	C	T	S	E			T	H	F		R	U	A		F	I	R
I	T	E	E	O	F	I	S		H	E	A	T	P	O	E	E		C	O	B
R	L	V	H	S	T	R	N	T	H	A	S	T	R	E	E	A	H	U	U	N
S	I	C	I	S	U	I	A	E	L	S	N	F	R	H	M	L	L	A	A	S

Puzzle #50

Napoleon Bonaparte

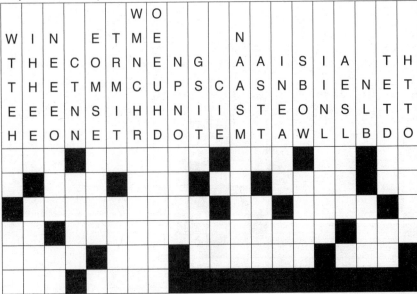

			W	O															
W	I	N		E	T	M	N		N								T		H
T	H	E	C	O	R	M	E	G	N	A	A	I	S	I	A		T		T
T	H	E	T	M	M	C	U	P	S	C	A	S	N	B	I	E	N	E	T
E	E	N	S	I	H	H	N	I	I	S	E	A	N	O	N	S	L	T	D
H	E	O	N	E	T	R	D	O	T	E	M	T	A	W	L	L	B	D	O

152   Puzzle Baron's Big Book of Puzzles

Puzzle #51

Katharine Hepburn

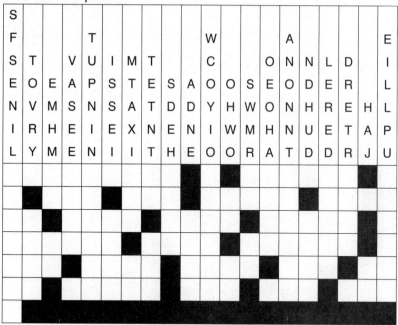

Puzzle #52

Cicero

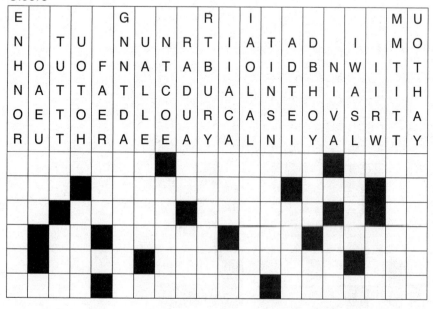

Puzzle #53

Theodore Roosevelt

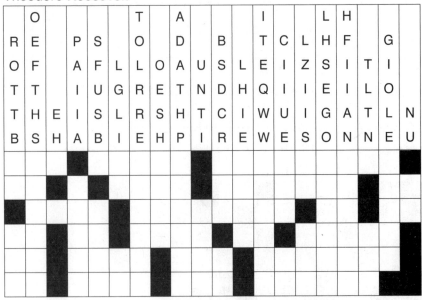

Puzzle #54

John Ruskin

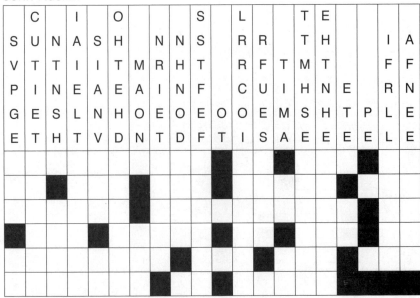

Puzzle #55

Helen Rowland

R																			
A				A			F							E	H				
O	S	G	A	N		C	I		H		E	I		T	E			O	G
C	C	M	H	S		O	C	E	A	B	T	C	O	L	H		S	A	A
I	T	O	N	A	T	M	M	N	R	E	S	W	I	W	L	E	F	E	I
A	S	C	T	O	R	C	H	E	H	R	A	H	O	M	L	E	M	P	U
L	U	C	H	T	H	O	T	H	G	I	L	C	T	T	R	I	S	T	H
S	N	S	U	T	L	A	A	N	D	I	S	O	T	T	N	E	B	T	E
	■				■				■							■			■
										■			■				■		
					■			■				■				■			
			■					■			■					■			
		■			■								■					■	
	■									■							■		
						■													
		■	■	■	■	■	■	■	■	■	■	■	■	■	■	■	■	■	■

Logic Puzzles

Introduction

Logic puzzles (also known as logic grid puzzles) require you to use logic and reasoning to deduce the relationships among different people, places, or things based on a limited number of clues. Using only the prompts provided, you must fill in the grid with X's and O's to determine the unique solution.

Always keep in mind that each item on the puzzle belongs to one and only one set. No item is ever paired with more than one item in each group.

Puzzle #1

Orangutan Sanctuary

Vikram Allindra has set up a small orangutan sanctuary in the Borneo rainforest, where injured and abandoned orangutans are cared for and eventually released back into the wild. Using only the clues provided, match each orangutan at the sanctuary with its age and handler, and determine where each animal originated.

1. Merah is 9 years older than the animal Calliope works with.

2. Rajesh is 10 years old.

3. Merah is either the animal Dolly works with or the 7-year-old.

4. Pemson is 9 years older than Beatrice's orangutan.

5. The youngest animal is named Ofallo.

6. The 13-year-old isn't cared for by Eva.

7. Merah is the oldest orangutan in the sanctuary.

		Orangutans					Handlers				
		Merah	Ofallo	Pemson	Quirrel	Rajesh	Beatrice	Calliope	Dolly	Eva	Francine
Ages	4										
	7										
	10										
	13										
	16										
Handlers	Beatrice										
	Calliope										
	Dolly										
	Eva										
	Francine										

Ages	Orangutans	Handlers
4		
7		
10		
13		
16		

Puzzle #2

Strongman Contest

It's time for this year's Strongman "Dead Lift" contest! Using only the clues here, match each contestant to his home country and the order in which he will participate, and determine the total weight (in pounds) each will lift.

1. The American won't lift 880 pounds.

2. Jeremy is either the man who will lift 920 pounds or the American.

3. Vincent is Canadian.

4. The Swede's weight will be 40 pounds heavier than Brent's, who will lift 920 pounds.

5. The Dane's weight will be 80 pounds heavier than Oliver's.

		Brent	Jeremy	Nicola	Oliver	Vincent	American	Canadian	Dane	South African	Swede
Weights	880 pounds										
	920 pounds										
	960 pounds										
	1,000 pounds										
	1,040 pounds										
Nationalities	American										
	Canadian										
	Dane										
	South African										
	Swede										

Weights	Competitors	Nationalities
880 pounds		
920 pounds		
960 pounds		
1,000 pounds		
1,040 pounds		

Puzzle #3

Rainforest Pharmaceuticals

Pravanox Pharmaceuticals has spent decades scouring the world's rainforests for new sources of medical drugs, and this year a number of these new drugs have been officially approved by the Food and Drug Administration. Using only the clues provided, match each drug to the condition it treats, the month it was approved, and the source from which its main ingredient is derived.

1. The medicine approved in March came from an extract found in palm trees. It isn't used to combat asthma.

2. The drug made from bromeliads treats either arthritis or asthma.

3. The drug that treats heart disease was approved one month before Damasol.

4. Gravon wasn't approved in April.

5. The medicine sourced from a palm tree was approved sometime after the one that treats diabetes.

6. The drug approved in January treats heart disease.

7. Of Hamzell and the diabetes drug, one was approved in January, and the other is sourced from a fig orchid.

		Drugs				Conditions				Sources			
		Damasol	Gravon	Hamzell	Pluniden	Arthritis	Asthma	Diabetes	Heart Disease	Bromeliad	Frog	Fig Orchid	Palm Tree
Months	January												
	February												
	March												
	April												
Sources	Bromeliad												
	Frog												
	Fig Orchid												
	Palm Tree												
Conditions	Arthritis												
	Asthma												
	Diabetes												
	Heart Disease												

Months	Drugs	Conditions	Sources
January			
February			
March			
April			

Puzzle #4

Sushi Rolls

Ben works at Nemo Sushi, and he needs to figure out the total bill for a number of different customers, each of whom ordered two different types of sushi rolls. Using only the clues here, match each order (two types of rolls) to its price, and determine the name of each customer.

1. Pam paid $2 less than the person who ordered the Hawaiian roll.

2. Of Nicole and whoever had the summer roll, one paid $9.50, and the other paid $13.50.

3. The Hawaiian roll and the spider roll were both in Nicole's order.

4. Whoever ordered the California roll paid $2 more than Seth.

5. The most expensive order included either the Hawaiian roll or the dragon roll, but not both. The tiger roll wasn't part of this order.

		Rolls				Rolls				Customers			
		Boston	California	Dragon	Hawaiian	Spider	Summer	Teriyaki	Tiger	Eleanor	Nicole	Pam	Seth
Prices	$9.50												
	$11.50												
	$13.50												
	$15.50												
Customers	Eleanor												
	Nicole												
	Pam												
	Seth												
Rolls	Spider												
	Summer												
	Teriyaki												
	Tiger												

Prices	Rolls	Rolls	Customers
$9.50			
$11.50			
$13.50			
$15.50			

Puzzle #5

Hotel Bookings

Help Diana sort out her next several hotel guests by matching each guest to his or her room number, home state, and length of stay.

1. Of Mrs. Quinn and the person from Utah, one will stay for four days, and the other will be in room 117.

2. Mr. Zamora's stay is somewhat longer than that of the customer from Pennsylvania, but it is one day shorter than the Utah native's reservation.

3. The client from Florida won't be in room 114.

4. Mr. Watkins will be staying in room 209.

5. Whoever is staying for five days will be in room 320.

		Guests				Rooms				States			
		Quinn	Tran	Watkins	Zamora	114	117	209	320	Florida	Hawaii	Pennsylvania	Utah
Days	2												
	3												
	4												
	5												
States	Florida												
	Hawaii												
	Pennsylvania												
	Utah												
Rooms	114												
	117												
	209												
	320												

Days	Guests	Rooms	States
2			
3			
4			
5			

Puzzle #6

Manatee Watching

Minnetonka Manatee Company sent out a number of different boats today on manatee viewing tours. Using only the clues given, match each boat to its captain and determine the total number of manatees seen by each as well as each boat's destination.

1. Captain Armstrong's group didn't go to Silver Springs.

2. Captain Preston's tour saw two more manatees than the one that went to Betty Beach, but it saw fewer manatees than the *Samantha*.

3. Of the *Benny II* (captained by Jim Jacobson) and the *Sea Cow,* one saw five manatees, and the other went to Betty Beach.

4. The *Watery Pete*, the boat that saw five manatees, and Captain Armstrong's boat are three separate vessels.

5. The group that went to Yellow Bend saw five manatees.

		Boats				Captains				Locations			
		Benny II	Samantha	Sea Cow	Watery Pete	Armstrong	Jacobson	Preston	Romero	Betty Beach	Silver Springs	Trey's Tunnel	Yellow Bend
Manatees	3												
	4												
	5												
	6												
Locations	Betty Beach												
	Silver Springs												
	Trey's Tunnel												
	Yellow Bend												
Captains	Armstrong												
	Jacobson												
	Preston												
	Romero												

Manatees	Boats	Captains	Locations
3			
4			
5			
6			

Puzzle #7

Grandkids' Birthdays

Mary has 42 different grandchildren, and it seems like barely a week goes by when she doesn't have to send out a birthday card! Help her sort out this month's cards by matching each grandchild to his or her birthday, age, and hometown.

1. The child from Thurman has his or her birthday sometime after Johanna's and four days before Nathaniel's.

2. The grandchild from Orange City has a birthday sometime after the child from West Okoboji (who isn't 6 years old).

3. Of the two birthdays on April 11 and 15, one is Nathaniel's, and the other is that of the boy or girl who lives in Thurman.

4. The 18-year-old's birthday is four days after that of the grandchild who lives in Orange City (who isn't 14 years old).

5. Isaac is either the child from Orange City or 6 years old.

				Grandchildren				Ages				Towns			
		Isaac	Johanna	Nathaniel	Sadie	6	9	14	18	Le Mars	Orange City	Thurman	West Okoboji
Birthdays	April 3												
	April 7												
	April 11												
	April 15												
Towns	Le Mars												
	Orange City												
	Thurman												
	West Okoboji												
Ages	6												
	9												
	14												
	18												

Birthdays	Grandchildren	Ages	Towns
April 3			
April 7			
April 11			
April 15			

Puzzle #8

Bridge Inspections

Mortimer Jones, a well-respected engineer, is regularly called in to do safety inspections of some of the most famous bridges all around the world. Help him prepare for his next several trips by matching each of the bridges to its length, type, and location.

1. North Bridge is in Oslo.

2. Of the bridge in Luxembourg and North Bridge, one is 13,000 feet long, and the other is the cantilever bridge.

3. The 8,500-foot bridge, North Bridge, and the one in Tallinn are three different structures.

4. The suspension bridge is 3,000 feet longer than Sandy Bridge.

5. Gorem Bridge is 10,000 feet long.

6. The truss bridge is shorter than the bridge in Luxembourg.

		Bridges				Types				Locations			
		Bay Bridge	Gorem Bridge	North Bridge	Sandy Bridge	Bowstring	Cantilever	Suspension	Truss	Luxembourg	Madrid	Oslo	Tallinn
Lengths	8,500 feet												
	10,000 feet												
	11,500 feet												
	13,000 feet												
Locations	Luxembourg												
	Madrid												
	Oslo												
	Tallinn												
Types	Bowstring												
	Cantilever												
	Suspension												
	Truss												

Lengths	Bridges	Types	Locations
8,500 feet			
10,000 feet			
11,500 feet			
13,000 feet			

Puzzle #9

Oscar Nominations

This year's Oscar nominations were announced this morning! Using only the clues provided, match each of the films to its director and total number of nominations received, and determine the genre of each.

1. *The Illusion,* the film that received two nominations, and the film directed by Maddie Mintz are in three different genres.

2. The comedy film titled *Sea of Dreams* received one fewer nomination than *The Illusion,* but it still garnered more nominations than the action film.

3. *The Illusion* is either the action film or the one that received four nominations.

4. *Maximum Risk* received two fewer nominations than the film directed by Danny Trevor.

5. The drama (which didn't get exactly four nominations), the film that received two nominations, and the film directed by Virgil Katz are three different projects.

		Movies				Directors				Genres			
		Bold Service	Maximum Risk	Sea of Dreams	The Illusion	Adrienne Day	Danny Trevor	Maddie Mintz	Virgil Katz	Action Film	Comedy	Drama	Musical
Nominations	2												
	3												
	4												
	5												
Genres	Action Film												
	Comedy												
	Drama												
	Musical												
Directors	Adrienne Day												
	Danny Trevor												
	Maddie Mintz												
	Virgil Katz												

Nominations	Movies	Directors	Genres
2			
3			
4			
5			

Puzzle #10

Superfood Smoothies

Rebecca works at Superfood Smoothies, and she's got a long line of customers waiting for their orders. Using only the clues here, match each customer to his or her order type and price.

1. Gene asked for quinoa in his smoothie. He didn't pay $7.75.

2. The person who wanted blueberries, Nellie, and whoever requested quinoa paid three different prices.

3. Of Paulette (who requested flaxseed) and Mercedes, one wanted bananas, and the other paid $8.75.

4. The four people were Nellie, Paulette, whoever requested strawberries, and the customer who paid $9.75.

5. The ginger smoothie cost $1 more than Paulette's.

	Customers				Superfoods				Fruits			
	Gene	Mercedes	Nellie	Paulette	Flaxseed	Ginger	Quinoa	Wheat Grass	Bananas	Blueberries	Raspberries	Strawberries
Prices $6.75												
$7.75												
$8.75												
$9.75												
Fruits Bananas												
Blueberries												
Raspberries												
Strawberries												
Superfoods Flaxseed												
Ginger												
Quinoa												
Wheat Grass												

Prices	Customers	Superfoods	Fruits
$6.75			
$7.75			
$8.75			
$9.75			

Puzzle #11

Vintage Pinball Machines

Curtis collects vintage pinball machines, and he's been looking at several currently for sale at his local game shop. Help him narrow down his choices by matching each pinball machine to the year it was built, the company that made it, and its current price.

1. Of Voyager Hero and the $1,750 machine, one was released in 1975, and the other was made by Hayco, Inc.

2. The $3,750 pinball machine came out sometime before the one made by Maxigame.

3. Bowling Alley was released in 1974.

4. The system produced by Waverly Toys is either the $1,500 pinball machine or Zany Circus.

5. Maxigame's pinball machine came out in 1975.

6. The machine released in 1976 costs more than $1,500.

7. The pinball game made by Hayco, Inc., came out sometime before Zany Circus.

		Machines				Companies				Prices			
		Archer Quest	Bowling Alley	Voyager Hero	Zany Circus	Dow Games	Hayco, Inc.	Maxigame	Waverly Toys	$1,500	$1,750	$3,750	$6,400
Years	1974												
	1975												
	1976												
	1977												
Prices	$1,500												
	$1,750												
	$3,750												
	$6,400												
Companies	Dow Games												
	Hayco, Inc.												
	Maxigame												
	Waverly Toys												

Years	Machines	Companies	Prices
1974			
1975			
1976			
1977			

Puzzle #12

Spelling Bee

Stride Elementary School held a spelling bee this week. Each contestant was from a different English class, and each was given a different word during the final round of the contest. Using only the clues provided, match each child to his or her English teacher, their final word, and the order in which they finished the contest.

1. The contestant whose final word was *bulwark*, the student from Mrs. Yeffer's class, and the student who finished in fourth place are three different people.

2. The word given to Mrs. Witte's student was two letters shorter than Floyd's.

3. Bessie didn't finish in second place.

4. Zachary is either the contestant from Mrs. Witte's class or the one who finished in fifth place.

5. Of Jill and the child from Mrs. Manzella's class, one had to spell *bulwark,* and the other was given the word *consommé*.

6. The word given to the fifth-place finisher was two letters longer than the one given to Mrs. Yeffer's student.

		Students				Teachers				Places			
		Bessie	Floyd	Jill	Zachary	Manzella	Steuben	Witte	Yeffer	Second	Fourth	Fifth	Sixth
Words	Anemic												
	Bulwark												
	Consommé												
	Duplicity												
Places	Second												
	Fourth												
	Fifth												
	Sixth												
Teachers	Manzella												
	Steuben												
	Witte												
	Yeffer												

Words	Students	Teachers	Places
Anemic			
Bulwark			
Consommé			
Duplicity			

Puzzle #13

Paper Airplanes

Mrs. Drammel's fifth-grade class held a paper airplane contest this afternoon. Using only the clues here, determine the color of each airplane, its maximum flight distance, and the order in which each was thrown.

1. The plane that was thrown first didn't go as far as Margo's (which wasn't the third throw).

2. Of the black plane and the one thrown second, one was Ella's, and the other went 45 feet.

3. The airplane that flew 55 feet (which wasn't green), Aaron's design, the blue plane, and the silver airplane were four different entries.

4. Valerie's design flew 10 feet shorter than the one that was thrown first.

5. Of Ella's design and the silver airplane, one went 25 feet, and the other was thrown fifth.

6. Of the green plane and the one Ella designed, one was thrown last, and the other went 25 feet.

		Students					Colors					Order				
		Aaron	Ella	Margo	Roderick	Valerie	Black	Blue	Green	Silver	Yellow	1	2	3	5	6
Distances	15 feet															
	25 feet															
	35 feet															
	45 feet															
	55 feet															
Order	1															
	2															
	3															
	5															
	6															
Colors	Black															
	Blue															
	Green															
	Silver															
	Yellow															

Distances	Students	Colors	Order
15 feet			
25 feet			
35 feet			
45 feet			
55 feet			

Puzzle #14

Shopping for Drones

Max has decided to buy a new flying drone for himself, but he hasn't quite figured out which one. Help him with the decision-making process by matching each possible drone to its price, and determine its maximum range (in feet) and total flying time per charge (in minutes).

1. The Werril 23A doesn't have a maximum range of 150 feet.

2. Of the two drones that cost $675 and $450, one has a maximum range of 100 feet, and the other is the Belhino 5.

3. The drone that costs $675 can fly for up to 15 minutes.

4. The Suzutake doesn't cost $600.

5. The $525 machine can fly for up to 30 minutes.

6. The machine that can fly for 60 minutes costs $225 more than the drone with a maximum range of 350 feet.

7. The Eldang-X costs less than the drone with a maximum range of 350 feet.

8. Of the $750 drone and the one that can fly for 20 minutes, one is the Werril 23A, and the other is the Suzutake.

9. The $600 drone doesn't have a maximum range of exactly 250 feet.

10. The Suzutake, the drone that can fly for 30 minutes, and the one with a maximum range of 150 feet are three different devices.

		Drones					Ranges					Flying Times				
		Belhino 5	Eldang-X	Motomiya	Suzutake	Werril 23A	100 feet	150 feet	250 feet	350 feet	1,000 feet	10 minutes	15 minutes	20 minutes	30 minutes	60 minutes
Prices	$450															
	$525															
	$600															
	$675															
	$750															
Flying Times	10 minutes															
	15 minutes															
	20 minutes															
	30 minutes															
	60 minutes															
Ranges	100 feet															
	150 feet															
	250 feet															
	350 feet															
	1,000 feet															

Prices	Drones	Ranges	Flying Times
$450			
$525			
$600			
$675			
$750			

Puzzle #15

Bookmobiles

Garrett County has set up a number of successful mobile libraries known as bookmobiles. Using only the clues given here, match each bookmobile to its driver and vehicle type, and determine the total number of books each offers.

1. The vehicle with 300 books, Books-4-U, and the Airstream are three different bookmobiles.

2. Ready Reader boasts 400 books.

3. Of the vehicle with 350 books and the Mack Truck, one is Lit on Wheels, and the other is driven by Terri.

4. Of the Sheryl's bookmobile and the Greyhound bus, one has 450 books and the other has 350.

5. Terri's vehicle is either Ready Reader or the one with 300 books and has more books than Jaime's bookmobile.

6. The Mack Truck has 150 more books than Explore More.

7. The Airstream has 50 more books than the one Patsy drives (which isn't the ambulance).

		Books-4-U	Explore More	Lit on Wheels	Ready Reader	Words to Go	Jaime	Kimberly	Patsy	Sheryl	Terri	Airstream	Ambulance	Greyhound Bus	Ice Cream Truck	Mack Truck
Books	250															
	300															
	350															
	400															
	450															
Vehicles	Airstream															
	Ambulance															
	Greyhound Bus															
	Ice Cream Truck															
	Mack Truck															
Drivers	Jaime															
	Kimberly															
	Patsy															
	Sheryl															
	Terri															

Books	Bookmobiles	Drivers	Vehicles
250			
300			
350			
400			
450			

Puzzle #16

Parking Violations

Sal, a newly hired police officer, has written a number of parking violations this week. Help him sort out his paperwork by matching each fine to its associated vehicle, license plate number, and state.

1. The $50 fine went to either the Grandero or the car from Mississippi.

2. The $100 fine went either to the car with the FRZ-192 plates (which was from Pennsylvania) or the car from Florida.

3. The Hornet doesn't have the RBD-337 plates.

4. The Fierro's fine was $75 cheaper than the Grandero's.

5. Of the Dartson and the car with the BMG-831 plates, one is from South Dakota, and the other is from Florida.

6. The car from Florida was given a fine that was $75 more than the one written for the Fierro.

7. The Dartson, the car that got the $25 fine, and the one with the RBD-337 plates are three different vehicles.

8. The Dartson wasn't fined $75.

9. The car from Pennsylvania was fined $25 less than the one with the MRT-628 plates.

	Cars					License Plates					States				
	Dartson	Fierro	Grandero	Hornet	Injitsu	BMG-831	FRZ-192	GGZ-007	MRT-628	RBD-337	Florida	Louisiana	Mississippi	Pennsylvania	South Dakota
$25															
$50															
$75															
$100															
$125															
Florida															
Louisiana															
Mississippi															
Pennsylvania															
South Dakota															
BMG-831															
FRZ-192															
GGZ-007															
MRT-628															
RBD-337															

Fines	Cars	License Plates	States
$25			
$50			
$75			
$100			
$125			

Puzzle #17

Nature Reserves

The Alabama Wildlife Fund has successfully lobbied to have a number of nature reserves established across the state to protect the habitats of certain endangered animals. Using only the clues provided, match each park to the year it was established and the animal that lives within it, and determine the county in which each is located.

1. Elm Park wasn't established in 2012, and it isn't in Pickens County.

2. The reserve established in 2006 isn't in Lamar County.

3. The park established in 2010 is either Riverside Glen (which is home to the sandy hare) or the one in Talladega County.

4. The reserve in Bibb County was established 4 years after the one that protects the atlas otter.

5. Of the pygmy beaver's reserve and the one in Bibb County, one was established in 2008, and the other is Howard Park.

6. The park devoted to the western gull wasn't established in 2012.

7. Of Riverside Glen and Howard Park, one is in Bibb County, and the other was established in 2010.

8. Foxtail Bend was established 4 years before Howard Park.

9. The reserve established in 2006 isn't in Pickens County.

Years	Reserves	Animals	Counties
2004			
2006			
2008			
2010			
2012			

Puzzle #18

Rugby Games

Michael has been teaching himself the basics of rugby and gone to watch a number of recent games near his hometown. Using only the clues here, match each game to its final score, date, and winning team, and determine the town in which each game was held.

1. The October 7 match didn't finish with a score of 20–13.

2. The game with the White Rhinos wasn't in Island Falls.

3. The game in Coachella was sometime before the one in Humeston.

4. Of the two games that ended with scores of 20–13 and 34–7, one was held on October 15, and the other was in Humeston.

5. The game with the Eagles wasn't on October 11.

6. The White Rhinos game wasn't on October 15.

7. The game that finished with a score of 13–9 was held 8 days after the match with the Dragons, but not in Edinburg.

8. Of the two games held on October 3 and October 19, one was with the Dragons, and the other was held in Avila Beach.

9. The game in Avila Beach ended with a score of either 24–21 or 13–9.

10. The game with the Tuscanos was on October 19.

	Teams					Scores					Towns				
	Dragons	Eagles	Rams	Tuscanos	White Rhinos	13–9	20–13	24–21	28–10	34–7	Avila Beach	Coachella	Edinburg	Humeston	Island Falls
October 3															
October 7															
October 11															
October 15															
October 19															
Avila Beach															
Coachella															
Edinburg															
Humeston															
Island Falls															
13–9															
20–13															
24–21															
28–10															
34–7															

Dates	Teams	Scores	Towns
October 3			
October 7			
October 11			
October 15			
October 19			

Puzzle #19

Legal Eagles

Samantha works to help recent law-school graduates find jobs in the legal industry. Using only the clues here, match each of her latest placements to the date they were hired and the name of the law firm that hired them, as well as the law school from which they graduated.

1. Abel was hired by Barr & Cobb.

2. Ingram & Kemp didn't hire anyone on March 12.

3. Of Rosalie and the person hired on March 15, one graduated from Northridge College, and the other was accepted to the Barr & Cobb firm.

4. Kelvin was hired by Haynes, Inc., but not on March 18.

5. The Rutherford College graduate was hired sometime after Kelvin.

6. The Faraday College graduate was hired 3 days after Gabriel but sometime before Kelvin.

7. Gabriel didn't graduate from Summit College.

8. Rosalie was hired sometime before the person hired by Leach & Mccall.

		Names					Law Firms					Colleges				
		Abel	Gabriel	Kelvin	Rosalie	Zachary	Barr & Cobb	Haynes, Inc.	Ingram & Kemp	Leach & Mccall	Velez & York	Faraday	Northridge	Riverview	Rutherford	Summit
Dates	March 12															
	March 15															
	March 18															
	March 21															
	March 24															
Colleges	Faraday															
	Northridge															
	Riverview															
	Rutherford															
	Summit															
Law Firms	Barr & Cobb															
	Haynes, Inc.															
	Ingram & Kemp															
	Leach & Mccall															
	Velez & York															

Dates	Names	Law Firms	Colleges
March 12			
March 15			
March 18			
March 21			
March 24			

Puzzle #20

Paintball League

The Gerber County Paintball League has just completed its tenth season. Help the league secretary finalize this year's standings by matching each team to its color, hometown, and final ranking.

1. The purple team is ranked one spot behind the orange team.

2. The team from Armona doesn't use orange paintballs.

3. Of the team that finished third and the one from Yucca Valley, one is the Splat Squad, and the other uses white paintballs.

4. The Oil Crew is from Libertyville.

5. The group from Libertyville, the team that finished fifth, and the Splat Squad are three different teams.

6. The Pea Shooters aren't from Evansdale.

7. The yellow team is ranked first, ahead of the squad from Forest City.

8. The Oil Crew is ranked somewhere behind the orange team.

9. The five teams are the Night Ninjas; the group from Yucca Valley; and the three teams ranked first, fourth, and fifth.

		Teams					Colors					Hometowns				
		Night Ninjas	Oil Crew	Pea Shooters	Splat Squad	Target Bombs	Green	Orange	Purple	White	Yellow	Armona	Evansdale	Forest City	Libertyville	Yucca Valley
Rankings	First															
	Second															
	Third															
	Fourth															
	Fifth															
Hometowns	Armona															
	Evansdale															
	Forest City															
	Libertyville															
	Yucca Valley															
Colors	Green															
	Orange															
	Purple															
	White															
	Yellow															

Rankings	Teams	Colors	Hometowns
First			
Second			
Third			
Fourth			
Fifth			

Puzzle #21

Angie's Birthday

A bunch of Angie's friends threw her a surprise party this evening. Using only the clues shared, determine what each friend brought, what time they arrived, and what town they came from.

1. Whoever arrived at 4:40 pm brought the potato chips.

2. Grant didn't arrive at 4:45 pm.

3. Of the two people from Fairfield and El Segundo, one brought the pork rinds, and the other is Eunice.

4. Of the friend from Pine Valley and Julie, one arrived at 4:50 pm, and the other brought the hummus.

5. Julie arrived 10 minutes before the person from Martensdale (who brought the soda).

6. The partygoer from El Segundo didn't bring the potato chips.

7. Sergio is either the person who brought the onion dip or the one who arrived at 4:40 pm.

		Eunice	Grant	Julie	Nelson	Sergio	Hummus	Onion Dip	Pork Rinds	Potato Chips	Soda	El Segundo	Fairfield	Kernville	Martensdale	Pine Valley
Times	4:30 pm															
	4:35 pm															
	4:40 pm															
	4:45 pm															
	4:50 pm															
Towns	El Segundo															
	Fairfield															
	Kernville															
	Martensdale															
	Pine Valley															
Brought	Hummus															
	Onion Dip															
	Pork Rinds															
	Potato Chips															
	Soda															

Times	Friends	Brought	Towns
4:30 pm			
4:35 pm			
4:40 pm			
4:45 pm			
4:50 pm			

Puzzle #22

Skee-Ball Superstars

Buckner's Boardwalk held a Skee-Ball contest this weekend. Using only the clues given, determine each player's final score and the lane they played in, along with their hometown.

1. Of the person who scored 300 points and the player in lane 3, one was Esther, and the other was from Elk Grove.

2. Hope wasn't from Bristol.

3. The contestant in lane 4 scored 620 points.

4. Whoever played in lane 2 finished with 460 points.

5. Zachary scored fewer points than the person from Pacific Grove.

6. The person in lane 1 scored 80 more points than Esther.

7. Hope scored 80 more points than the contestant from Cutler.

8. Of Alberta and the person in lane 6, one scored 300 points and the other 380.

9. The player from Cutler scored 80 more points than the Fort Kent native.

		Alberta	Esther	Hope	Irma	Zachary	1	2	3	4	6	Bristol	Cutler	Elk Grove	Fort Kent	Pacific Grove
Scores	300															
	380															
	460															
	540															
	620															
Towns	Bristol															
	Cutler															
	Elk Grove															
	Fort Kent															
	Pacific Grove															
Lanes	1															
	2															
	3															
	4															
	6															

Scores	Players	Lanes	Towns
300			
380			
460			
540			
620			

Puzzle #23

Crop Duster

Michael Matry owns a small crop-dusting business. Local farmers from all over Karab County regularly hire him to spray their crops with fertilizers or pesticides. Using only the clues here, match each of Michael's jobs this week to the correct farm and town, and determine the type of each farmer's crop.

1. The farm that grows spinach is either the one Michael will dust on June 6 or the one in Kent.

2. Blackwater (which is scheduled for June 7) will be sprayed sometime after the farm in Kent, which will be dusted one day before the one in Meadowgrove.

3. The cucumber farm, which isn't in Kent, won't be dusted on June 8.

4. The farm in George is either the one that grows potatoes or the one scheduled for June 7.

5. The crops in Latimer will be dusted sometime before the spinach field.

6. Of the potato farm and the one in Big Bear Lake, one will be dusted on June 5, and the other is Lone Oak.

7. Lone Oak doesn't grow alfalfa.

8. Tall Pines will be sprayed one day before the location in Latimer.

9. Hanford farm isn't scheduled for June 8.

		Farms					Towns					Crops				
		Blackwater	Hazelwood	Lone Oak	Meadowgrove	Tall Pines	Big Bear Lake	George	Hanford	Kent	Latimer	Alfalfa	Beets	Cucumbers	Potatoes	Spinach
Days	June 4															
	June 5															
	June 6															
	June 7															
	June 8															
Crops	Alfalfa															
	Beets															
	Cucumbers															
	Potatoes															
	Spinach															
Towns	Big Bear Lake															
	George															
	Hanford															
	Kent															
	Latimer															

Days	Farms	Towns	Crops
June 4			
June 5			
June 6			
June 7			
June 8			

Puzzle #24

The Poker Game

A small group of people meets on the first Friday of every month for a friendly game of poker. Tonight each person in the game won one hand each. Using only the clues here, match each player to his or her winning hand and determine the total amount of money won in each pot.

1. Of Omar and the winner of the second hand, one won the $9.00 pot, and the other ran the table with a full house.

2. The third hand didn't have the $18.25 pot.

3. The $23.25 pot went to either Jana or the person who won with a flush.

4. Kelley's winning hand was immediately before the one with a full house.

5. Salvador didn't have any flushes tonight.

6. The hand that was won with just one pair was three games before Kelley's winning hand and one hand before Guillermo's.

7. The $9.00 pot wasn't won with a straight.

8. Salvador didn't win either the first or fourth hands.

9. The first hand, the one with the $23.25 pot, and the one won with the straight were three different hands.

10. Omar's winning hand earned him more than $6 but not $18.25.

		Guillermo	Jana	Kelley	Omar	Salvador	One Pair	Full House	Flush	Straight	Straight Flush	$5.25	$6.50	$9.00	$18.25	$23.25
Hands	First															
	Second															
	Third															
	Fourth															
	Fifth															
Pots	$5.25															
	$6.50															
	$9.00															
	$18.25															
	$23.25															
Hands	One Pair															
	Full House															
	Flush															
	Straight															
	Straight Flush															

Hands	Players	Hands	Pots
First			
Second			
Third			
Fourth			
Fifth			

Puzzle #25

Reunion King

A 20-year reunion took place at Applebury High School this evening, and votes were taken on who would be crowned King of the Reunion. Using only the clues given, match each contestant to the sport he played in high school, the number of votes he received, and his current occupation.

1. Of the waiter and the person who got 32 votes, one is Marco, and the other played soccer.

2. The doctor received 14 fewer votes than Eduardo.

3. Of the lacrosse player and the dentist, one was Guillermo, and the other received 4 votes.

4. The hockey player is either the doctor or the contestant who got 25 votes.

5. The person who got 32 votes, Guillermo, and the soccer player are three different people.

6. Guillermo has never played basketball.

7. Of Wesley and the garbage man, one received 32 votes and the other 25.

		Contestants					Sports					Occupations				
		Eduardo	Guillermo	Marco	Nathaniel	Wesley	Basketball	Football	Hockey	Lacrosse	Soccer	Dentist	Doctor	Garbage Man	Lawyer	Waiter
Votes	4															
	11															
	18															
	25															
	32															
Occupations	Dentist															
	Doctor															
	Garbage Man															
	Lawyer															
	Waiter															
Sports	Basketball															
	Football															
	Hockey															
	Lacrosse															
	Soccer															

Votes	Contestants	Sports	Occupations
4			
11			
18			
25			
32			

Puzzle #26

Zip Lines

As a reward for getting an A+ on his sixth-grade history exam, Alan's parents are taking him to a local adventure park for some high-flying zip-lining fun. The park offers several different zip lines. Using only the clues given, match each zip line (A, B, C, etc.) to its maximum height, speed, and overall length.

1. Line E goes higher than 25 feet.

2. Neither line D nor line E has a maximum height of 45 feet.

3. Of line F and the line with a maximum speed of 30 MPH, one is 40 feet tall, and the other is 650 feet long.

4. The line that tops out at 55 MPH is 50 feet shorter in length than the one that only goes up to 35 MPH.

5. Line F, the fastest zip line, and the one with a maximum height of 45 feet are three separate lines.

6. The 25-foot-tall line is 150 feet longer than the one with a maximum height of 40 feet.

7. The slowest zip line is 50 feet shorter than the one that goes up to 50 MPH.

8. The 650-foot-long line is either line E or the one that tops out at 30 feet in height.

9. The 700-foot line is neither line D nor line F.

10. Line C is 50 feet longer than line F.

		Zip Line					Heights					Max Speeds				
		Line A	Line C	Line D	Line E	Line F	25 feet	30 feet	40 feet	45 feet	55 feet	30 MPH	35 MPH	45 MPH	50 MPH	55 MPH
Lengths	650 feet															
	700 feet															
	750 feet															
	800 feet															
	850 feet															
Max Speeds	30 MPH															
	35 MPH															
	45 MPH															
	50 MPH															
	55 MPH															
Heights	25 feet															
	30 feet															
	40 feet															
	45 feet															
	55 feet															

Lengths	Zip Line	Heights	Max Speeds
650 feet			
700 feet			
750 feet			
800 feet			
850 feet			

Puzzle #27

Wedding Gifts

Ally's going to get married in a few weeks, and a bunch of her friends have gotten together to discuss what gifts they are getting her for the wedding. Using only the clues shared here, match each wedding attendee to the gift they purchased, and determine how much they paid and what town they live in.

1. The person from Sun City spent $75 less than Ora Osborne.

2. Of Mitch Mayo and whoever gave Ally the toaster, one lives in Twin Peaks and the other in Eustis.

3. The planter cost $25 less than the gift the Fruitland native purchased.

4. The Eustis attendee didn't bring the most expensive gift.

5. Kit Kelley didn't buy the Blu-ray player.

6. The laptop cost $50 more than what the person from Sun City purchased.

7. Of Mitch Mayo and whoever bought the juicer, one lives in Jonesboro, and the other spent $450.

8. The Blu-ray player cost $25 more than Ned Norris's gift.

9. The planter cost $75 less than the juicer.

		Attendees					Gifts					Towns				
		Kit Kelley	Mitch Mayo	Ned Norris	Ora Osborne	Pam Powell	Blu-ray Player	Juicer	Laptop	Planter	Toaster	Eustis	Fruitland	Jonesboro	Sun City	Twin Peaks
Prices	$400															
	$425															
	$450															
	$475															
	$500															
Towns	Eustis															
	Fruitland															
	Jonesboro															
	Sun City															
	Twin Peaks															
Gifts	Blu-ray Player															
	Juicer															
	Laptop															
	Planter															
	Toaster															

Prices	Attendees	Gifts	Towns
$400			
$425			
$450			
$475			
$500			

Puzzle #28

Antique Maps

Patterson Kelly has a number of antique maps for sale in his shop. Using only the clues provided, match each of these maps to its cartographer, subject matter, publication year, and price.

1. The $545 map was published sometime after the map of Corsica, which came out in 1731.

2. The $1,100 map was published 36 years before Muenster's.

3. Bleux's print came out sometime after 1720.

4. The $545 print is either the map of Tuscany or the one by Lafiori.

5. The most expensive map isn't of Scandinavia.

6. Jenson's map, which came out in 1785, is priced at either $250 or $1,100.

7. The Corsican map was published 18 years before the one of Scandinavia.

8. The Warsaw map came out sometime before 1770.

9. The Tuscany map was published 18 years after Waldemuller's print.

		Cartographers					Subjects					Prices				
		Bleux	Jenson	Lafiori	Muenster	Waldemuller	Corsica	Denmark	Scandinavia	Tuscany	Warsaw	$250	$545	$750	$1,100	$2,500
Years	1713															
	1731															
	1749															
	1767															
	1785															
Prices	$250															
	$545															
	$750															
	$1,100															
	$2,500															
Subjects	Corsica															
	Denmark															
	Scandinavia															
	Tuscany															
	Warsaw															

Years	Cartographers	Subjects	Prices
1713			
1731			
1749			
1767			
1785			

Puzzle #29

The Art Thief

Michael Marceau, a notorious art thief, has finally been captured! While searching his home, investigators discovered a hidden trove of long-lost paintings, each by a different famous artist. Using only the clues here, match each painting to its artist and the year in which it was painted, and determine how many years each priceless piece has been missing.

1. Of Arim Aleen's painting and the one that's been missing for 22 years, one is *Hoxley Hills,* and the other was finished in 1905.

2. Rilania's painting hasn't been missing for more than 10 years.

3. The 1897 masterpiece isn't titled *Clockwork.*

4. *Hoxley Hills* was painted sometime between 1900 and 1925.

5. Dray D'Amici didn't paint anything in 1913.

6. *Tantrum* wasn't painted by Xesobe or Rilania.

7. The five paintings are *Willow Bend,* the painting that's been missing for 19 years, the two painted in 1897 and 1929, and the piece by Arim Aleen.

8. Of Yeust's painting and the one that's been missing for 20 years, one is *Willow Bend,* and the other was finished in 1921.

9. Rilania's missing masterpiece was painted 8 years before Yeust's.

	Artists					Paintings					Years Missing				
	Arim Aleen	Dray D'Amici	Rilania	Xesobe	Yeust	Clockwork	Hoxley Hills	Orange Sky	Tantrum	Willow Bend	10	19	20	22	25
1897															
1905															
1913															
1921															
1929															
10															
19															
20															
22															
25															
Clockwork															
Hoxley Hills															
Orange Sky															
Tantrum															
Willow Bend															

Years	Artists	Paintings	Years Missing
1897			
1905			
1913			
1921			
1929			

Puzzle #30

Candlemakers

The Hominyville Craft Fair features a candle cornucopia, where several different local candle-makers are offering their top-selling candles for sale. Using only the clues here, match each candle's two fragrances to its price and candlemaker.

1. Francisco's product costs $1 less than the peach candle.

2. The fig candle is less expensive than the freesia one.

3. Terry's candles are $2 cheaper than Luke's.

4. Kari has never used vanilla in any of her products and insists that all her products cost less than $8 each.

5. The $6.50 candle is either Francisco's or the one with freesia in it.

6. The pear candle, the freesia candle, Terry's product, and the one that costs $7.50 are four different candles.

7. Luke's candle is either the one priced at $6.50 or the pear-scented one.

8. The fig candles cost more than the apple-scented ones.

9. The ginger candles aren't the most expensive.

10. Of Luke's candle and the fig-scented product, one costs $6.50, and the other contains sandalwood.

11. None of the candles combine coconut and ginger.

		Sellers					Fragrances					Fragrances				
		Courtney	Francisco	Kari	Luke	Terry	Cinnamon	Freesia	Ginger	Sandalwood	Vanilla	Apple	Coconut	Fig	Peach	Pear
Prices	$4.50															
	$5.50															
	$6.50															
	$7.50															
	$8.50															
Fragrances	Apple															
	Coconut															
	Fig															
	Peach															
	Pear															
Fragrances	Cinnamon															
	Freesia															
	Ginger															
	Sandalwood															
	Vanilla															

Prices	Sellers	Fragrances	Fragrances
$4.50			
$5.50			
$6.50			
$7.50			
$8.50			

Multimedia Ad Agency

The Donner & Donner ad agency has released a number of new ads this month for one of its top clients. Using only the clues here, match each ad type to its creative director and total budget, and determine the total number of responses each received.

1. The direct mailer was produced by Faith Fowler.

2. The campaign produced by Hal Hopkins brought in 150 fewer responses than the one with the $15,000 budget, which wasn't made by Kenneth Kirby.

3. Faith Fowler's direct mailer campaign brought in 300 more responses than the newspaper ad.

4. The campaign with the $30,000 budget is either the one with 625 responses or the newspaper ad.

5. Of the campaign with the $90,000 budget and the campaign with 625 responses, one is the radio spot, and the other was produced by Faith Fowler.

6. The campaign with the $50,000 budget (which isn't the billboard) is either the ad with 1,075 responses or the one produced by Eddie Evans.

7. Neither Kenneth Kirby nor Eddie Evans worked on the radio spot.

8. The magazine ad has brought in 925 responses.

		Ad Type					Directors					Budgets				
	Billboard	Direct Mailer	Magazine Ad	Newspaper Ad	Radio Spot	Eddie Evans	Faith Fowler	Hal Hopkins	Julie Jordan	Kenneth Kirby	$15,000	$20,000	$30,000	$50,000	$90,000
Responses 625															
775															
925															
1,075															
1,225															
Budgets $15,000											
$20,000											
$30,000											
$50,000											
$90,000											
Directors Eddie Evans											
Faith Fowler											
Hal Hopkins											
Julie Jordan											
Kenneth Kirby											

Responses	Ad Type	Directors	Budgets
625			
775			
925			
1,075			
1,225			

Puzzle #32

Tech Startups

Angel Investors, Inc., regularly makes million-dollar investments in up-and-coming tech startup companies. Using only the clues provided, match its latest investments to each company, and determine the founder and product focus of each.

1. Madinkz.com, which was started by Fred Frost, received $1,000,000.

2. The five businesses are the one that received the $4,000,000 investment, Byxby.com, the camera retailer, Madinkz.com, and the one started by Vicky Velez.

3. The robot startup is either the one started by Betty Becker or Zetafish.com.

4. Madinkz.com received $1,000,000 less than the business that sells video games.

5. The startup that received the $4,000,000 investment wasn't founded by Addie Abrams.

6. Of the business that sells cameras and the startup that received the $4,000,000 investment, one is Zetafish.com, and the other was started by Pat Padilla.

7. Of the startup started by Addie Abrams and Pritecha.com, one sells sports gear, and the other received $5,000,000.

Investments	Startups	Founders	Products
$1,000,000			
$2,000,000			
$3,000,000			
$4,000,000			
$5,000,000			

Puzzle #33

Astronaut Missions

A fresh group of astronaut candidates has just completed training, and NASA has assigned each of them their first official launch mission. Using only the clues here, match each astronaut to his or her mission and launch date, and determine the research subject they will be focused on.

1. Mercedes won't be on mission GX-13.

2. The plant enzyme study, which isn't Wade's mission, will launch sometime before WB-664.

3. Neither Mercedes nor Wade will study gamma rays.

4. The radiation study will launch 2 months before ZF-15.

5. Mission CR-260 launches in January.

6. The plant enzymes study will launch 1 month after the radiation mission (which isn't Wade's focus) and 1 month before Francis's mission.

7. Of the April and May missions, one is ZF-15, and the other will be a study of gamma rays.

8. The solar storm mission is either WB-664 or the one launching in January.

9. Mission TV-412 won't launch in March.

10. Rose's mission isn't launching in May.

	Astronauts					Missions					Subjects				
	Francis	Katherine	Mercedes	Rose	Wade	CR-260	GX-13	TV-412	WB-664	ZF-15	Ant Colonies	Gamma Rays	Plant Enzymes	Radiation	Solar Storms
January															
February															
March															
April															
May															
Ant Colonies															
Gamma Rays															
Plant Enzymes															
Radiation															
Solar Storms															
CR-260															
GX-13															
TV-412															
WB-664															
ZF-15															

Months	Astronauts	Missions	Subjects
January			
February			
March			
April			
May			

Puzzle #34

Dutch Windmills

The Dutch are famous for their windmills, many of which have now been converted into homes. Julie is researching several for her upcoming trip. Help her with her research by matching each of these windmills to their current owner, town, and the date they were built.

1. The five windmills are the one built in 1706, Doesmolen, Grosmolen, and the two owned by the Smit and Van Den Berg families.

2. The Van Den Berg windmill was built 46 years after Grosmolen.

3. The Visser's home wasn't built in 1706.

4. The windmill in Moerkapelle isn't owned by the Bakker family.

5. The structure in Aarlanderveen was built 46 years before Zemelmolen.

6. Doesmolen was built sometime after the Smit family's mill.

7. Grosmolen isn't owned by the Bakker family.

8. Of the mill in Leiderdorp and the Smit family's home, one is Vlietmolen, and the other was built in 1775.

9. The Moerkapelle mill isn't owned by the Smit family.

10. Doesmolen is either the home in Schiedam or the one owned by the Smit family.

		Windmills					Families					Towns				
		Doesmolen	Grosmolen	Oostmolen	Vlietmolen	Zemelmolen	Bakker	De Vries	Smit	Van Den Berg	Visser	Aarlanderveen	Den Bommel	Leiderdorp	Moerkapelle	Schiedam
Years	1683															
	1706															
	1729															
	1752															
	1775															
Towns	Aarlanderveen															
	Den Bommel															
	Leiderdorp															
	Moerkapelle															
	Schiedam															
Families	Bakker															
	De Vries															
	Smit															
	Van Den Berg															
	Visser															

Years	Windmills	Families	Towns
1683			
1706			
1729			
1752			
1775			

Puzzle #35

Honey Shop

Beverly Beatrix runs The Honey Shop, a specialty store that sells a wide variety of locally produced honeys. Using only the clues here, match each item in her inventory to its price per jar, nectar source, local provider, and the town from which it is sourced.

1. The honey made in Fowler costs $1 more than the basswood honey, which costs $2 less than the honey made in Kellerton.

2. The clover honey costs $1 less than the lemon blossom honey.

3. Of Midge Mintz's product and the one that costs $7.50, one comes from Unity, and the other is made from lemon blossom nectar.

4. The alfalfa honey, the one that sells for $7.50, and Heddy Heath's honey are three different products.

5. Linda Lynn charges less than $9 for her product.

6. Heddy Heath's honey costs more than Midge Mintz's.

7. The honey from Troy is either the honey made from lemon blossom nectar or Jim Joyner's product.

8. The Nevada honey costs $1 more than the sage honey.

	Nectars					Providers					Towns				
	Alfalfa	Basswood	Clover	Lemon Blossom	Sage	Heddy Heath	Jim Joyner	Linda Lynn	Midge Mintz	Nick Norris	Fowler	Kellerton	Nevada	Troy	Unity
$5.50															
$6.50															
$7.50															
$8.50															
$9.50															
Fowler															
Kellerton															
Nevada															
Troy															
Unity															
Heddy Heath															
Jim Joyner															
Linda Lynn															
Midge Mintz															
Nick Norris															

Prices	Nectars	Providers	Towns
$5.50			
$6.50			
$7.50			
$8.50			
$9.50			

Puzzle #36

Mathematics Textbooks

Kendra works at the local college bookstore, and she needs to sort out the Mathematics textbooks. Help her with her task by matching each book's author to its subject and price, and determine the year in which each was published.

1. The Set Theory book is either the one that sells for $24.99 book or the one published in 2007.

2. Steve Spark has never written an Algebra book.

3. The 2010 book costs $10 less than the Algebra textbook.

4. Pat Peterson didn't have any of his books published in 2005.

5. The Set Theory textbook costs $5 more than the Trigonometry book.

6. The $29.99 book is either the one published in 2015 or the Pre-Calculus title.

7. Mina Morton's book is either the one priced at $29.99 or the Trigonometry book.

8. Of the Calculus book and the one released in 2008, one costs $24.99, and the other was written by Steve Spark.

9. The book written by Tara Tyne costs $15 less than the one published in 2015.

		Fields					Authors					Years				
		Algebra	Calculus	Pre-Calculus	Set Theory	Trigonometry	Mina Morton	Pat Peterson	Steve Spark	Tara Tyne	Velma Vintz	2005	2007	2008	2010	2015
Prices	$24.99															
	$29.99															
	$34.99															
	$39.99															
	$44.99															
Years	2005															
	2007															
	2008															
	2010															
	2015															
Authors	Mina Morton															
	Pat Peterson															
	Steve Spark															
	Tara Tyne															
	Velma Vintz															

Prices	Fields	Authors	Years
$24.99			
$29.99			
$34.99			
$39.99			
$44.99			

Puzzle #37

Supreme Court Cases

Sandra is compiling an article on some of the most recent Supreme Court decisions. Help her with her research by matching each case to its date, and determine the final decision (yes votes and no votes) as well as the name of the justice who wrote the majority opinion.

1. Justice Hatfield didn't write the majority opinion on *Ayers* v. *Byrd*.

2. *Short* v. *Metz* took place 1 week after the 7–2 decision.

3. *Watts* v. *Yang* was heard sometime after the case in which Justice Quinn wrote the majority opinion, and 1 week before the case in which Justice Hatfield wrote the majority opinion.

4. The 7–2 decision was either *Ayers* v. *Byrd* or *Zamora* v. *Pibb*.

5. The 5–4 decision took place 2 weeks after the 4–5 decision.

6. Of the case in which Justice Caldwell wrote the majority opinion and *Zamora* v. *Pibb*, one was the 2–7 decision, and the other was heard on March 31.

7. *Watts* v. *Yang* was heard sometime before *Ayers* v. *Byrd*.

8. Justice Larson didn't write the majority opinion for the March 10 case.

	Cases					Decisions					Justices				
	Ayers v. Byrd	Carson v. Dunn	Short v. Metz	Watts v. Yang	Zamora v. Pibb	2–7	3–6	4–5	5–4	7–2	Caldwell	Hatfield	Larson	Olson	Quinn
March 3															
March 10															
March 17															
March 24															
March 31															
Caldwell															
Hatfield															
Larson															
Olson															
Quinn															
2–7															
3–6															
4–5															
5–4															
7–2															

Dates	Cases	Decisions	Justices
March 3			
March 10			
March 17			
March 24			
March 31			

194   **Puzzle Baron's Big Book of Puzzles**

Puzzle #38

Girl Scout Badges

Today the mayor of Witleyville held a ceremony in which he awarded a number of local Girl Scouts their merit badges. Using only the clues here, determine the order in which each award was given, and match each girl to her badge and troop number.

1. Of Kendra and the girl in Troop 4031, one earned the leadership badge, and the other was awarded fourth.

2. The leadership badge was handed out sometime after the girl from Troop 4443 received her badge.

3. The girl from Troop 4781 was given her badge two spots after Wendy.

4. Of Gayle and whoever was given the first badge, one was in Troop 4443, and the other earned the dance badge.

5. The Girl Scout from Troop 5025 earned the theater badge.

6. Neither Gayle nor Kendra is in Troop 5025.

7. The ceramics badge was handed out two spots after the girl from Troop 4443 received her award.

8. Dolores didn't receive the third badge.

9. The second badge was given to either Kendra or Wendy.

		Girls					Badges					Troops				
		Dolores	Gayle	Kendra	Ollie	Wendy	Ceramics	Dance	Leadership	Swimming	Theater	3094	4031	4443	4781	5025
Orders	First															
	Second																
	Third																
	Fourth																
	Fifth																
Troops	3094																
	4031																
	4443																
	4781																
	5025																
Badges	Ceramics																
	Dance																
	Leadership																
	Swimming																
	Theater																

Orders	Girls	Badges	Troops
First			
Second			
Third			
Fourth			
Fifth			

Puzzle #39

Yoga Studio

Dave has opened a studio in downtown Boulder that offers classes in a number of different types of yoga. Using only the clues provided, match each class to its leader and scheduled time, and determine the total number of students in each.

1. Bikram yoga begins 3 hours before Teresa's Vinyasa yoga class.

2. The Ashtanga yoga class starts 2 hours after the session with 12 people.

3. Marilyn's session starts sometime after Hatha yoga.

4. The Bikram yoga class is either the class with six people or Marilyn's class.

5. The class with 9 people in it starts 2 hours after the one with 6 students.

6. Of the smallest class and the Hatha yoga class, one is led by Sandra and the other by Teresa.

7. The 11:30 am session is either Marilyn's or the class with 12 people.

8. Opal's class is either prenatal yoga or the one at 11:30 am.

		Yoga Types					Leaders					Class Sizes				
		Ashtanga	Bikram	Hatha	Prenatal	Vinyasa	Leah	Marilyn	Opal	Sandra	Teresa	5	6	9	12	14
Times	9:30am															
	10:30am															
	11:30am															
	12:30pm															
	1:30pm															
Class Sizes	5															
	6															
	9															
	12															
	14															
Leaders	Leah															
	Marilyn															
	Opal															
	Sandra															
	Teresa															

Times	Yoga Types	Leaders	Class Sizes
9:30am			
10:30am			
11:30am			
12:30pm			
1:30pm			

Puzzle #40

Backpacking Trip

Howie, a professional nature guide, is taking a group of campers on a week-long backpacking trip through the Gros Ventre Wilderness in Wyoming. Using only the clues provided, help Howie match each camper to his or her bag by determining the size (in liters), manufacturer, and color of each.

1. Of the 45-liter pack and the Pinkster, one is purple, and the other is Betty's.

2. The silver pack is 5 liters smaller than the Grennel.

3. The orange pack is 5 liters smaller than the Pinkster, which isn't gray.

4. Of the purple pack and the 30-liter backpack, one is Gene's, and the other is made by Adironda.

5. Freddie's 25-liter pack isn't made by Lugmor, and it isn't orange.

6. The five packs are the 40-liter pack, Gene's backpack, the silver pack, Salvador's pack, and the one made by Adironda.

		Names					Brands					Colors				
		Betty	Freddie	Gene	Myrna	Salvador	Adironda	Bistric	Grennel	Lugmor	Pinkster	Blue	Gray	Orange	Purple	Silver
Pack Size	25 liter															
	30 liter															
	35 liter															
	40 liter															
	45 liter															
Colors	Blue															
	Gray															
	Orange															
	Purple															
	Silver															
Brands	Adironda															
	Bistric															
	Grennel															
	Lugmor															
	Pinkster															

Pack Size	Names	Brands	Colors
25 liter			
30 liter			
35 liter			
40 liter			
45 liter			

Mathdoku

Introduction

Mathdoku puzzles are a mix between math puzzles and sudoku puzzles. You're given a partially filled-in grid, and you must enter the numbers 1 through 9 into each empty white square, using each number exactly once, so all six mathematical equations on the grid are fulfilled.

Each puzzle has one and only one unique solution, and all puzzles can be solved using only pure logical deduction.

Puzzle #1

	−		−		=	1
−		×		+		
	÷		+		=	10
+		+		+		
	×		−		=	30
=		=		=		
14		6		18		

Puzzle #2

	×		+		=	33
×		×		−		
	×		+		=	29
−		+		+		
	+		−		=	4
=		=		=		
67		18		6		

Puzzle #3

	×		−		=	2
×		×		÷		
	+		−		=	13
−		+		−		
	+		−		=	7
=		=		=		
2		76		0		

Puzzle #4

	×		+		=	45
−		÷		×		
	−		−		=	2
+		+		−		
	×		−		=	44
=		=		=		
4		12		11		

Puzzle #5

	÷		+		=	10
×		×		+		
	+		+		=	12
+		+		+		
	×		+		=	51
=		=		=		
47		10		14		

Puzzle #6

	+		−		=	7
×		×		+		
	÷		+		=	8
−		−		−		
	+		+		=	21
=		=		=		
0		1		2		

Puzzle #7

	−		+		=	8
÷		×		×		
	×		−		=	4
+		+		+		
	×		−		=	3
=		=		=		
7		29		74		

Puzzle #8

	−		+		=	5
+		+		×		
	+		−		=	4
−		−		+		
	×		−		=	51
=		=		=		
4		2		8		

Puzzle #9

	+		+		=	11
−		×		+		
	×		+		=	14
+		−		+		
	×		+		=	49
=		=		=		
4		6		16		

Puzzle #10

	×		−		=	50
−		×		+		
	×		+		=	22
−		−		−		
	+		+		=	13
=		=		=		
2		31		5		

Puzzle #11

	×		−		=	4
+		×		+		
	+		+		=	17
+		−		+		
	÷		−		=	3
=		=		=		
18		29		15		

Puzzle #12

	+		−		=	2
+		−		−		
	−		+		=	10
+		−		+		
	+		+		=	13
=		=		=		
12		5		8		

Puzzle #13

	×		+		=	22
+		×		×		
	−		−		=	1
+		+		−		
	×		+		=	37
=		=		=		
16		22		1		

Puzzle #14

	+		+		=	13
×		×		−		
	−		−		=	0
−		+		+		
	+		−		=	0
=		=		=		
17		18		10		

Puzzle #15

	×		−		=	3
+		×		−		
	+		+		=	15
+		−		−		
	−		−		=	2
=		=		=		
22		3		1		

Puzzle #16

	×		−		=	4
+		×		+		
	+		+		=	8
+		+		−		
	−		+		=	11
=		=		=		
12		11		3		

Puzzle #17

	×		−		=	11
+		+		×		
	−		+		=	1
−		−		−		
	×		+		=	21
=		=		=		
6		11		13		

Puzzle #18

	×		+		=	15
+		×		×		
	+		−		=	2
+		−		+		
	+		−		=	7
=		=		=		
12		4		43		

Puzzle #19

	×		+		=	43
+		+		×		
	+		+		=	17
−		−		+		
	+		+		=	14
=		=		=		
13		6		13		

Puzzle #20

	+		+		=	15
+		+		+		
	×		+		=	25
−		+		+		
	÷		+		=	11
=		=		=		
7		11		15		

More or Less

Introduction

In more or less puzzles, your task is to uncover the unique solution in which all greater than (>) equations are satisfied, using only the numbers 1 through n, where n is the size of the puzzle you're working on. So if you're working on a 6 × 6 puzzle, you'll use the numbers 1 through 6. In a 7 × 7 puzzle, you'll use the numbers 1 through 7, and so on.

Each number is used once and only once in each row and column. And each pair of numbers surrounding a > sign must adhere to that requirement. Every puzzle has only one solution, which can be reached using pure logic alone. The more difficult puzzles often require you to use commonly used sudoku techniques to find the solution.

Note: The absence of a > sign between any two numbers signifies nothing. It does not preclude one number from being greater than the other.

Puzzle #1

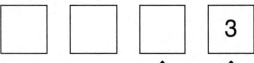
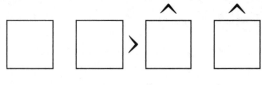
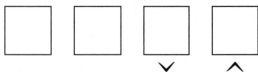
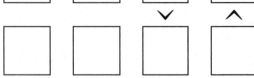

Puzzle #2

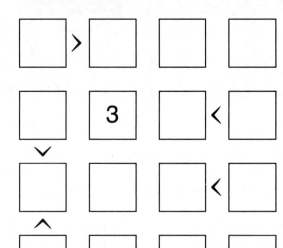

Puzzle #3

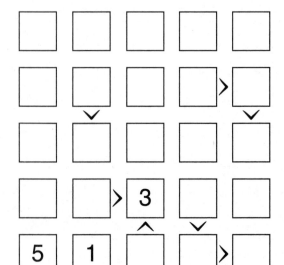

Puzzle #4

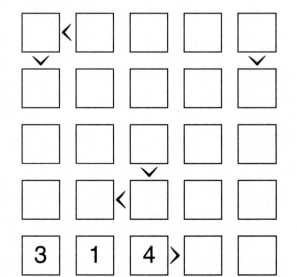

Puzzle #5

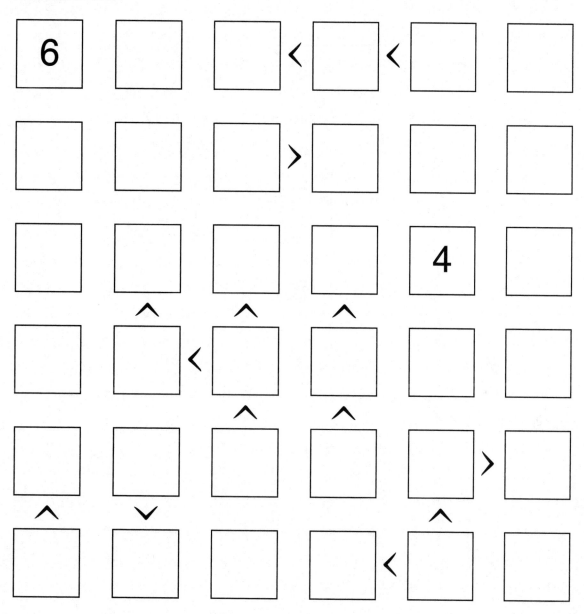

Puzzle #6

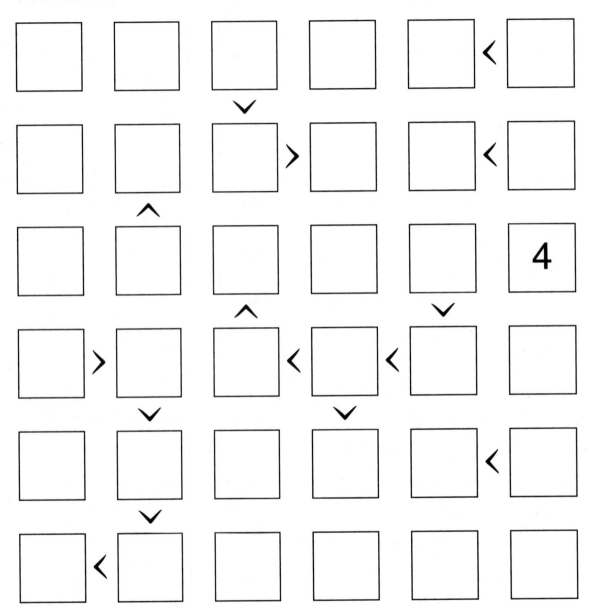

Puzzle #7

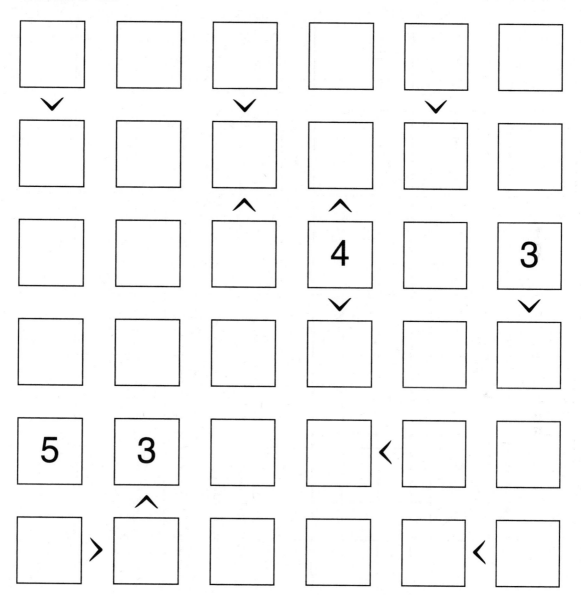

Puzzle #8

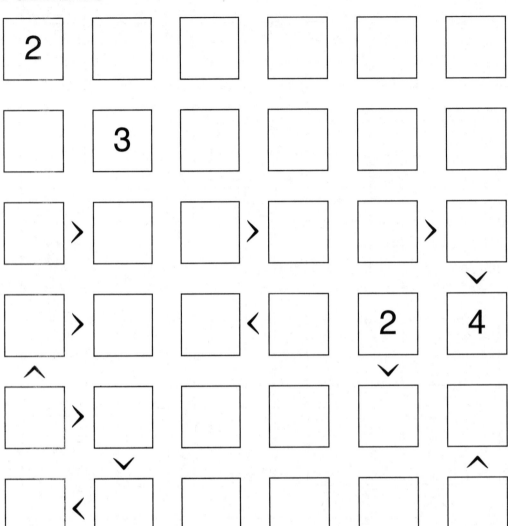

Puzzle #9

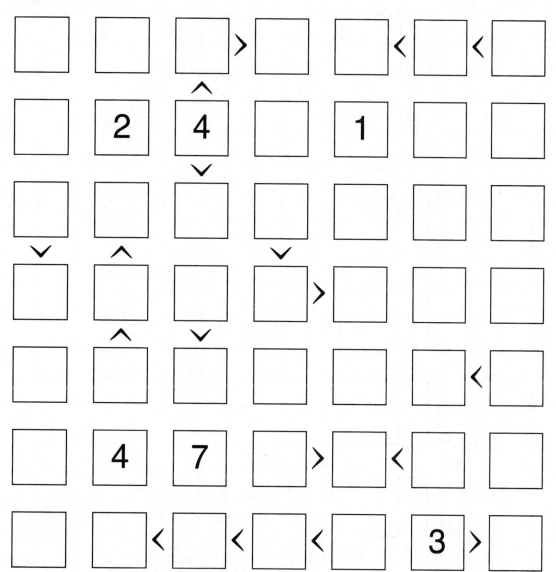

Puzzle #10

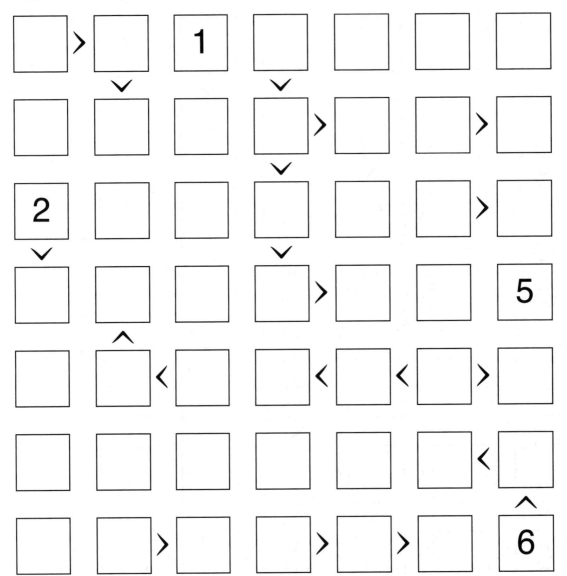

Puzzle #11

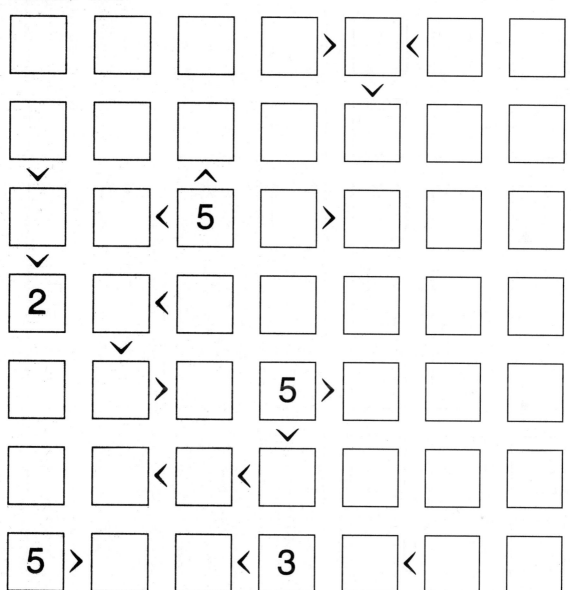

Puzzle #12

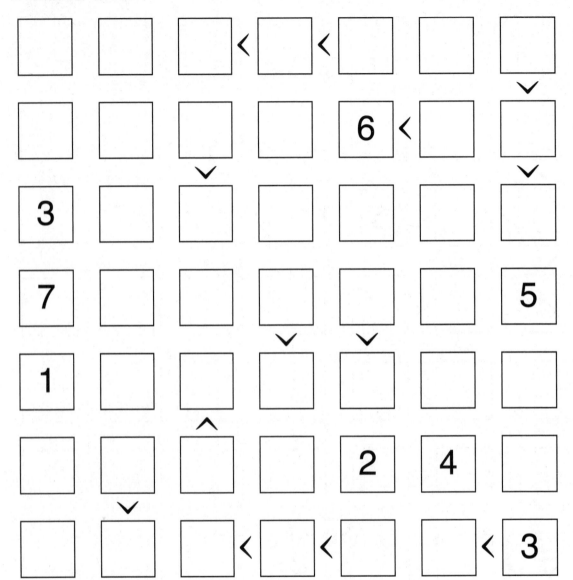

Neighbors

Introduction

In neighbor puzzles, your task is to work out the unique solution in which all "neighbor" requirements are satisfied using only the numbers 1 through *n*, where *n* is the size of the puzzle you're working on. So if you're working on a 6 × 6 puzzle, you'll use the numbers 1 through 6. In a 7 × 7 puzzle, you'll use the numbers 1 through 7, and so on.

Each number is used once and only once in each row and column. And each pair of numbers with a black bar between them must be "neighbors" on the number line—meaning one number is either one digit higher or lower than the other. For example, the neighbors of 3 are 2 and 4, and the neighbors of 5 are 4 and 6. The number 1 has only one neighbor, 2, and the highest number in any puzzle, *n*, has only one neighbor, *n* – 1.

Every puzzle has only one solution, and each solution can be reached using pure logic alone. The more difficult puzzles often require you to use commonly used sudoku techniques to find the solution.

Note: Unlike more or less puzzles, the absence of a black neighbor bar between any two numbers is significant. It means those two numbers are definitely *not* neighbors. Be sure to keep this in mind!

Puzzle #1

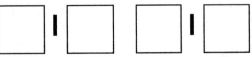
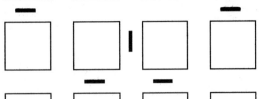

Puzzle #2

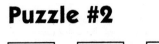
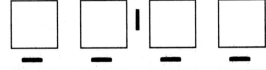
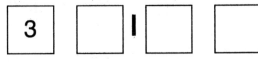
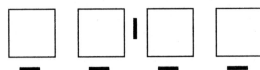
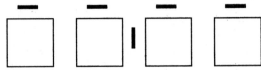

Puzzle #3

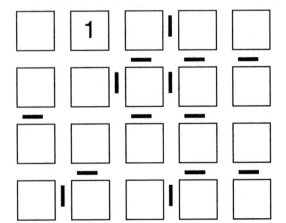

Puzzle #4

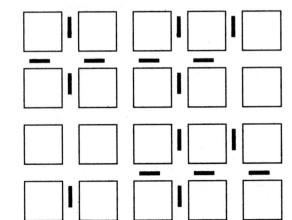

Puzzle #5

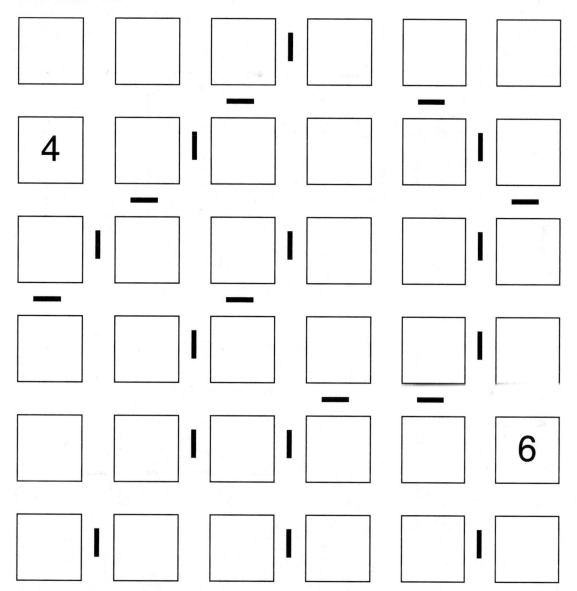

Puzzle #6

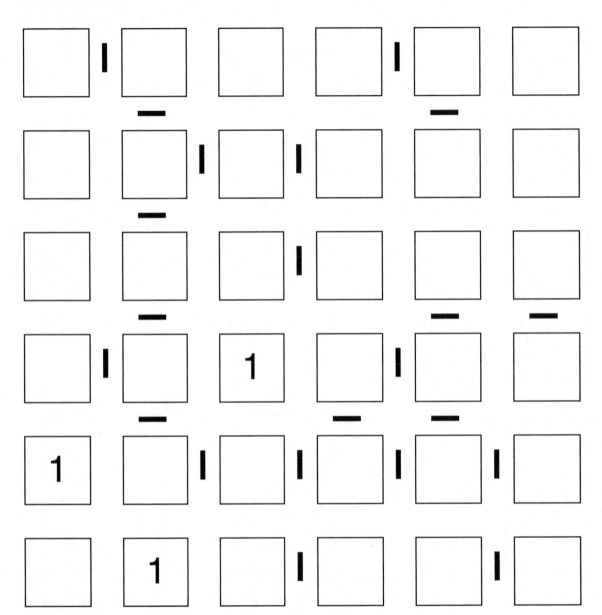

Puzzle #7

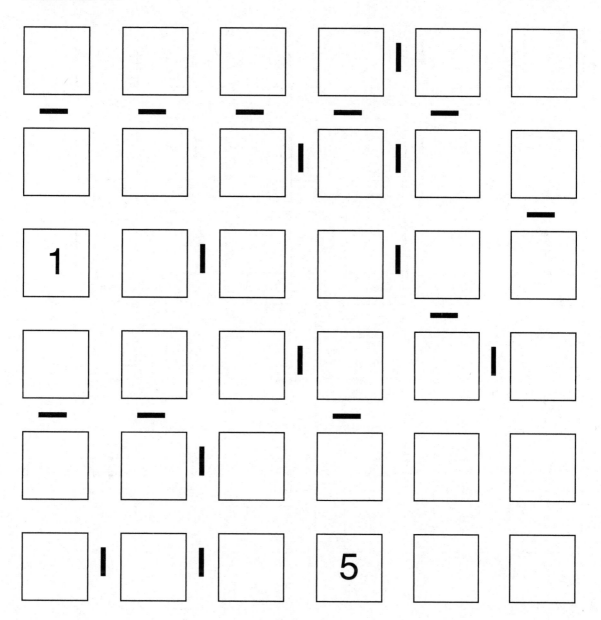

Puzzle #8

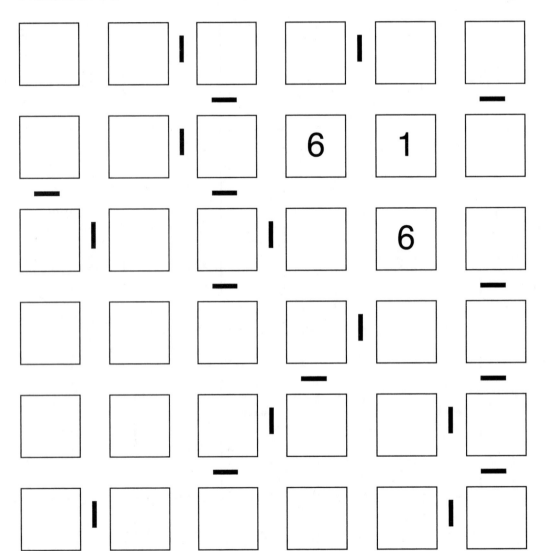

Puzzle #9

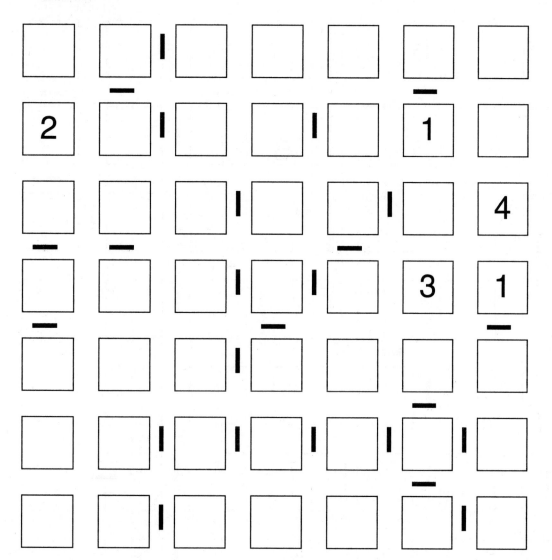

Puzzle #10

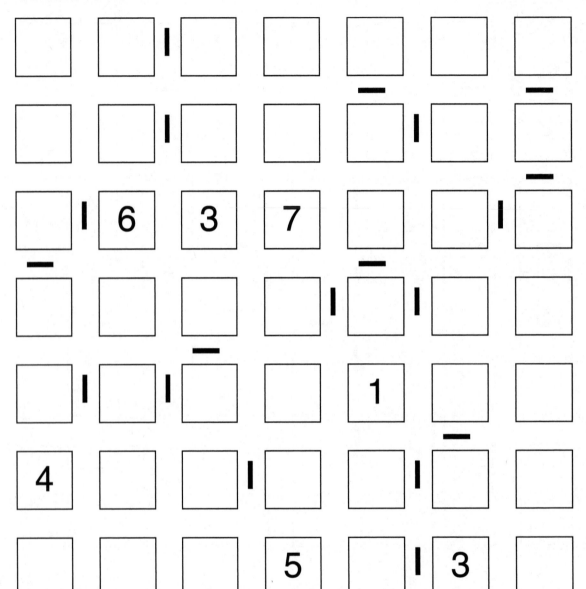

Puzzle #11

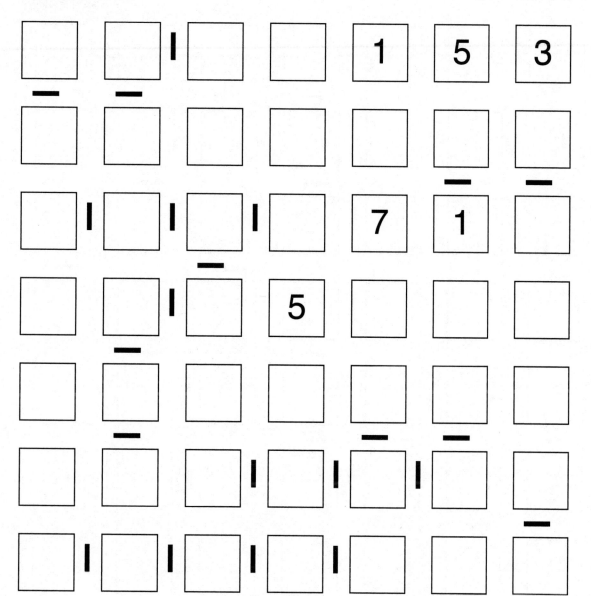

Puzzle #12

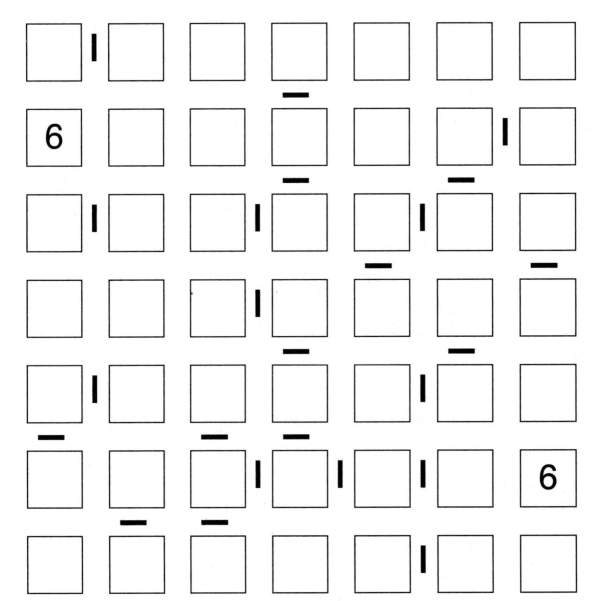

Puzzle #13

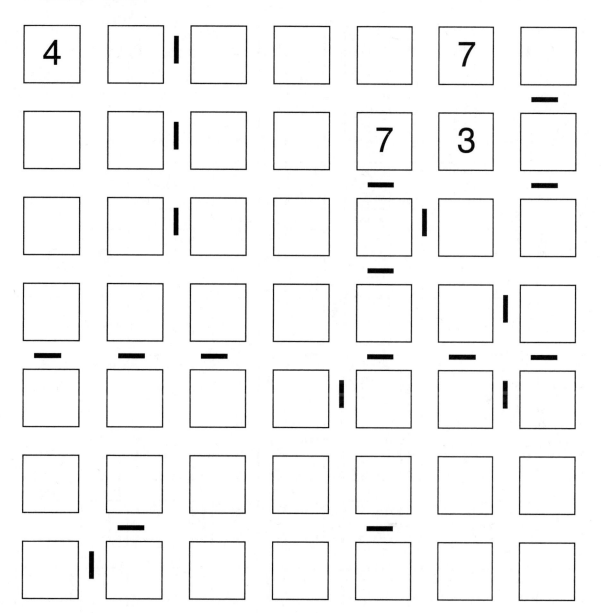

Puzzle #14

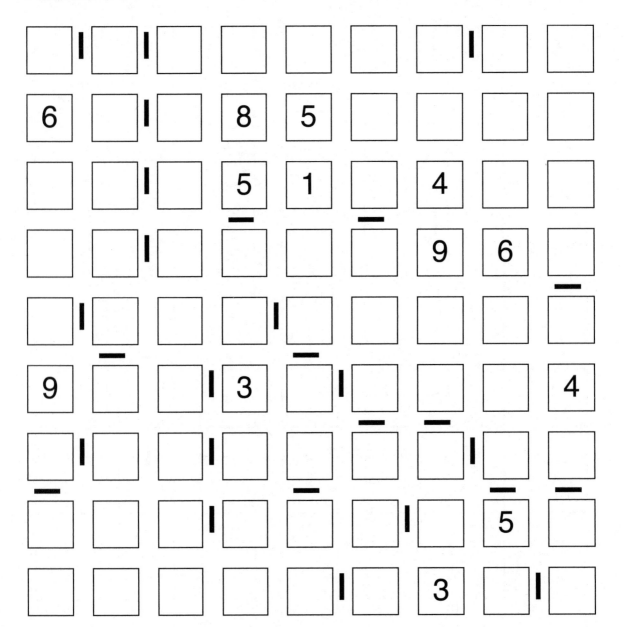

Puzzle #15

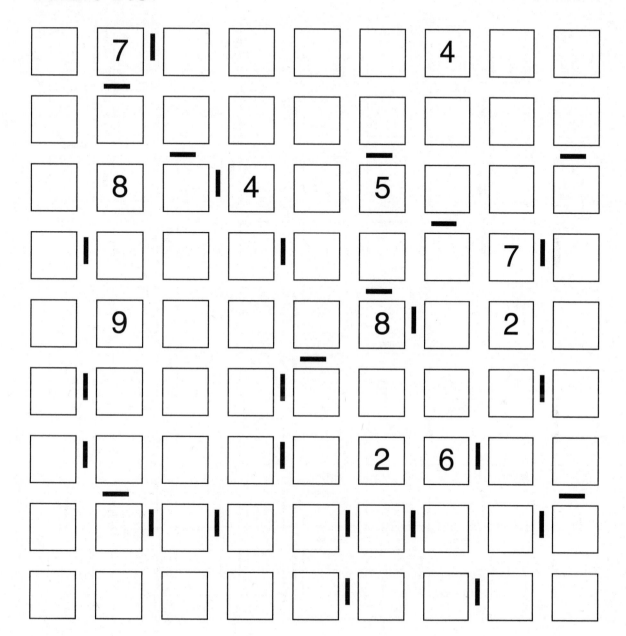

Puzzle #16

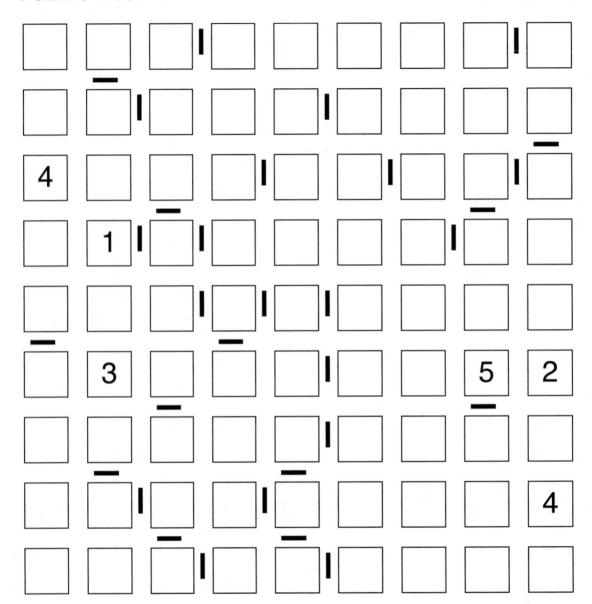

Puzzle #17

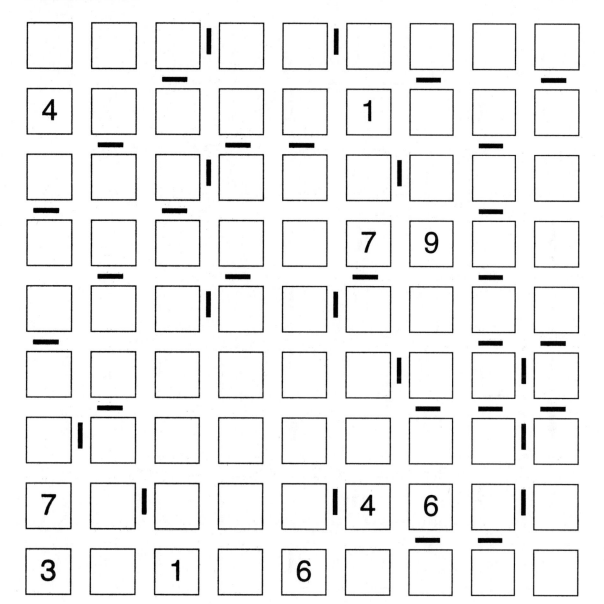

Puzzle #18

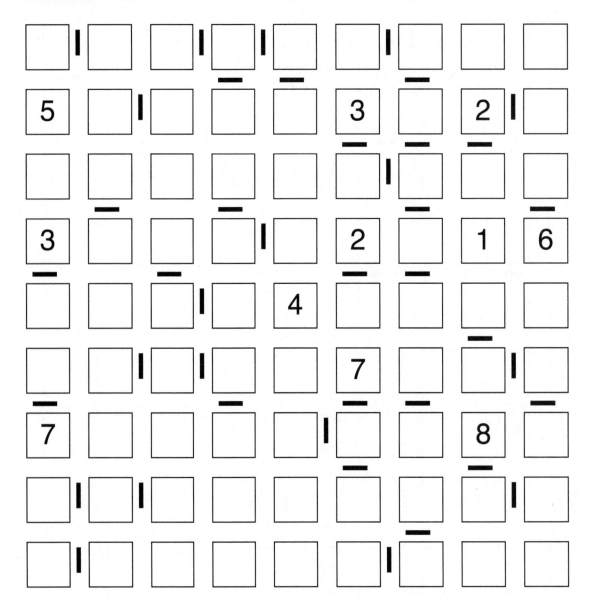

Reverse Word Searches

Introduction

Reverse word search puzzles are very similar to regular word searches. You are given a grid and a list of words, just like in a normal word search puzzle, except the letter grid contains only a handful of circled letters. Each of these circled letters is the first letter of one or more words. Your task is to place every word from the list onto the grid in such a way that every square in the grid holds one letter and every circled letter is used as the first letter of one or more words. Only one unique solution satisfies all the requirements for each puzzle.

Guessing is never required. Each reverse word search puzzle can be solved using logical deduction alone.

Puzzle #1

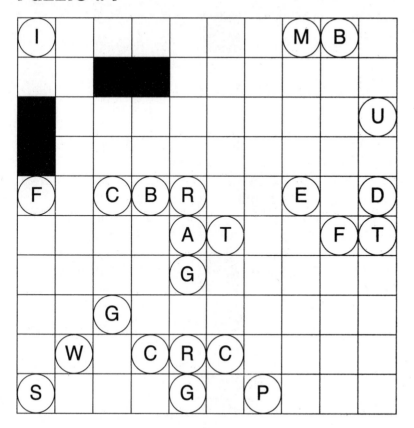

Aback	Great
Bastes	Gregarious
Bills	Imposes
Castigate	Matte
Chugs	Patchworks
Crowbar	Rabbi
Doubt	Races
Eerier	Sheds
Flops	Taint
Flurry	Theft
Genes	Ultra
Gourd	Worlds

Puzzle #2

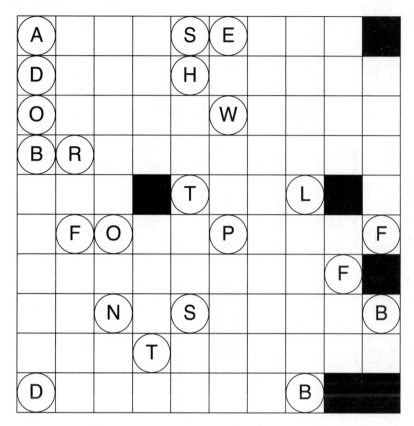

Adobe	Horses	Whopper
Advised	Least	
Beadier	Nosed	
Breathless	Okays	
Brides	Ounce	
Buoys	Peers	
Dices	Reopen	
Ditch	Scare	
Erase	Sonic	
Fireproofs	These	
Flier	Tornado	
Floppy	Wears	

Puzzle #3

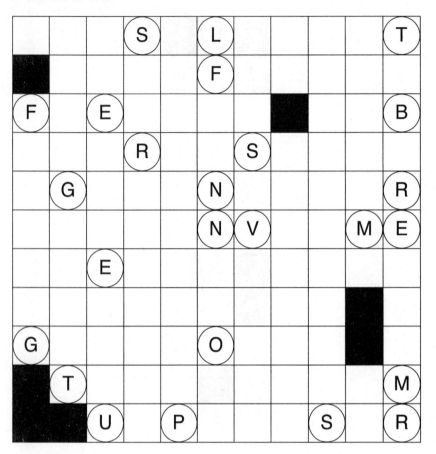

Bravely	Mugger	Taming
Eight	Noise	Tents
Elites	Nylon	Tribal
Excuse	Oxides	Unite
Facial	Psychology	Vexes
Faithless	Reaps	
Forges	Riser	
Gable	Roosters	
Gaily	Rouge	
Glucose	Sauce	
Lashed	Snout	
Merger	Spiritually	

Puzzle #4

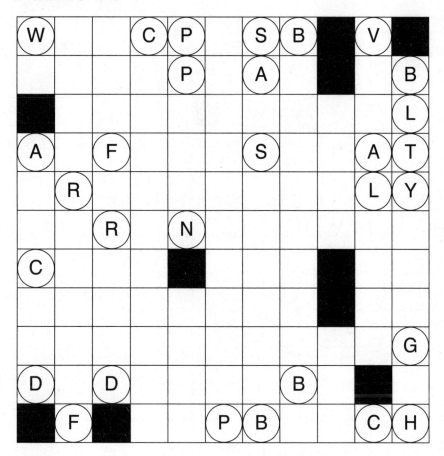

Along	Dunce	Repay
Answer	Fender	Salve
Array	Fleas	Sting
Backers	Guard	Tauts
Banning	Hugged	Viral
Beech	Laser	Waive
Brunette	Liner	Yawns
Brute	Named	
Caper	Pants	
Cared	Paradoxical	
Conveyances	Polar	
Decay	Refill	

Puzzle #5

	T					B			T
C	B							F	
							P		
C			S						N
	T		R	L					N
			C		P				I
	D		L	B					
		O	G	N					H
		P		B		D			
D									
	A			V					
E	G								E

Aides	Endorse	Papas
Beret	Energy	Placated
Binds	First	Polar
Blurts	Gassed	Radio
Broiling	Guide	Stepped
Caches	Hurrying	Taken
Chugs	Inexplicable	Thigh
Clear	Largely	Typed
Dicing	Loaned	Verbs
Distinctions	Nights	
Drills	Nones	
Ebony	Optic	

Puzzle #6

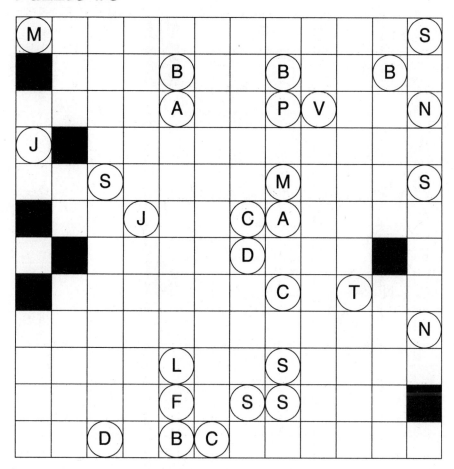

Abate	Duller	Sigma
Alloy	Fetch	Since
Badly	Fossils	Slacker
Baggie	Furry	Slays
Blobs	Jambs	Sputter
Bowed	Joyful	Swept
Boyhoods	Learn	Toppled
Collaborator	March	Valve
Couple	Muster	
Crams	Nested	
Crazier	Nonchalantly	
Dogmas	Purify	

Puzzle #7

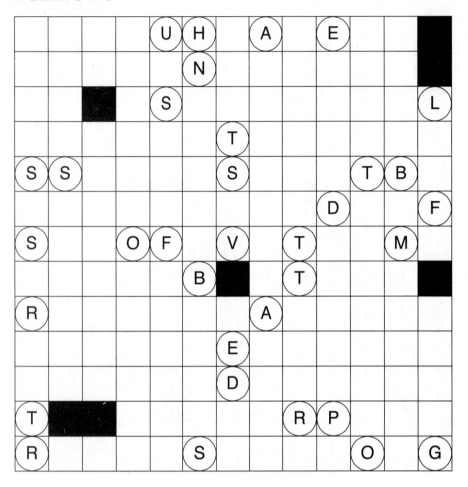

Accommodation	Growing	Risers	Union
Auditor	Heavens	Sears	Vestige
Bards	Hoots	Slice	
Beaks	Hushes	Slide	
Deport	Loafs	Sowed	
Diets	Matador	Surly	
Eaten	Nosed	Swept	
Edited	Oaths	Taken	
Feint	Observant	Teams	
Forms	Provoke	Tester	
Fundamentally	Remittances	Timer	
Gawks	Rider	Trestle	

Puzzle #8

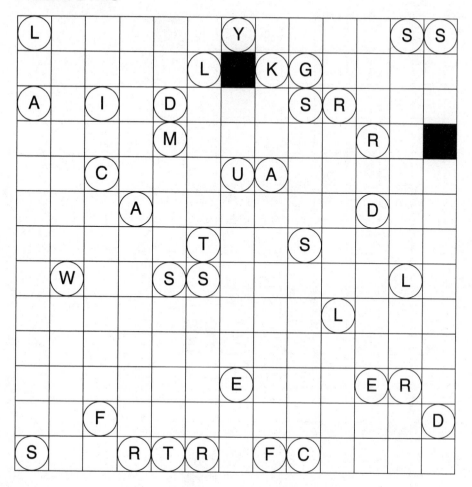

Aping	Feinting	Replenishes	Traps
Asked	Feted	Riser	Unpacked
Atlas	Greet	Rivet	Watts
Class	Incur	Saint	Wreaks
Curfews	Koala	Scold	Yokels
Deign	Landed	Sense	
Diced	Leases	Servants	
Doodled	Lousy	Sewing	
Dryly	Lures	Shack	
Dwelling	Minks	Swirls	
Ensuing	Realistically	Tattoos	
Eyelid	Remunerations	Teens	

Puzzle #9

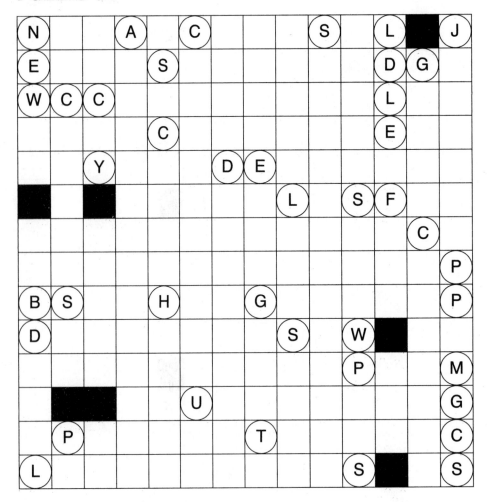

Altos	Erupted	Mapped	Steel
Boast	Examine	Newly	Torque
Cacaos	Field	Penultimate	Utter
Chaps	Gather	Philanthropist	Wayward
Collaboration	Grandchildren	Piled	Wells
Connotes	Greedily	Pretext	Yowls
Coral	Hedge	Seeps	
Crowd	Jarred	Sighed	
Dears	Lance	Slaughters	
Dinner	Lanes	Sneers	
Dooms	Lasses	Spats	
Earls	Loved	Spleen	

Puzzle #10

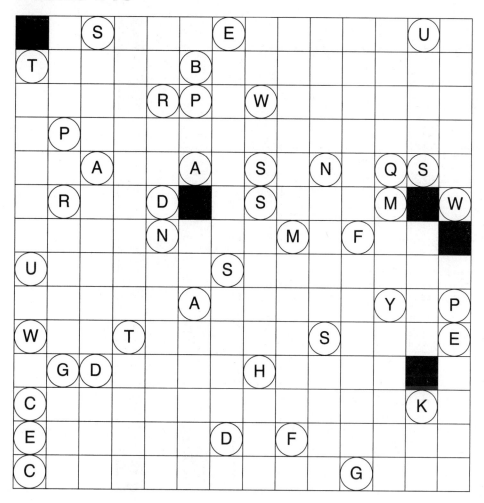

Adhere	Error	Pawning	Stylish
Alien	Esteems	Price	Super
Annals	Fleas	Psychoanalysis	Topic
Basest	Forts	Quips	Tunics
Crept	Gains	Roars	Units
Cricket	Gyrate	Ropes	Unsatisfactory
Debts	Heath	Scarecrows	Uppers
Defines	Knelt	Scenting	Waited
Disagrees	Meets	Sixes	Winner
Dissonances	Merits	Slave	Wiping
Dozens	Nasal	Slurs	Yawned
Edgier	Notch	Spade	

Puzzle #11

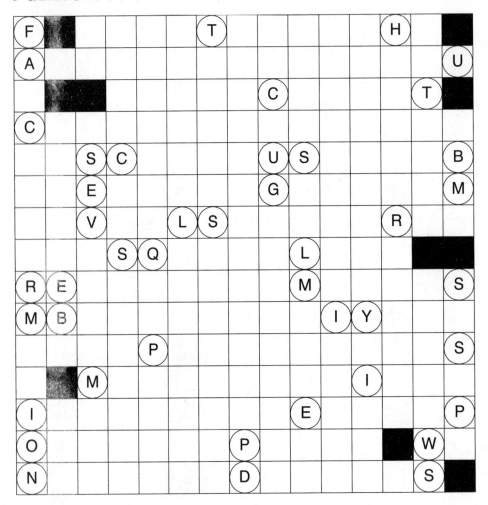

Annoyingly	Gavel	Onomatopoeia	Slams
Barge	Hooter	Paged	Smear
Bestow	Icings	Parka	Sober
Comprehensively	Ingratiate	Peremptory	Split
Conclusions	Iotas	Posts	Sweet
Confirmation	Lance	Queen	Taxes
Cuddle	Loudest	Reimbursements	Thuds
Dismal	Marking	Retort	Uncle
Entrap	Mature	Scram	Uneasy
Evading	Median	Seashores	Vials
Exact	Moors	Shrine	Write
Falcon	Narrated	Sixes	Yielded

Puzzle #12

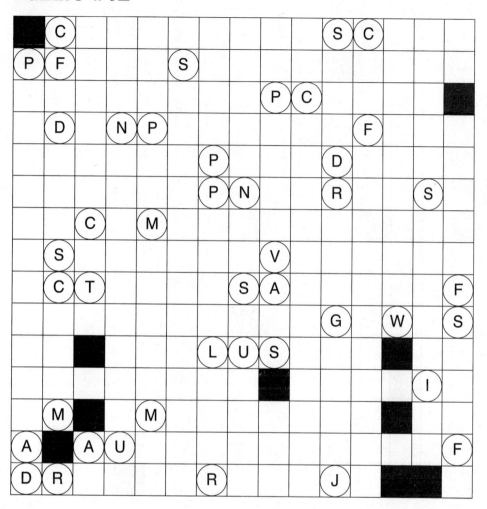

Acids	Fasts	Natural	Skulk
Amalgamations	Fifty	Palms	Slants
Austerity	Flinch	Peculiarly	Smite
Carol	Folding	Pipes	Snuffs
Clinically	Goody	Plausible	Sonic
Commanders	Invades	Posts	Stinks
Confidentiality	Juror	Rated	Tucked
Curly	Laser	Resale	Usage
Daisy	Masked	Rifts	Utilitarianism
Doors	Mimics	Safer	Vagary
Downs	Mocks	Scrub	Voted
Dresser	Nailed	Skewer	Wafts

Puzzle #13

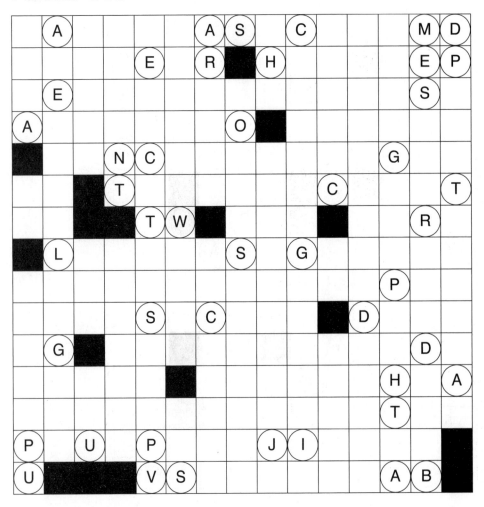

Added	Drizzled	Longs	Schoolchildren
Adorning	Dryer	Messier	Snipe
Alludes	Eager	Nudge	Study
Annuity	Elicit	Ogres	Sucks
Anthropological	Ended	Parks	Telegram
Audio	Gosling	Plied	Tickle
Badge	Grind	Point	Tiger
Casting	Grips	Pours	Types
Crisp	Hares	Preconception	Unpick
Crown	Horror	Rhyme	Upping
Curly	Irony	Rigidity	Vinyls
Deceives	Jails	Scarfed	Winner

Puzzle #14

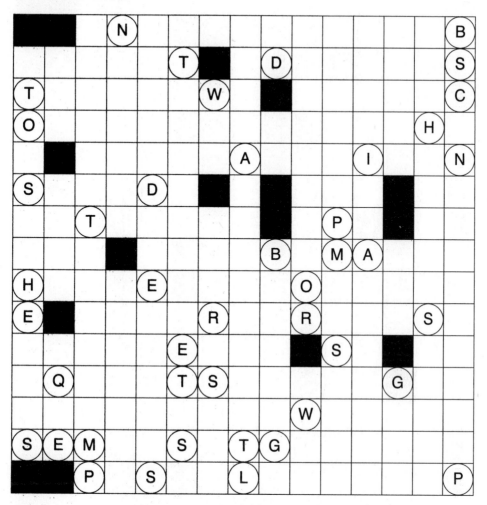

Aback	Grandest	Pasty	Souls
Agree	Haven	Powerless	Speed
Bankers	Hellos	Precisely	Spring
Bowed	Howled	Prompts	Steer
Chuck	Inhabit	Quiets	Styles
Dikes	Label	Raids	Tenders
Dividend	Makes	Robin	Thermodynamics
Emits	Mourn	Scenes	Thirty
Expel	Needs	Seduced	Thuds
Exterminate	Notification	Sides	Tousle
Exult	Olden	Sinuses	Waist
Goalie	Origin	Softer	Warden

Puzzle #15

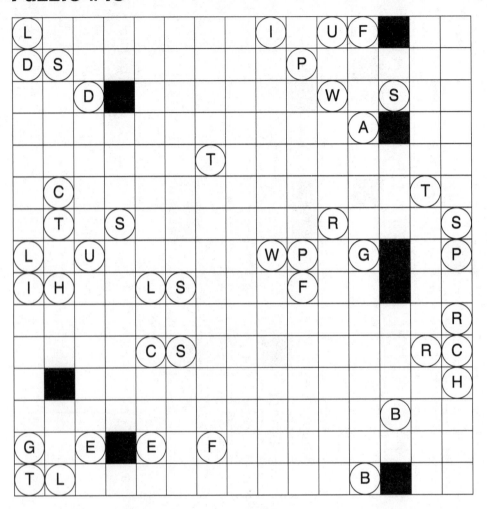

Arose	Fowling	Paired	Stark
Bemused	Gladden	Parch	Steward
Blares	Greedily	Plane	Supermarkets
Canopy	Hatchets	Rabbi	Thermodynamics
Caste	Hauls	Radiator	Thread
Chafe	Hooding	Rehabilitation	Tinge
Darns	Inert	Remittances	Tonic
Drain	Insides	Routs	Unity
Edict	Lards	Sewage	Usable
Exist	Lasers	Sheaf	Wafts
Flashy	Lauds	Skimping	Woods
Flosses	Luckily	Soloist	Worded

Puzzle #16

Agony
Aorta
Balder
Befell
Caulk
Chaps
Cover
Depots
Detail
Dikes
Dully
Edges

Fatal
Faultier
Felts
Flirt
Flower
Forked
Freshly
Fries
Furls
Impressively
Joker
Later

Looms
Mitten
Obsessed
Organ
Plank
Plutonium
Predispositions
Psychologically
Ravaged
Replaced
Rival
Runes

Sneer
Snipers
Spats
Stanches
Strike
Tells
Tiptoed
Toothpick
Vases
Vintage
Voiced
Yowls

Puzzle #17

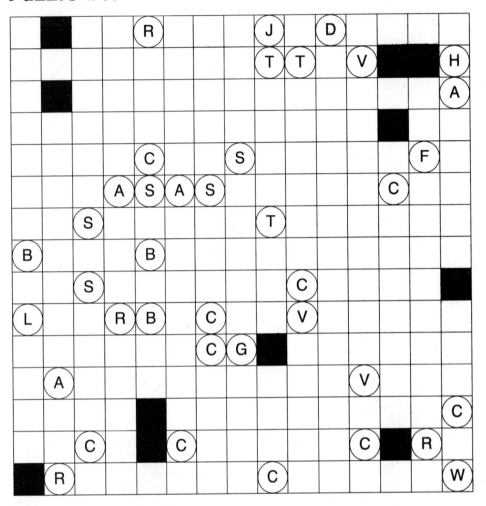

Acrylic	Chase	Groom	Sheathe
Acting	Clicks	Handles	Shoes
Anger	Clone	Judging	Stormy
Artful	Connect	Lauds	Tailed
Atlas	Constellations	Rarely	Teams
Baits	Convenes	Rates	Toots
Belongs	Corners	Rotate	Tuxedos
Blues	Covenant	Royals	Value
Blurts	Crags	Ruins	Veterinarian
Bossier	Creek	Sacks	Vetoes
Canon	Discouragement	Scaling	Wicker
Caste	Faiths	Screw	Wreaks

Puzzle #18

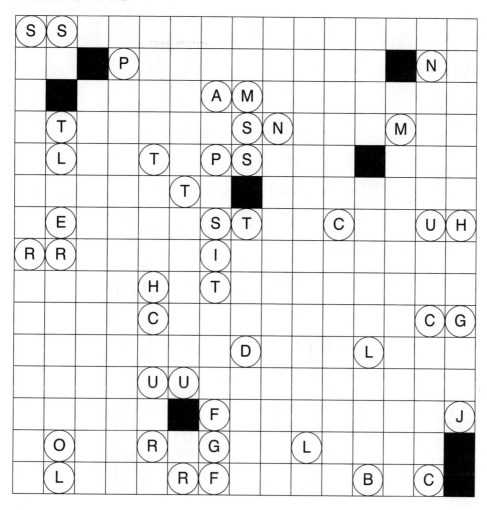

Aspect	Harshly	Nether	Squander
Backlog	Hitching	Nicking	Straw
Cabaret	Icons	Outraged	Struck
Coupons	Jargon	Petrol	Thwarts
Crony	Leaky	Plurality	Tipped
Crush	Leers	Rehabilitation	Tones
Doing	Leper	Repel	Twigs
Entrust	Lined	Reserves	Twirl
Fazes	Loafer	Rides	Unborn
Frolics	Maybe	Scientifically	Uncharitable
Grins	Mumble	Shaped	Unfits
Grocer	Mustiest	Snort	Unison

Puzzle #19

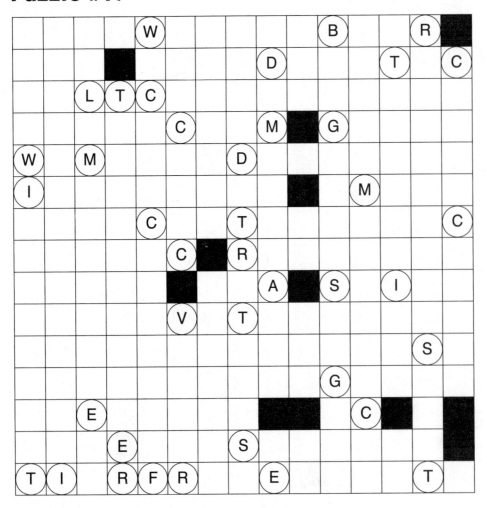

Acres

Bishop

Cavorts

Chafe

Chide

Choir

Climb

Comma

Condor

Courts

Diligent

Dough

Effort

Eldest

Erudite

Erupt

Filches

Froze

Fruit

Goats

Grunts

Inability

Inconsequential

Instep

Intellectuals

Lather

Macho

Martin

Mists

Mourned

Reluctance

Retry

Reverent

Riser

Rivets

Safety

Staff

Swatted

Taming

Theft

Tights

Timidly

Trots

Turtles

Vanes

Whale

Whine

Wicks

Puzzle #20

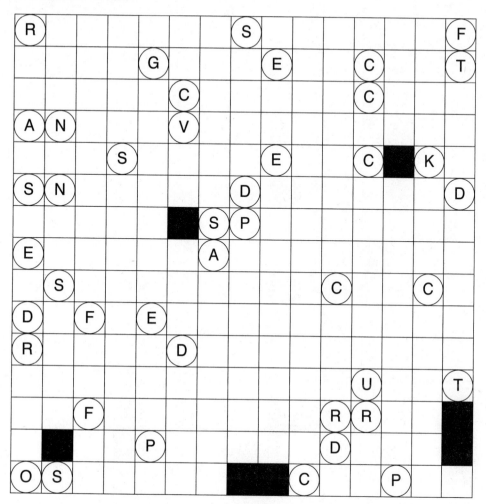

Answer	Dinner	Going	Rinds
Aspire	Dodges	Kiwis	Runts
Attorneys	Drift	Nomads	Safest
Canoes	Droves	Nonstandard	Sermon
Clues	Dulls	Otter	Sling
Clump	Easel	Parasite	Slivers
Collars	Edict	Pared	Submerge
Comply	Eject	Petulant	Sucks
Counsel	Equal	Prowled	Tanks
Cured	Finesse	Repents	Twice
Debugs	Flees	Rhododendrons	Unanimous
Differentiation	Flush	Rifle	Video

Sudoku

Introduction

Using only the numbers 1 through 9, fill in each sudoku grid so no number is repeated in any row, column, or grid. Each puzzle has one, and only one, unique solution, and each can be solved using pure logic. Guessing and trial and error are never required.

Puzzle #1

	5	6	7				3	
		2	4	5				9
			2				6	1
7						4		
1	8	4	3				2	
		5			1			6
2		8						
	3					6		
	9		1	2	4			3

Puzzle #2

			9	6		1	3	
		4	3				6	
	6	2						
		3			5	8	1	
	7				3			2
2	9	1	6	7		3		5
8	3							
	5		1					
	2		5			7		

Puzzle #3

	1		8	3	5			
	9			1	2			
4		7					5	2
	5	1						
					6			
				9		2		1
9	6		3	5		8		
	8			4				5

Puzzle #4

				4	7		1	
		4		5			8	2
		6	8					
1					3			
6		5	1	8			2	7
		7			5			6
		2						
					9	3		
			7	3				4

Puzzle #5

		8	9					4
	9		6				7	
								1
			7	1				
8	5				2		4	
1		4			8			9
9						3		
			7				1	
	2						8	7

Puzzle #6

4			6		7	8		
				9		1		
	9					7		
	3				5			6
			7					
		5					7	4
2		7	1		8			
	6	8	3					
9						6		8

Puzzle #7

			2		3			8
				5			7	9
	5	6						
			9	1			2	
5				3		7		1
3	8						4	
1			8					
	9		1					2
					6			

Puzzle #8

				5			9	
	9		6	1	2		3	
			3			2		6
				9			5	
		5	8		6			3
	2	8			5			
	5			2			1	4
	6							
7						5		

Puzzle #9

	8		6	1			3	
				3		8		
				5	1	6		
		1						
3		7	6					
	5	6						4
		4		9				
1	3	2			8			
5		7	4					

Puzzle #10

	7	3		5	8			2
5				2				
		6						7
		8		2				
1	5		4	7				9
							4	3
					5			
9				1		3		
		7		6				

Puzzle #11

	7		8	5		2		
	1					7		
	2	3			1			
	9				8		7	4
		5			2		3	1
							6	
		1		2				
					4		9	
	3		6	9				

Puzzle #12

			8				3	4
2				1				
								9
5					3			
		3	7					2
1					9		5	7
	2		1					
6		5				9	8	
9	4		3					

Puzzle #13

6			9					3
		2		7	8		4	
		9	4					
			1		6		7	
		7			9		5	6
					2			
5			6					4
9								
8	2	4						

Puzzle #14

7		1		4				
				8	1		4	5
					2			1
4				6	7			
	5	6		2			9	
1					9			4
2	7					6	1	
		9					3	
6								

Puzzle #15

	2		3			4		
9	1				6			
			1					8
			2			8	3	
					7			
		6		5	8			
3				4			6	
		7			3	2		
	9			6				4

Puzzle #16

1		4		2				9
8		9		3			4	7
		2			9			
					1		5	3
	6	1			5	8		
				7				
						4		
		3		9	7			6
						9		

Puzzle #17

				6	8			
7								9
	2					5		7
						2		
5			9			4		
9		1		3				
		4						3
1		8						
	4			8	7			2

Puzzle #18

				7		1		
		7			3			
8	1				3			7
2						8		
6	3		9			2		
		8			5			
	9			2				
		5		4	9	6		
			6			2		

Puzzle #19

3	2				4			
						5		1
	1							
	3	7		2				
6			7				2	
			4	9	5	7		
						1		
					8			6
5			1		3		4	7

Puzzle #20

			1			9		5
	2	3			5		6	1
				4				
	1							9
	3		4		2			
		5		9	3		2	
5			6					
								2
		7			9	5		6

Word Search

Introduction

Word search puzzles are fairly straightforward. You're given a list of words to find within a grid of seemingly random letters. Every word in the list appears once and only once in the grid, although they can be placed horizontally, diagonally, or vertically and can read left to right, right to left, top to bottom, or bottom to top.

Puzzle #1

```
I  L  A  M  C  O  M  O  R  O  S  N  A  R  I
L  E  D  L  A  D  O  W  G  L  A  P  E  N  A
G  S  N  P  B  U  D  R  E  O  R  T  D  N  R
A  O  G  A  P  A  G  W  E  B  T  I  D  I  U
M  T  A  R  M  E  N  I  A  A  A  O  D  J  B
B  H  A  A  A  O  I  I  S  H  R  T  G  S  A
I  O  L  G  L  G  K  W  A  R  L  I  B  Y  A
A  T  G  U  D  P  D  Q  A  A  A  T  W  Y  X
A  M  E  A  I  S  E  A  A  I  O  E  L  T  U
A  A  R  Y  V  U  T  C  N  N  S  A  L  L  M
R  C  I  N  E  D  I  Q  G  I  T  I  A  H  T
F  A  A  O  S  A  N  A  A  I  H  V  C  H  C
I  U  T  B  M  N  U  P  E  R  U  C  U  N  H
J  I  T  A  B  I  R  I  K  T  I  C  B  F  A
I  Y  J  G  Q  N  E  W  Z  E  A  L  A  N  D
```

Albania	Gambia	Libya	Togo
Algeria	Guam	Macau	Tonga
Andorra	Haiti	Maldives	Tuvalu
Armenia	India	Mali	United Kingdom
Aruba	Iran	Malta	
Bahrain	Iraq	Nepal	
Chad	Israel	New Zealand	
China	Italy	Oman	
Comoros	Jamaica	Paraguay	
Cuba	Kiribati	Peru	
Fiji	Laos	Qatar	
Gabon	Lesotho	Sudan	

Puzzle #2

```
E G U L G Y M N A S T I C S G
B J Q S P E E D S K A T I N G
N O T N I M D A B B O X I N G
S W B B B A U S G A K W B I N
H H B S A W L J U Q O O G R I
Y E O J L S T A H R J S N U M
C R Y T U E E E I G F B I G M
R U E L P D D B N A I I C B I
I E K H I U O G A N J H N Y W
C N C S C W T N S L I W E G S
K P O C L R Q I Q P L S F Z A
E J H I O C A V U K A R A T E
T B N T S S B I A T H L O N G
A G T K T B E D S R D A R T S
Q F L O G F I S H I N G R U C
```

Archery	Darts	Jai Alai	Speed Skating
Badminton	Diving	Judo	Squash
Baseball	Fencing	Karate	Surfing
Biathlon	Fishing	Luge	Swimming
Bobsled	Golf	Rowing	Tennis
Bowling	Gymnastics	Rugby	
Boxing	High Jump	Shot Put	
Cricket	Hockey	Soccer	

Puzzle #3

```
O R H N A Q U A M A R I N E O
L C S M D B R O W N U S S L W
P A H L W E P U A T B C I O L
E C O R A L U Y M V Y V L R I
A G I C E T C S N M E L V E L
C E M K R H E V E U E N E D A
H R A U A A E V E Y B S R N C
J U U D I H H N R Z O L A E T
C Z V H N B K C G R N H T V S
O A E P D R E B M A E O N A A
P Q E G I E B L F X P O R L L
P Q D V G N U V P Y O M L B M
E T O N O R K K T R A W A U O
R R F U C H S I A J U R L H N
Y P P E R S I M M O N P G S C
```

Amber	Coral	Lavender	Puce
Aquamarine	Cyan	Lilac	Purple
Azure	Ecru	Maroon	Rose
Beige	Fuchsia	Mauve	Ruby
Bone	Gold	Ochre	Salmon
Bronze	Gray	Olive	Silver
Brown	Green	Peach	Slate
Champagne	Indigo	Persimmon	Taupe
Charcoal	Ivory	Pink	Teal
Copper	Khaki	Plum	Yellow

Puzzle #4

```
E G K E H S U L E B O K U R D
S U T S P H E L L I P S I S K
U I A U I I S X B R A C K E T
B L H N R R P A P U R H Z M P
S L Y D O L E X H G L N G A U
C E P E P L W T D V Q L M B F
R M H R E O O R S R W M E S X
I E E S R D H C M A O R B T K
P T N C C E L S I C F L D Z N
T X L O E D T I A M A L O G O
Q I F R N X K E T D E Q I Y E
P K P E T C M Q R R M S R U C
A M P E R S A N D A T E E C A
E H P O R T S O P A C P P C P
D G K R A M N O I T S E U Q S
```

Ampersand	Comma	Percent	Space
Apostrophe	Ellipsis	Period	Subscript
Asterisk	Em Dash	Pilcrow	Tilde
At Sign	Guillemet	Pipe	Underscore
Bracket	Hash	Question Mark	
Bullet	Hyphen	Semicolon	
Caret	Obelus	Slash	

Puzzle #5

```
F  L  I  N  T  R  E  H  C  P  O  T  A  S  H
C  U  P  U  C  G  E  O  D  E  B  N  M  G  Q
S  O  F  R  E  I  Y  D  W  V  D  U  L  A  L
G  A  B  B  R  O  A  P  P  E  I  D  A  L  Q
J  A  O  A  G  E  B  S  R  D  G  O  L  D  D
M  A  R  B  L  E  A  I  A  U  S  A  C  I  M
S  T  S  N  U  T  T  B  M  S  M  H  J  U  X
A  S  E  P  E  E  E  I  I  A  A  N  A  M  G
N  C  S  T  E  T  X  L  N  L  F  L  N  L  N
D  H  U  I  I  R  I  G  K  A  F  V  T  E  E
S  I  L  E  K  C  A  W  Y  E  R  G  I  T  I
T  S  F  V  A  N  L  W  P  P  N  G  M  I  S
O  T  U  Q  E  Q  U  A  R  T  Z  X  O  R  S
N  G  R  S  P  U  M  I  C  E  Y  O  N  Y  X
E  R  E  P  P  O  C  X  R  L  X  S  Y  P  W
```

Agate	Copper	Gypsum	Pyrite
Andesite	Flint	Jade	Quartz
Antimony	Gabbro	Jasper	Sandstone
Barium	Gallium	Lead	Schist
Basalt	Garnet	Manganese	Shale
Calcite	Geode	Marble	Silica
Chalk	Gneiss	Mica	Sulfur
Chert	Gold	Onyx	Tufa
Coal	Granite	Potash	
Cobalt	Greywacke	Pumice	

Puzzle #6

```
T R E E H C Y L D U P E T A D
L H M N A G N O L D P L S U E
A I M Q J K L E M O N E U E N
L N E C T A R I N E L C A O A
Q N A T U B M A R O N A L C T
U A O N H C O H Q T O E J S H
I I H Y A U D U T K M G E T W
N R R G M B A O G U M R N N S
C U J S P T C A U N I S I A R
E D K I W I O P A E S J P R M
M U L P R N V P V R R G A R G
R D K P H U A L A T E R P U U
E T A N A R G E M O P A A C P
O R A N G E P P T K V P Y V H
Y R R E B L U M M A R E A S E
```

Apple	Guava	Melon	Plum
Apricot	Kiwi	Mulberry	Pluot
Avocado	Lemon	Nectarine	Pomegranate
Banana	Lime	Orange	Quince
Currant	Longan	Papaya	Raisin
Date	Loquat	Peach	Rambutan
Durian	Lychee	Pear	
Grape	Mango	Persimmon	

Puzzle #7

```
E C H O C T A W O J I B W A K
T G N I O O U S H A W N E E S
O P A Q M Q I E G Q A J E H N
U K E S I O U X L R N R O O G
Q O E H O W T X R A C S O G R
E O N I D Q Y A V X H T N M O
P M I D W Q G A W O K O H A S
M A M A X A J F N A J O P R V
I L O T N O M E A D T E U I E
A L N S H D O P H A O O T C N
M I E A K M O H A W K T P O T
I T M M I E Q Y M N H P Z P R
T P E N O B S C O T O P I A E
C A T A W B A M I C M A C M Q
A K W B A N N O C K G V G J A
```

Aleut	Kiowa	Nootka	Shawnee
Bannock	Maricopa	Ojibwa	Shoshone
Catawba	Menominee	Omaha	Sioux
Choctaw	Miami	Osage	Tillamook
Creek	Micmac	Penobscot	Wampanoag
Gros Ventre	Mohawk	Pequot	Wyandot
Hidatsa	Narragansett	Pima	
Hopi	Navajo	Potawatomi	

Puzzle #8

```
H O A D R O F R E H T U R N R
A P N L I N N A E U S M S R V
W Q E E S B N I E T S N I E H
K M W Z Y E R U E T S A P G N
I A T I N V T D A R W I N N A
N X O N H O O K E L N O L I G
G W N B K S B Q L D K E N D A
R E M I E H N E P P O L E O S
W L D E P F D E L M X I G R F
K L O L L N A I F N E L T H O
H U Y G E N S R P P L A N C K
M F V M R R U U A J D G O S T
N A M N Y E F C X D T Z R W D
B U N S E N I L K N A R F R U
Y S E D E M I H C R A Y N X Y
```

Archimedes	Galileo	Maxwell	Rutherford
Bunsen	Hawking	Mendel	Sagan
Curie	Hooke	Newton	Schrodinger
Darwin	Huygens	Nobel	Tesla
Einstein	Kepler	Oppenheimer	
Faraday	Leibniz	Pasteur	
Feynman	Linnaeus	Planck	
Franklin	Lister	Rontgen	

Puzzle #9

```
A  M  E  E  A  T  I  V  R  O  B  R  A  T  J
D  A  L  H  L  J  E  C  U  R  P  S  I  U  L
M  H  P  N  E  P  S  A  E  P  P  W  O  N  A
R  O  P  A  B  F  A  D  W  A  L  N  U  T  R
I  G  A  M  I  F  L  M  H  B  H  M  Q  S  C
F  A  H  E  R  A  D  E  C  P  E  A  E  E  H
M  N  I  R  O  Y  Z  Y  R  N  M  E  S  H  B
A  Y  C  I  L  S  Q  D  I  E  L  B  C  C  S
S  O  K  C  I  P  Y  P  B  Z  O  N  Y  H  W
L  C  O  A  V  H  D  C  Y  W  C  R  P  R  E
A  L  R  N  E  E  B  L  A  C  K  O  A  K  E
B  J  Y  E  R  H  W  I  R  M  P  H  S  E  T
W  I  L  L  O  W  L  F  G  L  O  F  Z  D  G
U  N  Y  M  U  U  V  U  A  J  M  R  S  H  U
D  O  G  W  O  O  D  R  Z  S  L  E  E  G  M
```

Alder	Cedar	Mahogany	Sycamore
American Elm	Chestnut	Maple	Walnut
Apple	Dogwood	Olive	Willow
Arborvitae	Gray Birch	Poplar	
Aspen	Hemlock	Red Pine	
Balsam Fir	Hickory	Sequoia	
Beech	Hornbeam	Spruce	
Black Oak	Larch	Sweetgum	

Puzzle #10

```
J U N E A U W C A U G U S T A
S U B M U L O C Q I D N Y D P
L N P O Z N D E S M O I N E S
P H I I C A R S O N C I T Y L
H E E O A K A A I P M Y L O I
O K R U W L C T N O T N E R T
E D R E E P S U C I P Z F O T
N J E M V U Q D T S T P A U L
I N D I A N A P O L I S T I E
X B A N E L E H P V A Z N B R
Q N O T S O B D E V E C A G O
M A D I S O N W K B O R S X C
J A C K S O N R A L E I G H K
Y X X Z O E N E N N E Y E H C
A L B A N Y L A N S I N G R A
```

Albany	Concord	Lansing	Salem
Augusta	Denver	Lincoln	Santa Fe
Austin	Des Moines	Little Rock	St. Paul
Boise	Dover	Madison	Topeka
Boston	Helena	Olympia	Trenton
Carson City	Indianapolis	Phoenix	
Cheyenne	Jackson	Pierre	
Columbus	Juneau	Raleigh	

Puzzle #11

```
G P U N J A B I S P A N I S H
O M A N D A R I N L I M A T Q
L C Z T U V W G Y V J D W H U
A F P H A K K A R I S D N S E
G E S E N A V A J E U T C I C
A M H A R I C C V T E I C K H
T U O T H S A P C N B K F R U
R E M H K H I H T A R A M U A
K U R D I S H A R M K T K T W
T G F Y M I D A N E E E J U F
Z J S R P L N R D S B G R Y C
N A M R E G I F N E Z D B C T
K O R E A N S T E L U G U F C
Q V P E W E C R O M A N I A N
I T A L I A N H I L A G N E B
```

Amharic	Hakka	Marathi	Tagalog
Arabic	Hindi	Pashto	Tamil
Bengali	Italian	Persian	Telugu
Dutch	Javanese	Punjabi	Turkish
English	Khmer	Quechua	Urdu
French	Korean	Romanian	Uzbek
German	Kurdish	Sindhi	Vietnamese
Greek	Mandarin	Spanish	

Puzzle #12

```
P  L  A  R  E  T  A  L  I  U  Q  E  P  N  A
O  T  E  E  Z  L  N  F  B  A  E  R  A  P  Q
L  H  D  E  J  M  U  I  R  N  L  R  R  H  I
Y  P  I  I  E  Q  E  P  O  N  I  B  A  R  P
G  Y  O  R  T  B  W  C  Q  P  T  C  L  E  U
O  R  Z  S  U  B  M  O  H  R  Y  Z  L  T  S
N  A  E  C  C  Y  J  N  I  F  N  V  E  E  S
C  M  P  U  A  E  G  A  E  O  S  C  L  M  E
V  I  A  Y  S  P  N  G  G  N  Y  T  O  A  L
E  D  R  U  X  G  L  A  B  L  E  B  G  I  E
R  N  T  C  L  E  X  B  I  C  B  L  R  D  C
V  B  I  E  L  E  T  N  U  O  V  F  A  Z  S
O  N  J  L  H  E  D  R  O  H  C  F  M  C  O
S  Q  U  A  R  E  V  I  E  R  A  D  I  U  S
I  F  A  V  R  E  R  V  V  V  M  I  D  S  I
```

Acute	Diameter	Point	Trapezoid
Chord	Equilateral	Polygon	Triangle
Circle	Hexagon	Pyramid	Vertex
Cone	Isosceles	Radius	
Cube	Line	Rhombus	
Curve	Obtuse	Scalene	
Cylinder	Parallelogram	Square	

Puzzle #13

```
P K Q A O S R O C E N A C B H
G C H I N E S E S H A R P E I
S S P O O D L E L G A E B K F
M T W X A R M T W Q T T E A W
G L W C A E D H R S S E B U B
T P M U Z T H I H S S B D H V
X S A P M H U C O H Y R I A I
A V L U B K H M O Z S A V U K
S W T T O A E N L C R B F H U
L T I T X W D O W B K O F I L
O L P O E A L S Z I V A B H A
U B O L R Z K H Q L O P P C S
G I O P P A P I L L O N U O K
H U C O L L I E T T B V M L O
I X P O I N T E R A X R I P I
```

Akita	Chihuahua	Mutt	Saluki
Azawakh	Chinese Shar-pei	Papillon	Shih Tzu
Barbet	Cockapoo	Plott	Sloughi
Beagle	Collie	Pointer	Vizsla
Borzoi	Keeshond	Poodle	
Boxer	Kuvasz	Pug	
Cane Corso	Maltipoo	Puli	

Puzzle #14

```
D U G O N G N G N I R R E H G
H W M O D U S W P B L A D V C
C P R D T I S E A M G G C M E
E C E N O M E N A R A R O A R
A K W D C Y K R O B P L N N Z
E N A U T I L U S Q A R C A C
A G V H K I P P X N M S H T E
S T N R N E Z T K C N M S E K
E Q I O R I H M R O I X Q E A
A L J U P J O Y A P H L E S N
L D M U S S E L M E C C L U S
I J E L L Y F I S H R O K R A
O Y S T E R R X T Y U B C L E
N Y K N I H P L O D S I O A S
X Y B E S S A R W C Z A C W H
```

Anemone	Dugong	Marlin	Sea Lion
Bream	Grouper	Mussel	Sea Snake
Clam	Hake	Nautilus	Shrimp
Cobia	Herring	Orca	Sponge
Cockle	Jellyfish	Oyster	Urchin
Conch	Krill	Prawn	Walrus
Dolphin	Manatee	Sea Bass	Wrasse

Puzzle #15

```
C H E R V I L G G R K B O K W
Q C A Y E N N E P E P P E R C
N I G E L L A M Y A B E P L H
P O S S Y H S T R M R N H R I
P A P R I K A U X G O S K F V
N T N C B V G N U G N Y L R E
T P W O Q Y E N A A A Q C E S
R R T U R M E R I C G M C D Y
R E W O L F R E D L E A L N Y
W C G O D A F I U E R R O E O
A I M N T A L A M D O J V V C
S L H I I L R Y S R O O E A U
A R J O N G H C S O R R E L M
B A G K F T Y E C A M A L T I
I G T H A I B A S I L M B L N
```

Cayenne Pepper	Fenugreek	Mint	Sage
Chervil	Garlic	Nigella	Sorrel
Chives	Ginger	Nutmeg	Tarragon
Clove	Hyssop	Oregano	Thai Basil
Cumin	Lavender	Paprika	Thyme
Dill	Mace	Parsley	Turmeric
Elderflower	Marjoram	Saffron	Wasabi

Puzzle #16

```
E  S  T  R  O  M  B  O  N  E  T  Y  L  T  N
L  S  E  P  I  P  N  A  P  H  A  D  Y  X  B
T  S  D  G  V  A  O  N  A  I  P  B  D  J  C
S  Y  R  E  G  B  U  G  L  E  C  R  U  O  A
I  N  A  R  E  A  E  G  D  L  A  C  W  T  C
H  T  O  Y  P  N  I  S  U  T  R  B  O  A  I
W  H  B  L  T  J  C  T  I  W  E  S  W  L  N
Y  E  Y  E  C  O  E  S  I  L  C  E  B  P  O
N  S  E  D  Q  Y  F  C  L  D  O  M  U  E  M
N  I  K  T  E  P  M  U  R  T  R  I  K  N  R
E  Z  M  A  R  I  M  B  A  C  D  H  U  H  A
P  E  V  U  U  E  F  Z  A  Q  E  C  L  O  H
H  R  U  Y  P  O  Z  X  Z  L  R  L  E  R  E
A  L  O  I  V  B  A  S  S  O  O  N  L  N  O
Q  X  S  A  X  O  P  H  O  N  E  B  E  O  E
```

Alpenhorn	Cymbal	Organ	Sitar
Banjo	Harmonica	Panpipes	Synthesizer
Bassoon	Keyboard	Penny Whistle	Trombone
Bugle	Lute	Piano	Trumpet
Cello	Lyre	Piccolo	Tuba
Chimes	Marimba	Recorder	Ukulele
Cowbell	Oboe	Saxophone	Viola

Puzzle #17

```
K O C O R S I C A I B I Z A K
N G X X C Y P R U S S Y O E B
J A M A I C A D T E C Q Y O O
D B U A L B X K Y Q S W S E R
A O N R E L I C R E E H K N A
T T R K U T H E V S R A W I C
W S U I T E N A T A O R T T A
A J Q S L J E R I W Z U K R Y
W A B L E A M T C H A B Y A A
H U E U R N A I E R C A G M D
B S B Y A T J K L R E S S T U
A U D G G I O A A U C G I S M
L S N H F G R U N E Z S R J R
I O N M L U C A D C B O Z A E
T I U A M A A I R P A C N O B
```

Antigua	Corsica	Ischia	Nauru
Aruba	Crete	Jamaica	Roatan
Azores	Cyprus	Kauai	Seychelles
Bali	Elba	Key West	St. Kitts
Bermuda	Fiji	Luzon	St. Martin
Boracay	Ibiza	Majorca	Tobago
Capri	Iceland	Maui	Tonga

Puzzle #18

```
Y  B  S  Z  I  J  E  D  U  C  A  T  I  O  N
A  R  W  U  O  Q  K  U  J  Y  U  C  D  Y  Y
G  G  T  R  L  R  S  G  N  I  S  R  U  N  F
S  N  I  S  V  U  D  V  T  T  Q  I  A  T  D
C  I  I  B  I  C  C  W  B  R  T  M  R  E  B
I  T  D  R  F  M  D  L  E  O  I  I  C  A  M
T  N  P  G  E  N  E  C  A  N  J  N  H  S  R
S  U  A  H  T  E  O  H  N  C  A  O  I  G  Y
I  O  Y  C  Y  N  N  G  C  D  G  L  T  E  R
T  C  W  D  O  S  X  I  F  V  A  O  E  O  O
A  C  X  M  H  S  I  L  G  N  E  G  C  M  T
T  A  I  D  O  M  B  C  R  N  Z  Y  T  E  S
S  C  I  S  U  M  C  U  S  A  E  T  U  T  I
S  P  H  T  C  A  O  E  N  D  U  V  R  R  H
I  P  A  L  K  J  H  K  T  C  R  F  E  Y  U
```

Accounting	Dance	Geometry	Physics
Architecture	Economics	History	Statistics
Calculus	Education	Journalism	
Chemistry	Engineering	Music	
Criminology	English	Nursing	

Puzzle #19

```
S  U  R  E  B  R  E  C  G  F  G  C  T  E  B
O  D  O  P  P  E  L  G  A  N  G  E  R  I  B
N  M  Y  C  W  R  A  I  T  H  O  E  P  B  X
G  S  S  L  T  M  R  N  S  P  Q  M  V  M  Z
P  P  G  R  B  Y  V  D  P  M  H  G  E  O  B
V  O  O  I  P  A  T  P  H  Y  U  D  T  Z  H
O  L  I  B  N  R  N  X  I  N  E  O  H  P  C
L  C  P  N  E  O  C  E  N  T  A  U  R  A  T
T  Y  Y  N  G  E  M  D  X  U  U  R  R  S  A
O  C  P  R  R  K  H  E  R  Z  L  Y  O  U  U
O  O  O  I  V  O  S  S  D  A  T  H  A  D  Q
F  G  G  Z  X  X  C  I  N  A  G  O  G  E  S
G  Y  R  K  S  I  L  I  S  A  B  O  V  M  A
I  T  E  Y  J  E  E  J  N  Y  B  M  N  Z  S
B  O  G  E  Y  M  A  N  S  U  S  A  G  E  P
```

Banshee	Demon	Medusa	Satyr
Basilisk	Doppelganger	Nymph	Sphinx
Bigfoot	Dragon	Ogre	Troll
Bogeyman	Fairy	Pegasus	Unicorn
Centaur	Ghost	Phoenix	Wraith
Cerberus	Gnome	Pixie	Yeti
Cyclops	Gorgon	Sasquatch	Zombie

Puzzle #20

```
C S H E N I R E H T A C N J O
N A O J B I L L Y K D I A N A
Q L Y U Z Z A N E X N H S C
H O L I V I A I R I E P T A Y
B H L V C R E L Y T H E E R N
Y C G J O H N U P H P T A A T
L I L S N J R J U H L G W H H
L N X E B A W I A R A E E B I
I I K B H T Y N S E R C C H A
E B Y N R C I R A T O I A I U
S G O I A E A J N L I L R N S
Y M R C Q R N R D A M A G G I
Z B Q O A L F D R W M Q N R Z
Q I T L E J D L A U R A A E D
H E L E N G M H G M U S W I L
```

Alice	Frank	John	Rachel
Billy	Gary	Julia	Ralph
Brenda	George	Keith	Ryan
Catherine	Grace	Laura	Sandra
Christian	Helen	Maria	Sarah
Cynthia	Jacob	Nicholas	Stephanie
Diana	Janet	Nicole	Tyler
Ethan	Joan	Olivia	Walter

Solutions

Acrostics

Puzzle #1
A. LIGHTSHOW
B. ATTHATTIME
C. NOTEWORTHY
D. SUBURB
E. EYETEETH
F. NAIVETY
G. SHERMAN
H. THOUGHT
I. HAVETO
J. EASTEREGGHUNT
K. GUNGHO
L. INTERMINABLY
M. RUNONTHEBANK
N. LINER
O. STARTERS

The strangest thing about strange things is that they're only strange when you hear about them or think about them later, but never when you're living them. —Lori Lansens, *The Girls*

Puzzle #2
A. BAKESHOP
B. LEFTIN
C. UPSIDE
D. MYHUMPS
E. EDMONTON
F. TATTY
G. INTHEWAY
H. GOODYTWOSHOES
I. EASEDIN
J. RETOUCHES
K. ENDUP
L. YABBA
M. ETHNO
N. SOUTHPAW

Some changes happen deep down inside of you. And the truth is, only you know about them. Maybe that's the way it's supposed to be. —Judy Blume, *Tiger Eyes*

Puzzle #3
A. INHALE
B. SWATAT
C. ALDRICH
D. ACIDIFY
E. CHEWINGTHEFAT
F. SUITOR
G. DOSIDO
H. INTENTIONS
I. ATOMS
J. LEGATO
K. ONEMONTH
L. GORDONBROWN
M. UNKIND
N. ENFANT

The intention of dialogue is to reach new understanding and, in doing so, to form a totally new basis from which to think and act. —William Isaacs, *Dialogue*

Puzzle #4
A. WRISTWATCHES
B. INTERSTATE
C. LASTWISH
D. KITTEN
E. SHAPIRO
F. BEEHIVE
G. LAVIGNE
H. OTTAWAN
I. OBELI
J. DASHING
K. MOLEHILLS
L. ADEPTLY
M. GRAPHITE
N. IONIAN
O. CHITCHATTED

Lily hated politics. Grandmother said that was naive, that hating politics was like hating the weather. Pointless, since both were inevitable. —Eileen Wilks, *Blood Magic*

Puzzle #5
A. HUMPTY
B. EXCULPATORY
C. STUDIOUS
D. SEAWATER
E. EATFAT
F. SPOOKY
G. INTHEBUFF
H. DOUGH
I. DAWSON
J. HOCKEY
K. ALLEYCAT
L. REVELATION
M. TOUCHE
N. HOUSTON
O. AUTO

What could I say to you that would be of value, except that perhaps you seek too much, that as a result of your seeking you cannot find. —Hermann Hesse, *Siddhartha*

Acrostics (continued)

Puzzle #6

A. COIFFURE
B. ASONG
C. MOTIONS
D. UPSET
E. SLIPAWAY

F. TWEAKED
G. HOLYWAR
H. EYESWIDESHUT
I. PSHAW
J. LIPID

K. ARTES
L. GAWKS
M. UNCUT
N. EVENS

Stupidity has a knack of getting its way; as we should see if we were not always so much wrapped up in ourselves.
—Albert Camus, *The Plague*

Puzzle #7

A. PLAYOFFS
B. ITSABOY
C. PAWNS
D. EBBETS
E. RONWEASLEY

F. GOTINTHEWAY
G. RETRY
H. EXACT
I. YODELS
J. HARDTOP

K. OBLATE
L. UNTASTEFUL
M. NICEPUTT
N. DOGWOOD

Always try to be good to people, don't always put yourself first, and don't always expect things to be fair, because they won't be. —Steffan Piper, *Greyhound*

Puzzle #8

A. TENURES
B. ATEASE
C. MMMCCC
D. PROFFER
E. LABOHEME
F. INEFFECT

G. NEARHERE
H. MONIKER
I. YOUREALLWET
J. PHOEBES
K. HESIOD
L. AMBROSE

M. NOVELLAS
N. TRIESTE
O. ONEEYED
P. MUTINOUS

Remember, every performance will be the first for someone in the audience and the last for someone else. You must be sure to make each one special. —Anstance Tamplin, *My Phantom*

Puzzle #9

A. VAUNT
B. OFFHOURS
C. LILITH
D. TYPES
E. AMNESTY

F. IKNOWIT
G. REVELER
H. EAGLERAY
I. CAMPHOR
J. AFTERYOU

K. NORAHS
L. DINTY
M. IRISHPEOPLE
N. DEFORMATIONS
O. EMPLOY

Fools admire everything in an author of reputation. For my part, I read only to please myself. I like only that which serves my purpose. —Voltaire, *Candide*

Puzzle #10

A. CARTWHEEL
B. RICHE
C. OVEREATEN
D. STEPTWO
E. SLIWA
F. TAKEMEHOME

G. HOWNOW
H. ELLROY
I. STOWE
J. HABANA
K. EELPOT
L. POACH

M. HOHOHO
N. ETHENE
O. RELATIVE
P. DEFAMATION

At some point, we all come to a place where we have to choose whether to be the hero, the villain, or to walk away and remain one of the sheep. —Ethan Cross, *The Shepherd*

Acrostics (continued)

Puzzle #11

A. BYTHEBOOK
B. INVOKES
C. ROSEBUSH
D. DAMAGE
E. FALLOW
F. RABBITFOOD

G. OGLALA
H. MOOTED
I. THEAGE
J. HEADWAY
K. EATONS
L. FACETED

M. INUSA
N. REMADE
O. STEAMSHOVEL
P. TEMPEH

Life takes you a lot of places. Some good, some bad. I've always found that having a home somewhere makes the good better and the bad bearable. —Jessica Bird, *From the First*

Puzzle #12

A. FINESTHOUR
B. EDWARDS
C. EASYOUTS
D. HEADHONCHO
E. ATCHISON

F. NAILEDDOWN
G. MAHI
H. IVORYTOWER
I. NASTIEST
J. DOUBLEFEATURE

K. GENETICISTS
L. ARTHRO
M. MELDS
N. ENSUE

There were a thousand secrets in her eyes, a thousand wounds. A lifetime of distrust and betrayal. Isolation. How did one overcome such things? —Christine Feehan, *Mind Game*

Puzzle #13

A. DIATOM
B. ACTSOF
C. VATTED
D. INFANTRYMEN
E. DAFFIEST
F. SANANTONIO

G. OFFEREDUP
H. NINETEEN
I. TERREHAUTE
J. HITCHCOCK
K. ENCHANTED
L. LAYABET

M. EMMANUEL
N. DEARTH
O. GOODMAN
P. EXACTITUDE

The physical exertions and mental fortitude that the mountains demanded forced me to face fear, manage doubt, and take action, even in the face of uncertainty. —Jim Davidson, *The Ledge*

Puzzle #14

A. CHOPPIER
B. ACHESON
C. REWORKS
D. LIFESTYLE
E. SEETHED

F. ARCHIVIST
G. GNOMES
H. ASHTREE
I. NOSIREE
J. COFFEEPOT

K. ONTOPOFTHEWORLD
L. SITTINGS
M. MINNIE
N. OUIDA
O. STAID

Cosmos is a Greek word for the order of the universe. It is, in a way, the opposite of Chaos. It implies the deep interconnectedness of all things. —Carl Sagan, *Cosmos*

Puzzle #15

A. BOASTED
B. APANIC
C. RUTHENIUM
D. NOHELP
E. ENLIST

F. STIFFENS
G. ACCLIVITY
H. RAILTHIN
I. ITEMIZES
J. STAVE

K. TENTHS
L. OFFLINE
M. THESIS
N. LOWCAL
O. EMDASH

Happiness—that state of mind in which men realize themselves and flourish best—consists in a life of intellectual activity. —Jonathan Barnes, *Aristotle*

Acrostics (continued)

Puzzle #16

A. MONARCH
B. AFLUTTER
C. SNIPPET
D. LIGAMENT
E. ANNOTATE
F. COREYS
G. HEREIN
H. BITTER
I. UNCLES
J. ROPESOFF
K. NOPROB
L. ONEPIECE
M. UNIFORM
N. TEXTILE

More often than not, people interpret their experience of burnout as reflecting some basic personality malfunction. —Christina Maslach, *Burnout*

Puzzle #17

A. GALENA
B. LOONIEST
C. ANTENNA
D. DOODADS
E. WORKMANSHIP
F. ENTERINTO
G. LATTE
H. LEANONME
I. OVERAWE
J. UNHOOKS
K. THICKENERS
L. LOOSE
M. INOVER
N. ESSAYS
O. REHABILITATES
P. STANDOFF

He'd had to make his way alone, and no one—not rock stars, not professional athletes, not software billionaires, and not even geniuses—ever makes it alone. —Malcolm Gladwell, *Outliers*

Puzzle #18

A. CUTOFF
B. HANGOUT
C. ATTORNEYS
D. BOTFLY
E. OBITPAGE
F. NANNYGOAT
G. SUNBATHED
H. UNISON
I. MOTTLE
J. MEDITATE
K. EGGCREAM
L. RECRUIT
M. LAWTON
N. AMAST
O. NEARTHETOP
P. DAHLIA

The fundamental truth: a baseball game is nothing but a great slow contraption for getting you to pay attention to the cadence of a summer day. —Michael Chabon, *Summerland*

Puzzle #19

A. CRYPTOGRAPHY
B. HUMIDITY
C. OUTHOUSE
D. RETINUE
E. ONDAATJE
F. SHOE
G. TELEPATHY
H. RELATIONSHIP
I. ELEGISTS
J. BIWEEKLY
K. UNSETTLE
L. INTHENEARFUTURE
M. LEVIATHAN
N. THROWAWAYS

John Hull, a blind man, writes that while the eyes put you at the periphery of the universe—you are always at its edge, looking in—the ears put you at its center. —Michael Chorost, *Rebuilt*

Puzzle #20

A. HOMEBASE
B. UNBEATEN
C. FETCHING
D. FLETCHER
E. MMMCIII
F. ANGLEE
G. NONSMOKING
H. TRAVERSES
I. HIGHHEELS
J. REPOTS
K. OSTEND
L. WEIGHTINESS
M. AMBITION
N. WOWED
O. ARISTA
P. YELLED

Sometimes in life, there are pivotal moments. While seemingly benign on the surface, something within acknowledges that a bridge has been crossed. —Heather Huffman, *Throwaway*

Acrostics (continued)

Puzzle #21

A. IMMOBILE
B. YEOLDE
C. ETHYLS
D. RETWEETS
E. SHELTERED
F. UVLIGHT
G. NINEVEH
H. ASTHE
I. FIFTEENTH
J. TONNAGES
K. EMBLEMATIC
L. RANOUTOF
M. DONOTENTER
N. AWAITED
O. REGROWTH
P. KOWTOW

Confronted by the foreign, we grow newly attentive to the details of the world, even as we make out, sometimes, the larger outline that lies behind them. —Pico Iyer, *Sun After Dark*

Puzzle #22

A. PLETHORA
B. ABOVETHELAW
C. MONTHLY
D. UNCUFFED
E. KVETCH
F. MARTS
G. YEWTREE
H. NOTATION
I. AFTERWORK
J. MATADORS
K. EIGHT
L. INAWEOF
M. SHAREHOLDER
N. REDHOT
O. EYESFRONT
P. DAINTIER

Let me first state forthright that contrary to what we've often read in books and heard from preachers, when you are a woman, you don't feel like the Devil. —Orhan Pamuk, *My Name Is Red*

Puzzle #23

A. WAGEFREEZES
B. OSHKOSHBGOSH
C. OTHER
D. LAWNORNAMENTS
E. FACTSOFLIFE
F. NINETYFIVE
G. INBETWEEN
H. GRAPEFRUIT
I. HUSHPUPPIES
J. THEMISTOCLES
K. ASAMATTEROFFACT
L. NOTIFICATIONS
M. DWELLINTHEHEART
N. DELETION
O. ARTHRITIC
P. YOSEMITESAM

Raising his eyes for a moment from the face of his watch, he rested them upon the opposite bank, reflectively and not without a certain wistfulness, as if the sternness of their gaze were still capable of mitigation. —Virginia Woolf, *Night and Day*

Puzzle #24

A. BLOWTHEWHISTLE
B. REPATRIATION
C. OHIORIVER
D. NUMBEST
E. TOFUS
F. EACHONE
G. JACKASS
H. AFFECT
I. NUCLEOTIDES
J. EDWINDROOD
K. ENSOR
L. YIELDED
M. REFILLS
N. EREMITE

Prejudices, it is well known, are most difficult to eradicate from the heart whose soil has never been loosened or fertilised by education. —Charlotte Brontë, *Jane Eyre*

Puzzle #25

A. STEMSTHETIDE
B. HEATHERGRAHAM
C. ELWOODHAYNES
D. CARDPUNCH
E. KAZAKH
F. LESMIZ
G. EARLYWARNING
H. YELLOWKNIFE
I. MOONLIGHTING
J. ODDNUMBERED
K. ONETREEHILL
L. NEWFANGLED
M. BOOKMARKED
N. UNSUBSTANTIATED
O. RESERVES
P. NIGHTCLUBS

She nudged me with her tan and black muzzle, then pressed her full weight against my shoulder and arm, knocking me back on my heels. Like a lot of big dogs, rottweilers have an inbred desire to lean on the unwary. —Alisa Sheckley, *Moonburn*

Acrostics (continued)

Puzzle #26

A. CONTESTANTS
B. HISSING
C. INHERENT
D. LARGELY
E. DRAWINGABLANK
F. PULMONARY
G. HEADOFSTATE
H. INDEFINABLE
I. LAUNDRY
J. ODWALLA
K. TUTTI
L. HOUSEPLANT
M. ENTERING
N. AORTIC

She complained of no illness, but grew thinner and thinner, like a cloud gradually floating away, and retaining its transparent beauty to the last. —Lydia Maria Child, *Philothea*

Puzzle #27

A. CHICO
B. AFCWEST
C. RECTIFY
D. DONOT
E. HONEYS
F. INTERRACIAL
G. DEVASTATED
H. DHOW
I. EXCELIN
J. NSYNC
K. ELISHA
L. MANACLE
M. PUFFIN
N. ILYICH
O. RAINFORESTS
P. ELTONS

What is scientific fact? An oxymoron. Science does not deal in facts. It deals in hypotheses, which are never fully and finally correct. —Orson Scott Card, *Hidden Empire*

Puzzle #28

A. CHECKIN
B. ATGREATLENGTH
C. REDHOT
D. ROBOT
E. INASTEW
F. GLOATED
G. ESPOUSED
H. ROCKET
I. SATCHMO
J. OPTIMIZATION
K. UNCERTAIN
L. LANDOWNER
M. LAKES
N. ENTHUSED
O. SHORTHAND
P. SISYPHEAN

Her heart was doing crazy things, and she still could not locate her kneecaps. She took a deep breath and put some serious attention into tracking them down. —Gail Carriger, *Soulless*

Puzzle #29

A. LACAGEAUXFOLLES
B. AILMENT
C. RISKIT
D. SHODDIER
E. ORDERIN
F. NAILVARNISH
G. ENDPAPER
H. VICTORIASSECRET
I. OPEDS
J. LEAFEATING
K. UNAPPEALING
L. TRIPP
M. INUNIFORM
N. OUTOFMONEY
O. NIBLET

The origin of life and individual species posed a particular problem for Greeks intent on devising purely materialistic explanations for natural phenomena. —Edward J. Larson, *Evolution: The Remarkable History of a Scientific Theory*

Puzzle #30

A. PINCHED
B. ROCOCO
C. ONADIME
D. UNDAMAGED
E. SWIFT
F. TIBETAN
G. STREWED
H. WERNER
I. AFFIANCE
J. NDJAMENA
K. NEEDIER
L. SUFFICE
M. WATCHMAN
N. ATOMICWEIGHT
O. YELLOWHORNET

In my cowardice I became at once a man, and did what all we grown men do when face to face with suffering and injustice; I preferred not to see them. —Marcel Proust, *Swann's Way*

Clueless Crosswords

Puzzle #1

```
B O O   S U R P R I S E D   S E A
E A R S     A R E N A     T E A R
G R A C E   W I P E D   P H A S E
  S L A V E   Z   P   E R U P T
Q   R I N S E   T U X E D O   M
U   P   L E T   U   S P Y   R   U
O U R S   M A R S H A L   I T E M
T   O   O I L   E   G O T   S   M
E   J E W E L S   P E D A L   Y
  P E A L S   P   R   E B O N Y
P A C T S   O A S I S   S N O U T
A C T S     F R A N K     E T C H
Y E S   A F F E C T I O N   E K E
```

1	2	3	4	5	6	7	8	9	10	11	12	13
O	R	V	Z	Y	N	M	K	S	E	D	Q	T

14	15	16	17	18	19	20	21	22	23	24	25	26
A	C	I	U	B	W	F	X	G	H	L	P	J

Puzzle #2

```
D E F E C T   M A M A S   C     F
  I   U N I T E     J A W   E
A B S   X E N O N   K A R A T E
O P E N S   T O P   L I B E L E D
P E R I O D   R   R I M   E L M
T   P L E A   D E M O   R O P E
I   E   O B S E R V I N G   W   X
C A P S   T I N Y   T O U T     A
  B O P   O D D   Q   S Y S T E M
D E C L A R E   C U E   S A I L S
O T H E R S   S H E L F   R E F
Z   S E T   P A R K A   R
E   N   M E A T Y   R O U S E S
```

1	2	3	4	5	6	7	8	9	10	11	12	13
H	E	M	Z	C	B	I	F	U	T	K	S	R

14	15	16	17	18	19	20	21	22	23	24	25	26
N	G	J	A	X	W	L	D	Q	P	O	V	Y

Puzzle #3

```
  F E R V E N T   J A C K P O T
C O M A     A Z   Z   O   L I O N
O R B S     R A I S I N   A L T O
A D A P T E R   L   S E N S E S
X   R   H   O U C H   Q     E
E   K   U   W   H   P   U   R
D R E A M I E R   B R E A T H E S
    D   B   R   T O T E   E   E
S   E   S O W S   O   T   C
M A L A D Y   G   P U R P O S E
O K A Y   E N R A G E   A R I D
G I V E   T     S   C   P I L E
  N A S T I L Y   A T T R A C T
```

1	2	3	4	5	6	7	8	9	10	11	12	13
F	P	Y	X	V	K	U	T	Z	L	I	S	W

14	15	16	17	18	19	20	21	22	23	24	25	26
R	H	G	M	A	O	C	E	N	Q	D	B	J

Puzzle #4

```
  A G E   P A R I S H   S K I D
Q   O W E   U N C U T   I   W
U   V E N D   S P A M   A D S   I
A R E   D I S T U R B E D   U M P
R   R   G A I T   L   J O B   E
T A N   P I P E S   Y   U N T O
Z   M E A T   R   R   U S E R   N
  B E G S   T   T E M P T   A P E
E   N O T   R   A L O E   C   I
C A T   R E A C T I O N S   T U G
H   S L Y   D A T A   D E L I   H
O   O   F E L O N   T I N   S
  W A X Y   S L O T H S   E G G
```

1	2	3	4	5	6	7	8	9	10	11	12	13
I	S	N	E	Q	J	B	Y	T	U	A	D	K

14	15	16	17	18	19	20	21	22	23	24	25	26
F	R	Z	W	H	V	L	C	O	P	G	M	X

Puzzle #5

```
C L A S P   S O U P S   A F T E R
  S H A D O W   L I Q U O R
M O T O R   N E W E R   B R A V O
U N H O O K   D A D   Q U E U E D
G E M   L I D   X   O U R   M A D
  S A V E D   Y   I N H A L E
S   A   N O W   B I B   I   R
T I P T O E   Z   B A S I L
E R A   B Y E   O   E L F   N I B
M O R A S S   J O B   E R A S E R
S N A K E   B U S E S   A R E N A
  D I S C O S   E E R I E R
L I E N S   A T O N E   D A T E D
```

1	2	3	4	5	6	7	8	9	10	11	12	13
L	V	K	N	X	J	R	U	C	W	T	M	A

14	15	16	17	18	19	20	21	22	23	24	25	26
O	H	I	B	P	Y	G	E	Z	S	F	D	Q

Puzzle #6

```
G O A D S   S C Y T H E   I C Y
O   M Y   H E R E I N   H E M
R O P E D   R I S I N G   F E T A
E   E   O V E N   C   H A R E   N
S   D   U   J A C K E T   O R G Y
  D   A B L E   H   S H O W E R
Q U E L L   C H A R S   U N D E R
  E X T E N T   I   A N T S   W
B L U E   A S T R A Y   I   C   F
E   D R A B   H   B E E N   L   L
T H I S   B A R B E D   G L A Z E
S U N   R E T O R T   A S   F
  E G G   D E B A S E   T Y P E S
```

1	2	3	4	5	6	7	8	9	10	11	12	13
Z	I	J	C	T	S	U	L	G	O	R	Q	W

14	15	16	17	18	19	20	21	22	23	24	25	26
F	K	A	E	V	D	P	X	H	M	Y	B	N

Clueless Crosswords (continued)

Puzzle #7

Puzzle #8

Puzzle #9

Puzzle #10

Puzzle #11

Puzzle #12

Clueless Crosswords (continued)

Puzzle #13

```
JILTED   APATHY
MEDIA  BRAS  OAT
ALIEN  SLICK ANEW
PYLON  SQUAT ARKS
LOOM  FOUR  VISIT
A   S  RABBI DENSE
Z W GOES UMPS G  P
ASIDE  SHARP  G  O
PSALM  LEEK   LYNX
OHMS  PETAL  GOOEY
SOFA  BAYOU  DESKS
LUG  ICES   UNSET
LEANED   ABBEYS
```

1	2	3	4	5	6	7	8	9	10	11	12	13
A	C	H	V	L	B	Z	X	P	Y	M	Q	N

14	15	16	17	18	19	20	21	22	23	24	25	26
D	I	E	W	R	O	G	J	T	K	F	U	S

Puzzle #14

```
JUICY  CARATS  EBB
A TO   CAVEAT  LIE
PRAWN  ATTEND  REND
A L UNTO R ITEM G
N Y D TRUTHS VISE
E  SIZE L AMBUSH
FRONT NOTES REHAB
GRAYED R SKIS   M
SOAR ISRAEL  E Q W
A CLOG U LEAF U H
GELS HORRID  SLICE
ARE  STRAIT  AT A
ASK  YELPED  EXERT
```

1	2	3	4	5	6	7	8	9	10	11	12	13
H	L	E	Q	N	X	O	G	W	Y	R	V	D

14	15	16	17	18	19	20	21	22	23	24	25	26
Z	K	I	C	A	B	P	U	F	J	T	S	M

Puzzle #15

```
S ACRE  AXLES  ROAM
P  HOARD  OAT  E
R PASTED  TRUFFLES
ITALY F S D E P
GUNK  UNIT  ISRAEL
S EAST Z DOT R I
SKIDS  EVADE  ADEPT
E L KID B SARI  R
F N I I S T B I R S I I R
P  M C E A  TEAMS
SQUASHED  JIGSAW  A
G ERA  AREAS  L
SORE  DRYER  TREK M
```

1	2	3	4	5	6	7	8	9	10	11	12	13
I	T	V	Q	J	M	K	W	U	G	P	C	E

14	15	16	17	18	19	20	21	22	23	24	25	26
Z	O	B	Y	S	D	N	X	F	R	A	L	H

Puzzle #16

```
SLEAZY   PASTAS
EQUAL  SASH  SAT
CURSE  MUSHY SPIT
SHAKY  GUSTY DULL
TOTE  DASH  LIMIT
O D  FEIGN SENSE
I J TOFU RUGS G X
CLASH  EMBED  A I
INLAY  LASSO  DEBT
VIEW  AMUSE  OVALS
YETI  SCARY  OBESE
DOG  UNIT  HONED
RHYMED   COMETS
```

1	2	3	4	5	6	7	8	9	10	11	12	13
F	K	A	U	Z	X	W	P	Q	T	H	C	M

14	15	16	17	18	19	20	21	22	23	24	25	26
V	D	L	E	O	R	Y	G	I	J	N	B	S

Puzzle #17

```
JAGGED  ADMIT  S  G
R  INFER   FOE  A
YEA PUFFS  KENNEL
LEASH NIT WIZARDS
UNTIES X SAD  TAG
N AMPS  AKIN  AGES
A K PENKNIVES E T
RUNS  LAID  EYES E
POP  LID Q  SATIRE
COLONEL  CUE  TIDAL
UNLOAD  CLING  RIG
R SKY  OUTDO  O
B S GLOBS  BOTTLE
```

1	2	3	4	5	6	7	8	9	10	11	12	13
T	I	J	O	M	D	L	Q	V	R	P	W	K

14	15	16	17	18	19	20	21	22	23	24	25	26
U	C	A	B	G	F	X	H	S	E	Z	N	Y

Puzzle #18

```
RUBBER  SAVVY  C H
O  UNCLE  JAB  E
WOW GUILT  BANANA
CHEAT TOY RUMORED
ZODIAC N AID  EGO
A FLOP  FROG  SENT
R Q COLLECTED D W
SOUR  LAID  STAY I
DIE  END B  SMARTS
MOLLUSK  BOB  SKIRT
ARTIST  TOXIC  SPY
T SEE  HYENA  E
S S ABYSS  TRUNKS
```

1	2	3	4	5	6	7	8	9	10	11	12	13
S	J	G	K	F	P	V	R	L	A	M	H	W

14	15	16	17	18	19	20	21	22	23	24	25	26
N	I	Z	C	U	B	Y	Q	E	D	X	T	O

Clueless Crosswords (continued)

Puzzle #19

| 1 C | 2 K | 3 O | 4 R | 5 A | 6 U | 7 T | 8 P | 9 N | 10 B | 11 Y | 12 Q | 13 W |
| 14 Z | 15 I | 16 D | 17 M | 18 E | 19 F | 20 X | 21 V | 22 J | 23 G | 24 L | 25 S | 26 H |

Puzzle #20

| 1 I | 2 S | 3 O | 4 A | 5 Y | 6 G | 7 H | 8 X | 9 Z | 10 B | 11 P | 12 L | 13 N |
| 14 E | 15 D | 16 V | 17 T | 18 M | 19 C | 20 W | 21 J | 22 Q | 23 K | 24 F | 25 U | 26 R |

Puzzle #21

| 1 L | 2 K | 3 N | 4 V | 5 D | 6 S | 7 A | 8 H | 9 I | 10 O | 11 Z | 12 F | 13 T |
| 14 B | 15 Q | 16 X | 17 J | 18 C | 19 G | 20 P | 21 Y | 22 M | 23 E | 24 W | 25 R | 26 U |

Puzzle #22

| 1 U | 2 Z | 3 D | 4 Y | 5 G | 6 W | 7 N | 8 V | 9 S | 10 F | 11 H | 12 P | 13 R |
| 14 M | 15 K | 16 E | 17 I | 18 J | 19 C | 20 B | 21 X | 22 A | 23 L | 24 O | 25 Q | 26 T |

Puzzle #23

| 1 L | 2 F | 3 J | 4 G | 5 Y | 6 I | 7 W | 8 A | 9 S | 10 E | 11 X | 12 P | 13 R |
| 14 V | 15 C | 16 U | 17 O | 18 T | 19 H | 20 B | 21 N | 22 Z | 23 K | 24 D | 25 Q | 26 M |

Puzzle #24

| 1 Q | 2 E | 3 Z | 4 S | 5 K | 6 G | 7 I | 8 H | 9 L | 10 Y | 11 P | 12 D | 13 M |
| 14 B | 15 O | 16 T | 17 R | 18 V | 19 A | 20 U | 21 W | 22 N | 23 J | 24 X | 25 C | 26 F |

Clueless Crosswords (continued)

Puzzle #25

Puzzle #26

Puzzle #27

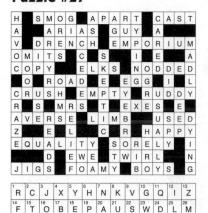

Puzzle #28

Puzzle #29

Puzzle #30

Crosswords

Puzzle #1

```
S O S O . S A S S . . . S I F T
P L E A . A D I E U . . A V E R
E L L S . L O A M S . . H O L E
C A L I F O R N I A G I R L S .
. . . S O O N . . . . A B Y S S
P T A . U N S A V E D . . . . .
O R G A N . . L A B . O P A L .
W O U L D N T I T B E N I C E .
S T E P . A W E . . G E N R E .
. . . S P O N S O R . E E K . .
B A S S O . . . U R E A . . . .
L I T T L E S A I N T N I C K .
A S E A . F O R T E . G L U E .
S L A B . T R I E R . S I R E .
T E D S . E D D Y . . T A L L .
```

Puzzle #2

```
I H O P . H O O P . . . H E D Y
P A R R . O U T I E . . A L I E
U S D O . N I H A O . . V I D A
T H O M A S J E F F E R S O N .
. . . O S H A . . . T E A K S .
E D S . A U S T R I A . . . . .
G U L A G . . Y O N . I D E O .
G R O V E R C L E V E L A N D .
S A G E . A D E . . N A R C O .
. . . T H E R M A L . . T E R .
A M B E R . . D N A S . . . . .
W I L L I A M M C K I N L E Y .
A L O E . O C A L A . I D B E .
S L A V . N A D I R . P L O W .
H I T S . N E V A . . S S N S .
```

Puzzle #3

```
A D O S . H A U L . . . C H E R
W A S H . A N T E S . . H O V E
O F L A . I O W A N . . A S I T
L E O N A R D O D A V I N C I .
. . . E R D E . . . . W R I T E
E S E . G O S S I P S . . . . .
S A N Y O . . T L S . G O R E .
E U G E N E D E L A C R O I X .
L D L S . S O I . . O F F A T .
. . . O C O N N O R . S A S . .
E P O C H . . . E F F S . . . .
T O U L O U S E L A U T R E C .
T I T O . S W I S H . O Y E Z .
A N I T . G E N O A . O N E A .
S T E S . D E N T . . D E E R .
```

Puzzle #4

```
H E M A N . A C T V . . L U G S
O M A H A . W I F I . . O T H E
N E G O T I A T O R . U I E S .
K E N T U C K Y . G U I L E S .
S R A . R E E . D I V S . . . .
. . . A R S . I N S I P I D . .
D O R A L . D E I . . A R L O .
C H I P . O U I D A . N E I N .
C O M P . C T Y . . B A K E S .
C H E L S E A . I B A . . . . .
. . . E L A H . N A H . I F I .
O R E G O N . A R K A N S A S .
H A R A . A B N O R M A L L Y .
I N I T . U L N A . E R A S E .
O I S E . T E E D . N Y M E T .
```

Puzzle #5

```
O R U . O N T O . . . T R U C E
C O R . H O E R . P O I R O T .
K A L A H A R I . E M P I R E .
. . D I A M O N D B A C K S . .
N O N O . . . L O A . . . . . .
A N O S . N E E D L E N O S E .
D E O . R E D S . . E A T O N .
Y A N K E E S . M A R L I N S .
A T A R I . I A G O . O N U . .
S A N A N T O N I O . I S E E .
. . . H T C . . . . . M E T S .
I L L E G I T I M A T E . . . .
N E A L O N . S E N A T O R S .
T I G E R S . O A T S . D I E .
I F S A Y . R T E S . . A P E .
```

Puzzle #6

```
M I C S . R E H A B . . H I T .
M C L I V . E A U D E . A D E .
C H O R E O G R A P H . N E A .
M A G E L L A N . E D S E L . .
L T S . C G I . D U A N E . . .
. . . F R A N C I S D R A K E .
S E E T O . A N D S . T O S . .
I N X S . E V I T A . P I K S .
T S O . A D A R . C O C O A . .
H E R N A N C O R T E S . . . .
. . C O M A S . E E L . R I A .
C H I L I . O V A T I O N S . .
O Y S . L E I F E R I C S O N .
O P T . N A D I R . C A I N E .
K O S . E R O D E . . N E E R .
```

Crosswords (continued)

Puzzle #7

```
E N T S █ █ O F T H E █ S S I
G O R E S █ C O R E A █ H A D
B L A C K P E P P E R █ O L E
D I S T I L L S █ █ L O W E D
F E H █ B A L █ L O O S E █ █
█ █ █ J U N I P E R B E R R Y
A S S A M █ █ A N N E █ C I V
F A T S █ H A U T E █ M A C E
I G A █ D I L L █ █ N A P E S
T O R T I L L A F L A T █ █ █
█ █ A O R T A █ I E R █ R C A
S I N C E █ █ E N A C T O R S
A R I █ C H I L I P O W D E R
G A S █ T U B E S █ S I E T E
E E E █ V E T C H █ █ T O E D
```

Puzzle #8

```
C R A N █ █ A B E █ █ D I E N
A U T O █ S C O T █ H I N D I
S T E P █ A H O T █ I M O N E
T H E R E F O R E █ T A R A █
█ █ █ O R E O S █ R O G █ █ █
A R A B I C █ █ B E N G A L I
S A K █ K O R E A N █ I N A T
A B E T S █ Y O S █ G O N N A
M A L E █ P A S H T O █ A A S
I T A L I A N █ A M E L I A █
█ █ █ L T S █ K H M E R █ █ █
█ B E L A █ C H E E R E D U P
T A M I L █ M A W R █ C O R E
A R M E Y █ I K E S █ T U D E
V E E S █ █ V I R █ █ S P U N
```

Puzzle #9

```
G I N A █ T E M P █ C U L L S
I S A N █ O P I E █ A R E A L
M A U D █ N I L E █ L A T H E
M A R I O N C O T I L L A R D
E C U █ C E S █ █ S O S █ █ █
█ █ █ H H S █ U C S F █ S S I
P E K O E █ E T T U █ E W A N
B A R B R A S T R E I S A N D
A R O O █ G A E L █ F A N T A
S L C █ S A U R █ P E I █ █ █
█ █ █ B A P █ W A L █ S I N █
S H I R L E Y M A C L A I N E
A W A I T █ E X G I █ M E L L
C A M E O █ A V O N █ O V A L
S N I F F █ S I N G █ K E Y S
```

Puzzle #10

```
E S P N █ H E C H E █ A P A L
T H E E █ A T E A R █ R O L O
C A D B U R Y C R E M E E G G
S H S █ D O P E █ █ U N S A Y
█ █ █ M O L E █ W E S T █ █ █
A L M O N D █ Y O R K █ S A M
S A U R █ D A N S E █ W V A █
T H R E E M U S K E T E E R S
R A K █ X E N I A █ S E I S █
O R Y █ O N E R █ N E S T L E
█ █ █ B T U S █ H A L O █ █ █
A C T I I █ E E N S █ A T S █
W H A T C H A M A C A L L I T
L I V E █ A M I T Y █ O A K Y
S A I S █ M O T H S █ T W I X
```

Puzzle #11

```
B Y M E █ N E L L █ A R E Y E
F E I N █ I V E Y █ S H E B A
F O R T U N E I S T H E R O D
S F O █ N E N A █ A C T O R S
█ █ █ O A T S █ M C A T █ █ █
A K I M B O █ B U O N █ M O R
B A N A L █ Y E S M █ M A C H
O F T H E W E A K A N D T H E
I K E A █ E N R Y █ U L T R A
L A R █ L I T A █ O T I S E S
█ █ █ D O R A █ H A J I █ █ █
O S G O O D █ G O T O █ C E L
S T A F F O F T H E B R A V E
H A I F A █ Y O U R █ S N A G
A B A S H █ I S M S █ S I N G
```

Puzzle #12

```
A H A B █ A F A R █ █ R A B E
N A C L █ T I C K █ E E R I E
W H A T O R A T O R S L A C K
R A B █ N O T V █ E M I L E █
█ █ █ R I S █ F L E E █ █ █ █
█ S H I A S █ M I A █ D A Y O
D I A L M █ C A S T S █ C I D
I N D E P T H T H E Y M A K E
V A I █ S O O T Y █ N O S E D
A I T S █ M P S █ B A S E S █
█ █ █ C P A S █ M O P █ █ █ █
█ E D O A T █ C O W S █ I O S
U P T O Y O U I N L E N G T H
M E E T S █ S A T E █ N O R A
S E N S █ █ M O E S █ W R A Y
```

Crosswords (continued)

Puzzle #13

```
O S S I E . A S H E . C A N A
C L I M E . S O A R . H O A R
H U M O R I S T H E F I R S T
O R I F I C E S . . L A T T E
. . L Y S . V E E . A Y S . .
F O R A Y . S E R E . . . . .
O P E D . L A T E N T . C E N
G I F T T O P E R I S H I N A
S E S . A T E A S E . M A G I
. . I T E M . W O O L F . . .
A M B . P O P . C L E . . . .
B O O N E . C H A I R M A N .
F O R E I G N L A N G U A G E
A L O E . O D E S . H E R E S
B A N S . S A F E . T R Y S T
```

Puzzle #14

```
I C A L . E C A R D . D E M S
R Y N E . D A L A I . I S O N
A R T S . D R U M S . T S A O
Q U I T T I N G S M O K I N G
I S S . W E E . A N A . . . .
. L I S . C A Y S . I C I . .
L U M E T . V O R E . E L I N
I S E A S Y I V E D O N E I T
E D H S . E R E S . C Y R I L
U A R . S S G T . B T O . . .
. M E W . M E E . S E E . . .
H U N D R E D S O F T I M E S
I B E X . C A N O E . M O L T
L E V I . A T A L L . A T E E
T R E X . N E P A L . M E R E
```

Puzzle #15

```
I C A N . O N U S . I M N O .
E L L A . N I L E S . B L I X
R E A M . E B E R T . E X G I
I F P E O P L E B E H A V E D
. O K I E . . E M I L E . . .
C P B . I N T E G R A . . . .
D R A W N . Y E A . Z E E S .
L I K E G O V E R N M E N T S
X M E N . B I O . I N C A N .
. R E D F E R N . E T S . . .
T Y P E A . L A C E . . . . .
Y O U D C A L L T H E C O P S
S U N G . R E S O W . O K R A
O N C E . T I A R A . N L E R
N T H S . A T O Y . O A T S .
```

Puzzle #16

```
G E T A . S P I T . D A D E .
A L O G . T O N E D . R I O S
R E N O . E G G E R . O N U S
B E I N T E R E S T I N G B E
. Y O L O . . B E E T S . . .
S S E . Y E M E N I S . . . .
T E M P O . W A N . N E A P .
E N T H U S I A S T I C A N D
P T S D . T N N . M O T I F .
. M U G S H O T . S T S . . .
A R E S O . I D O S . . . . .
D O N T T A L K T O O M U C H
A M O R . G I N S U . U C L A
M A L O . S P O O L . R A U L
S N A P . O W N S . F L E E .
```

Puzzle #17

```
F I D O . M E D O . D B A S .
E H O W . I V A N . Y E A R S
M O N E Y N E V E R M A D E A
A P T . A U R A . E C R U S .
. N T T . O V A L . . . . . .
A C A K E . E K E . Y E N S .
U N L I T . H E A R D . T A O
F O O L O F A N Y B O D Y I T
O U S . N A Z I S . G O P R O
S T E N . R E E . O F T E N .
. G I R D . M D I . . . . . .
S O U S A . S U E S . S E O .
O N L Y S H O W S T H E M U P
R O D E O . W I T T . M E L T
G W E N . S T Y E . P E A S .
```

Puzzle #18

```
I G G Y . G H E E . T R A N .
B R E E . R A C E . M Y E R S
M E N A R E M O S T A P T T O
S Y L . E T A L . R A I D S .
. . F E S . T I M S . . . . .
. A F O U L . N E S . T B A R
A L O N G . L E C H E . E M O
B E L I E V E W H A T T H E Y
E P I . S I F T S . O R A N G
D H O W . S T S . L I A R S .
. H A H S . I A L . . . . . .
R E I G N . A C U E . Y O U .
L E A S T U N D E R S T A N D
H U S K S . L I N E . U L N A
O P T S . E M I L . B U O Y .
```

306   Puzzle Baron's Big Book of Puzzles

Crosswords (continued)

Puzzle #19

B	R	A	Y		A	L	L	E			D	A	S	S
R	A	S	A		B	E	A	N		E	A	R	L	S
I	F	Y	O	U	H	A	V	E	A	L	W	A	Y	S
G	T	E		S	O	R	E		R	U	N	T	S	
			H	R	S		Y	A	L	E				
	A	G	N	E	S		O	U	R		D	O	W	D
A	M	O	U	R		A	N	N	A	S		R	H	O
D	O	N	E	I	T	T	H	A	T	W	A	Y	I	T
H	C	G		N	Y	L	O	N		A	D	O	P	E
D	O	S	T		C	A	T		C	L	A	U	S	
			E	C	O	S		D	A	L				
	O	R	A	L	B		O	E	N	O		A	B	S
I	S	P	R	O	B	A	B	L	Y	W	R	O	N	G
A	S	M	A	D		D	O	T	O		A	N	A	T
M	A	S	T			J	E	A	N		P	E	I	S

Puzzle #20

L	O	W	S		A	I	D	S			H	T	M	L
E	A	R	P		A	U	D	I		A	E	R	I	E
T	H	E	F	I	R	S	T	D	U	T	Y	O	F	A
S	U	N		N	O	E	S		N	A	D	I	A	
			S	N	D		D	I	D	A				
	T	O	O	T	S		B	I	S		Y	S	E	R
F	E	R	R	Y		S	O	D	O	M		A	D	O
R	E	V	O	L	U	T	I	O	N	A	R	Y	I	S
A	M	I		E	R	I	N	S		R	U	S	T	S
U	S	S	R		S	E	G		S	T	R	O	H	
			A	S	U	S		A	H	I				
	R	E	V	E	L		I	R	A	N		W	O	E
T	O	G	E	T	A	W	A	Y	W	I	T	H	I	T
I	C	O	N	S		D	E	A	L		H	O	L	T
C	A	N	S			S	A	N	S		Y	A	Y	A

Cryptograms

Puzzle #1
There is neither happiness nor unhappiness in this world; there is only the comparison of one state with another.
—Alexandre Dumas

Puzzle #2
The difference between the impossible and the possible lies in determination. —Tommy Lasorda

Puzzle #3
It is impossible to travel faster than the speed of light, and certainly not desirable, as one's hat keeps blowing off.
—Woody Allen

Puzzle #4
There are two insults no human being will endure—that he has no sense of humor, and that he has never known trouble. —Sinclair Lewis

Puzzle #5
The greatest gift a parent can give a child is unconditional love. There's nothing wrong with tough love, as long as the love is unconditional. —George Herbert Walker Bush

Puzzle #6
There is no road too long to the man who advances deliberately and without undue haste. —Jean de La Bruyère

Puzzle #7
Every day of our lives we are on the verge of making those slight changes that would make all the difference.
—Mignon McLaughlin

Puzzle #8
The only interesting answers are those which destroy the questions. —Susan Sontag

Puzzle #9
It has long been an axiom of mine that the little things are infinitely the most important. —Sir Arthur Conan Doyle

Puzzle #10
I believe that it is better to tell the truth than a lie. I believe it is better to be free than to be a slave. And I believe it is better to know than to be ignorant. —H. L. Mencken

Puzzle #11
The most important thing in communication is to hear what isn't being said. —Peter Drucker

Puzzle #12
It is one of the blessings of old friends that you can afford to be stupid with them. —Ralph Waldo Emerson

Puzzle #13
The hardest struggle of all is to be something different from what the average man is. —Charles Schwab

Puzzle #14
Every man should have a college education in order to show him how little the thing is really worth.
—Elbert Hubbard

Cryptograms (continued)

Puzzle #15
There are two things which will always be very difficult for a democratic nation: to start a war and to end it.
—Alexis de Tocqueville

Puzzle #16
The best thing about giving of ourselves is that what we get is always better than what we give. The reaction is greater than the action. —Orison Swett Marden

Puzzle #17
I never know what I think about something until I read what I've written on it. —William Faulkner

Puzzle #18
The trouble with eating Italian food is that five or six days later you're hungry again. —George Miller

Puzzle #19
There is always more misery among the lower classes than there is humanity in the higher. —Victor Hugo

Puzzle #20
There are two kinds of people, those who finish what they start and so on. —Robert Byrne

Puzzle #21
It is necessary to distinguish between the virtue and the vice of obedience. —Lemuel K. Washburn

Puzzle #22
The things we hate about ourselves aren't more real than things we like about ourselves. —Ellen Goodman

Puzzle #23
I can't understand why a person will take a year to write a novel when he can easily buy one for a few dollars.
—Fred Allen

Puzzle #24
There is nothing better for the spirit or the body than a love affair. It elevates the thoughts and flattens the stomachs. —Barbara Howar

Puzzle #25
History is the record of an encounter between character and circumstances. —Donald Creighton

Puzzle #26
There are two ways of exerting one's strength: one is pushing down, the other is pulling up.
—Booker T. Washington

Puzzle #27
There is nothing that will kill a man so soon as having nobody to find fault with but himself. —George Eliot

Puzzle #28
There are two things that one must get used to or one will find life unendurable: the damages of time and injustices of men. —Nicolas Chamfort

Cryptograms (continued)

Puzzle #29

It is better to rise from life as from a banquet—neither thirsty nor drunken. —Aristotle

Puzzle #30

The only reason some people get lost in thought is because it's unfamiliar territory. —Paul Fix

Puzzle #31

If the human brain were so simple that we could understand it, we would be so simple that we couldn't.
—Emerson M. Pugh

Puzzle #32

Nothing ever gets anywhere. The earth keeps turning round and round and gets nowhere. The moment is the only thing that counts. —Jean Cocteau

Puzzle #33

The best morale exists when you never hear the word mentioned. When you hear a lot of talk about it, it's usually lousy. —Dwight D. Eisenhower

Puzzle #34

People become attached to their burdens sometimes more than the burdens are attached to them.
—George Bernard Shaw

Puzzle #35

There is no kind of dishonesty into which otherwise good people more easily and frequently fall than that of defrauding the government. —Benjamin Franklin

Puzzle #36

There's no reason to be the richest man in the cemetery. You can't do any business from there. —Colonel Sanders

Puzzle #37

There was nothing wrong with Southern California that a rise in the ocean level wouldn't cure. —Ross Macdonald

Puzzle #38

Don't be afraid to talk to yourself. It's the only way you can be sure somebody's listening. —Franklin P. Jones

Puzzle #39

The difference between a job and a career is the difference between forty and sixty hours a week. —Robert Frost

Puzzle #40

One of the greatest delusions in the world is the hope that the evils in this world are to be cured by legislation.
—Thomas B. Reed

Puzzle #41

There's a fine line between fishing and just standing on the shore like an idiot. —Steven Wright

Puzzle #42

The best conversations with mothers always take place in silence, when only the heart speaks. —Carrie Latet

Cryptograms (continued)

Puzzle #43

One of the hardest things in life is having words in your heart that you can't utter. —James Earl Jones

Puzzle #44

That we can comprehend the little we know already is mind-boggling in itself. —Tom Gates

Puzzle #45

It is dangerous to be right in matters on which the established authorities are wrong. —Voltaire

Puzzle #46

The world has the habit of making room for the man whose actions show that he knows where he is going. —Napoleon Hill

Puzzle #47

Fishing tournaments seem a little like playing tennis with living balls. —Jim Harrison

Puzzle #48

The shepherd always tries to persuade the sheep that their interests and his own are the same. —Stendhal

Puzzle #49

This would be a much better world if more married couples were as deeply in love as they are in debt. —Earl Wilson

Puzzle #50

Every day I get up and look through the Forbes list of the richest people in America. If I'm not there, I go to work. —Robert Orben

Puzzle #51

There are perhaps no days of our childhood we lived so fully as those we spent with a favorite book. —Marcel Proust

Puzzle #52

Success is the necessary misfortune of life, but it is only to the very unfortunate that it comes early. —Anthony Trollope

Puzzle #53

Everything one invents is true, you may be perfectly sure of that. Poetry is as precise as geometry. —Gustave Flaubert

Puzzle #54

I suppose it is much more comfortable to be mad and know it than to be sane and have one's doubts. —G. B. Burgin

Puzzle #55

Everyone has talent. What is rare is the courage to follow the talent to the dark place where it leads. —Erica Jong

Puzzle #56

Self-pity is our worst enemy, and if we yield to it, we can never do anything good in the world. —Helen Keller

Cryptograms (continued)

Puzzle #57
Democracy consists of choosing your dictators after they've told you what it is you want to hear. —Alan Coren

Puzzle #58
We cannot control the evil tongues of others but a good life enables us to disregard them. —Cato the Elder

Puzzle #59
If you want to make certain a job gets done, give it to somebody who is really busy. They'll have their secretary do it. —Joe Moore

Puzzle #60
The way you overcome shyness is to become so wrapped up in something that you forget to be afraid.
—Lady Bird Johnson

Puzzle #61
Regret is an appalling waste of energy; you can't build on it; it's only good for wallowing in. —Katherine Mansfield

Puzzle #62
Laughing is the sensation of feeling good all over and showing it principally in one spot. —Josh Billings

Puzzle #63
When you encounter seemingly good advice that contradicts other seemingly good advice, ignore them both.
—Al Franken

Puzzle #64
The more sand has escaped from the hourglass of our life, the clearer we should see through it. —Jean Paul

Puzzle #65
The greater difficulty, the more glory in surmounting it. Skillful pilots gain their reputation from storms and tempests. —Epicurus

Puzzle #66
I became a good pitcher when I stopped trying to make them miss the ball and started trying to make them hit it. —Sandy Koufax

Puzzle #67
You should never have your best trousers on when you turn out to fight for freedom and truth. —Henrik Ibsen

Puzzle #68
Bankers know that history is inflationary and that money is the last thing a wise man will hoard. —Will Durant

Puzzle #69
Power is something of which I am convinced there is no innocence this side of the womb. —Nadine Gordimer

Puzzle #70
Do not allow people to dim your shine because they are blinded. Tell them to put on some sunglasses.
—Lady Gaga

Cryptograms (continued)

Puzzle #71
The worst thing about Europe is that you can't go out in the middle of the night and get a Slurpee. —Tellis Frank

Puzzle #72
What we do is less than a drop in the ocean. But if it were missing, the ocean would lack something.
—Mother Teresa

Puzzle #73
Master your instrument, master the music, and then forget all that crap and just play. —Charlie Parker

Puzzle #74
One of the most adventurous things left us is to go to bed. For no one can lay a hand on our dreams.
—Edward Verrall Lucas

Puzzle #75
Getting married is a lot like getting into a tub of hot water. After you get used to it, it ain't so hot. —Minnie Pearl

Puzzle #76
The whole history of physics proves that a new discovery is quite likely lurking at the next decimal place.
—F. K. Richtmyer

Puzzle #77
If the light in your life has changed to yellow, I recommend you floor it. It's safer than the alternative.
—Jeb Dickerson

Puzzle #78
Never think that war, no matter how necessary, nor how justified, is not a crime. —Ernest Hemingway

Puzzle #79
Temper never mellows with age, and a sharp tongue is the only edged tool that grows keener with constant use.
—Washington Irving

Puzzle #80
We cannot escape fear. We can only transform it into a companion that accompanies us on all our exciting
adventures. —Susan Jeffers

Puzzle #81
Whenever there is a conflict between human rights and property rights, human rights must prevail.
—Abraham Lincoln

Puzzle #82
A love for tradition has never weakened a nation, indeed it has strengthened nations in their hour of peril.
—Winston Churchill

Puzzle #83
Much unhappiness has come into the world because of bewilderment and things left unsaid.
—Fyodor Dostoyevsky

Cryptograms (continued)

Puzzle #84
Life is little more than a loan shark: It exacts a very high rate of interest for the few pleasures it concedes.
—Luigi Pirandello

Puzzle #85
All philosophies, if you ride them home, are nonsense, but some are greater nonsense than others.
—Samuel Butler

Puzzle #86
Mathematics is as much an aspect of culture as it is a collection of algorithms. —Carl Boyer

Puzzle #87
My kittens look at me like little angels, and always after doing something especially devilish. —Jamie Ann Hunt

Puzzle #88
A bride at her second marriage does not wear a veil. She wants to see what she is getting. —Helen Rowland

Puzzle #89
He who sees the truth, let him proclaim it, without asking who is for it or who is against it. —Henry George

Puzzle #90
Affirmations are like prescriptions for certain aspects of yourself you want to change. —Jerry Fankhauser

Puzzle #91
Poetry is just the evidence of life. If your life is burning, well, poetry is just the ash. —Leonard Cohen

Puzzle #92
One should be just as careful in choosing one's pleasures as in avoiding calamities. —Chinese proverb

Puzzle #93
If moral behavior were simply following rules, we could program a computer to be moral. —Samuel P. Ginder

Puzzle #94
When women are depressed, they either eat or go shopping. Men invade another country. —Elayne Boosler

Puzzle #95
Avoid the crowd. Do your own thinking independently. Be the chess player, not the chess piece. —Ralph Charell

Puzzle #96
The petty economies of the rich are just as amazing as the silly extravagances of the poor. —William Feather

Puzzle #97
After growing wildly for years, the field of computing appears to be reaching its infancy. —John Pierce

Puzzle #98
The hardest job kids face today is learning good manners without seeing any. —Fred Astaire

Cryptograms (continued)

Puzzle #99
Make three correct guesses consecutively and you will establish a reputation as an expert. —Laurence J. Peter

Puzzle #100
If equations are trains threading the landscape of numbers, then no train stops at pi. —Richard Preston

Puzzle #101
No person was ever honored for what he received. Honor has been the reward for what he gave.
—Calvin Coolidge

Puzzle #102
Drama is imagination limited by logic. Mathematics is logic limited by imagination. —Nathan Campbell

Puzzle #103
Strength of mind rests in sobriety; for this keeps your reason unclouded by passion. —Pythagoras

Puzzle #104
Life consists not in holding good cards but in playing those you hold well. —Josh Billings

Puzzle #105
An original writer is not one who imitates nobody, but one whom nobody can imitate. —Chateaubriand

Puzzle #106
Living at risk is jumping off the cliff and building your wings on the way down. —Ray Bradbury

Puzzle #107
Dealing with network executives is like being nibbled to death by ducks. —Eric Sevareid

Puzzle #108
Knowledge is gained by learning; trust by doubt; skill by practice; love by love. —Thomas Szasz

Puzzle #109
Let those who would write heroic poems make their life a heroic poem. —John Milton

Puzzle #110
Doctors think a lot of patients are cured who have simply quit in disgust. —Don Herold

Puzzle #111
Patriotism is often an arbitrary veneration of real estate above principles. —George Jean Nathan

Puzzle #112
Destiny has two ways of crushing us—by refusing our wishes and by fulfilling them. —Henri Frederic Amiel

Puzzle #113
Garner up pleasant thoughts in your mind, for pleasant thoughts make pleasant lives. —John Wilkins

Cryptograms (continued)

Puzzle #114

The only Zen you find on the tops of mountains is the Zen you bring up there. —Robert M. Pirsig

Puzzle #115

No cord or cable can draw so forcibly, or bind so fast, as love can do with a single thread. —Robert Burton

Drop Quotes

Puzzle #1
Youth is a wonderful thing. What a crime to waste it on children. —George Bernard Shaw

Puzzle #2
Everything is funny as long as it is happening to somebody else. —Will Rogers

Puzzle #3
It is easier to love humanity as a whole than to love one's neighbor. —Eric Hoffer

Puzzle #4
The trouble with the rat race is that even if you win you're still a rat. —Lily Tomlin

Puzzle #5
The destruction of the past is perhaps the greatest of all crimes. —Simone Weil

Puzzle #6
The pleasure that is in sorrow is sweeter than the pleasure of pleasure itself. —Percy Bysshe Shelley

Puzzle #7
The future belongs to those who believe in the beauty of their dreams. —Eleanor Roosevelt

Puzzle #8
Any man who does not accept the conditions of human life sells his soul. —Charles Baudelaire

Puzzle #9
Most people ignore most poetry because most poetry ignores most people. —Adrian Mitchell

Puzzle #10
Concentration comes out of a combination of confidence and hunger. —Arnold Palmer

Puzzle #11
The man who does not read good books has no advantage over the man who cannot read them. —Mark Twain

Puzzle #12
One does not get better but different and older and that is always a pleasure. —Gertrude Stein

Puzzle #13
Men are rich only as they give. He who gives great service gets great rewards. —Elbert Hubbard

Puzzle #14
One man practicing sportsmanship is far better than fifty preaching it. —Knute Rockne

Puzzle #15
A successful marriage is an edifice that must be rebuilt every day. —André Maurois

Drop Quotes (continued)

Puzzle #16
A general is just as good or just as bad as the troops under his command make him. —Douglas MacArthur

Puzzle #17
I never know whether to pity or congratulate a man on coming to his senses. —William M. Thackeray

Puzzle #18
All the extraordinary men I have known were extraordinary in their own estimation. —Woodrow Wilson

Puzzle #19
The only way to discover the limits of the possible is to go beyond them into the impossible. —Arthur C. Clarke

Puzzle #20
Science is the great antidote to the poison of enthusiasm and superstition. —Adam Smith

Puzzle #21
What gunpowder did for war the printing press has done for the mind. —Wendell Phillips

Puzzle #22
There is a road from the eye to the heart that does not go through the intellect. —G. K. Chesterton

Puzzle #23
It is in the character of very few men to honor without envy a friend who has prospered. —Aeschylus

Puzzle #24
It is sometimes important for science to know how to forget the things she is surest of. —Jean Rostand

Puzzle #25
Do not be afraid of defeat. You are never so near to victory as when defeated in a good cause. —Henry Ward Beecher

Puzzle #26
There is often more spiritual force in a proverb than in whole philosophical systems. —Thomas Carlyle

Puzzle #27
An intellectual is a man who takes more words than necessary to tell more than he knows.
—Dwight D. Eisenhower

Puzzle #28
Discovery consists of seeing what everybody has seen and thinking what nobody has thought. —Albert von Szent-Györgyi

Puzzle #29
As long as people believe in absurdities they will continue to commit atrocities. —Voltaire

Puzzle #30
Those who believe that they are exclusively in the right are generally those who achieve something. —Aldous Huxley

Drop Quotes (continued)

Puzzle #31
Talking with you is sort of the conversational equivalent of an out of body experience. —Bill Watterson

Puzzle #32
Take from the philosopher the pleasure of being heard and his desire for knowledge ceases. —Jean-Jacques Rousseau

Puzzle #33
Democracy is the recurrent suspicion that more than half of the people are right more than half of the time. —E. B. White

Puzzle #34
You are forgiven for your happiness and your successes only if you generously consent to share them. —Albert Camus

Puzzle #35
Never hold discussions with the monkey when the organ grinder is in the room. —Winston Churchill

Puzzle #36
Early in life I had noticed that no event is ever correctly reported in a newspaper. —George Orwell

Puzzle #37
People are usually more convinced by reasons they discovered themselves than by those found out by others. —Blaise Pascal

Puzzle #38
A thousand words will not leave so deep an impression as one deed. —Henrik Ibsen

Puzzle #39
Man was created a little lower than the angels and has been getting a little lower ever since. —Josh Billings

Puzzle #40
One of the advantages of being disorderly is that one is constantly making exciting discoveries. —A. A. Milne

Puzzle #41
Never tell people how to do things. Tell them what to do and they will surprise you with their ingenuity. —George S. Patton

Puzzle #42
The world is always ready to receive talent with open arms. Very often it does not know what to do with genius. —Oliver Wendell Holmes Sr.

Puzzle #43
Through perseverance many people win success out of what seemed destined to be certain failure. —Benjamin Disraeli

Puzzle #44
If you follow reason far enough it always leads to conclusions that are contrary to reason. —Samuel Butler

Drop Quotes (continued)

Puzzle #45
If men cease to believe that they will one day become gods then they will surely become worms. —Henry Miller

Puzzle #46
I thank fate for having made me born poor. Poverty taught me the true value of the gifts useful to life.
—Anatole France

Puzzle #47
Smell is a potent wizard that transports us across thousands of miles and all the years we have lived.
—Helen Keller

Puzzle #48
There are no greater wretches in the world than many of those whom people in general take to be happy.
—Seneca

Puzzle #49
It is in his pleasure that a man really lives; it is from his leisure that he constructs the true fabric of self.
—Agnes Repplier

Puzzle #50
The strong man is the one who is able to intercept at will the communication between the senses and the mind.
—Napoleon Bonaparte

Puzzle #51
Sometimes I wonder if men and women really suit each other. Perhaps they should live next door and just visit now and then. —Katharine Hepburn

Puzzle #52
Natural ability without education has more often raised a man to glory and virtue than education without natural ability. —Cicero

Puzzle #53
The first requisite of a good citizen in this republic of ours is that he shall be able and willing to pull his weight.
—Theodore Roosevelt

Puzzle #54
Punishment is the last and the least effective instrument in the hands of the legislator for the prevention of crime.
—John Ruskin

Puzzle #55
A man can become so accustomed to the thought of his own faults that he will begin to cherish them as charming little personal characteristics. —Helen Rowland

Logic Puzzles

Puzzle #1

4	Ofallo	Beatrice
7	Quirrel	Calliope
10	Rajesh	Eva
13	Pemson	Francine
16	Merah	Dolly

Puzzle #2

880 pounds	Vincent	Canadian
920 pounds	Brent	South African
960 pounds	Oliver	Swede
1,000 pounds	Jeremy	American
1,040 pounds	Nicola	Dane

Puzzle #3

January	Hamzell	heart disease	frog
February	Damasol	diabetes	fig orchid
March	Gravon	arthritis	palm tree
April	Pluniden	asthma	bromeliad

Puzzle #4

$9.50	Boston	summer	Seth
$11.50	California	tiger	Pam
$13.50	Hawaiian	spider	Nicole
$15.50	dragon	teriyaki	Eleanor

Puzzle #5

2	Quinn	117	Pennsylvania
3	Zamora	114	Hawaii
4	Watkins	209	Utah
5	Tran	320	Florida

Puzzle #6

3	*Benny II*	Jacobson	Betty Beach
4	*Watery Pete*	Romero	Silver Springs
5	*Sea Cow*	Preston	Yellow Bend
6	*Samantha*	Armstrong	Trey's Tunnel

Puzzle #7

April 3	Johanna	14	West Okoboji
April 7	Isaac	9	Orange City
April 11	Sadie	18	Thurman
April 15	Nathaniel	6	Le Mars

Puzzle #8

8,500 feet	Sandy Bridge	truss	Madrid
10,000 feet	Gorem Bridge	cantilever	Luxembourg
11,500 feet	Bay Bridge	suspension	Tallinn
13,000 feet	North Bridge	bowstring	Oslo

Logic Puzzles (continued)

Puzzle #9

2	*Maximum Risk*	Adrienne Day	action film
3	*Sea of Dreams*	Virgil Katz	comedy
4	*The Illusion*	Danny Trevor	musical
5	*Bold Service*	Maddie Mintz	drama

Puzzle #10

$6.75	Gene	quinoa	strawberries
$7.75	Nellie	wheat grass	raspberries
$8.75	Paulette	flaxseed	blueberries
$9.75	Mercedes	ginger	bananas

Puzzle #11

1974	Bowling Alley	Dow Games	$3,750
1975	Voyager Hero	Maxigame	$1,500
1976	Archer Quest	Hayco, Inc.	$1,750
1977	Zany Circus	Waverly Toys	$6,400

Puzzle #12

anemic	Bessie	Yeffer	sixth
bulwark	Jill	Witte	second
consommé	Zachary	Manzella	fifth
duplicity	Floyd	Steuben	fourth

Puzzle #13

15 feet	Valerie	silver	fifth
25 feet	Ella	black	first
35 feet	Aaron	green	sixth
45 feet	Margo	blue	second
55 feet	Roderick	yellow	third

Puzzle #14

$450	Eldang-X	100 feet	10 minutes
$525	Motomiya	350 feet	30 minutes
$600	Werril 23A	1,000 feet	20 minutes
$675	Belhino 5	150 feet	15 minutes
$750	Suzutake	250 feet	60 minutes

Puzzle #15

250	Explore More	Jaime	ambulance
300	Words to Go	Patsy	ice cream truck
350	Lit on Wheels	Sheryl	Airstream
400	Ready Reader	Terri	Mack Truck
450	Books-4-U	Kimberly	Greyhound bus

Logic Puzzles (continued)

Puzzle #16

$25	Fierro	FRZ-192	Pennsylvania
$50	Hornet	MRT-628	Mississippi
$75	Injitsu	RBD-337	Louisiana
$100	Grandero	BMG-831	Florida
$125	Dartson	GGZ-007	South Dakota

Puzzle #17

2004	Elm Park	atlas otter	Lamar
2006	Foxtail Bend	western gull	Wilcox
2008	Riverside Glen	sandy hare	Bibb
2010	Howard Park	pygmy beaver	Talladega
2012	Wanda Park	box python	Pickens

Puzzle #18

October 3	Dragons	28–10	Coachella
October 7	White Rhinos	34–7	Humeston
October 11	Rams	13–9	Island Falls
October 15	Eagles	20–13	Edinburg
October 19	Tuscanos	24–21	Avila Beach

Puzzle #19

March 12	Gabriel	Velez & York	Riverview
March 15	Abel	Barr & Cobb	Faraday
March 18	Rosalie	Ingram & Kemp	Northridge
March 21	Kelvin	Haynes, Inc.	Summit
March 24	Zachary	Leach & Mccall	Rutherford

Puzzle #20

first	Target Bombs	orange	Evansdale
second	Splat Squad	purple	Yucca Valley
third	Night Ninjas	white	Armona
fourth	Oil Crew	yellow	Libertyville
fifth	Pea Shooters	green	Forest City

Puzzle #21

4:30 pm	Grant	pork rinds	El Segundo
4:35 pm	Julie	hummus	Kernville
4:40 pm	Eunice	potato chips	Fairfield
4:45 pm	Nelson	soda	Martensdale
4:50 pm	Sergio	onion dip	Pine Valley

Puzzle #22

300	Esther	6	Bristol
380	Alberta	1	Fort Kent
460	Zachary	2	Cutler
540	Hope	3	Elk Grove
620	Irma	4	Pacific Grove

Logic Puzzles (continued)

Puzzle #23

June 4	Tall Pines	Kent	alfalfa
June 5	Meadowgrove	Latimer	potatoes
June 6	Hazelwood	Hanford	spinach
June 7	Blackwater	George	cucumbers
June 8	Lone Oak	Big Bear Lake	beets

Puzzle #24

first	Jana	one pair	$18.25
second	Guillermo	straight flush	$9.00
third	Salvador	straight	$5.25
fourth	Kelley	flush	$23.25
fifth	Omar	full house	$6.50

Puzzle #25

4	Nathaniel	lacrosse	doctor
11	Guillermo	football	dentist
18	Eduardo	soccer	waiter
25	Wesley	hockey	lawyer
32	Marco	basketball	garbage man

Puzzle #26

650 feet	line F	30 feet	45 MPH
700 feet	line C	40 feet	30 MPH
750 feet	line A	45 feet	50 MPH
800 feet	line E	55 feet	55 MPH
850 feet	line D	25 feet	35 MPH

Puzzle #27

$400	Ned Norris	planter	Sun City
$425	Pam Powell	Blu-ray player	Fruitland
$450	Mitch Mayo	laptop	Eustis
$475	Ora Osborne	juicer	Jonesboro
$500	Kit Kelley	toaster	Twin Peaks

Puzzle #28

1713	Lafiori	Warsaw	$2,500
1731	Bleux	Corsica	$1,100
1749	Waldemuller	Scandinavia	$750
1767	Muenster	Tuscany	$545
1785	Jenson	Denmark	$250

Puzzle #29

1897	Rilania	*Orange Sky*	25
1905	Yeust	*Willow Bend*	22
1913	Xesobe	*Clockwork*	19
1921	Arim Aleen	*Hoxley Hills*	20
1929	Dray D'Amici	*Tantrum*	10

Logic Puzzles (continued)

Puzzle #30

$4.50	Terry	ginger	apple
$5.50	Francisco	sandalwood	fig
$6.50	Luke	freesia	peach
$7.50	Kari	cinnamon	coconut
$8.50	Courtney	vanilla	pear

Puzzle #31

625	radio spot	Hal Hopkins	$30,000
775	newspaper ad	Julie Jordan	$15,000
925	magazine ad	Eddie Evans	$50,000
1,075	direct mailer	Faith Fowler	$90,000
1,225	billboard	Kenneth Kirby	$20,000

Puzzle #32

$1,000,000	Madinkz.com	Fred Frost	textbooks
$2,000,000	Atriano.com	Vicky Velez	video games
$3,000,000	Byxby.com	Betty Becker	robots
$4,000,000	Pritecha.com	Pat Padilla	sports gear
$5,000,000	Zetafish.com	Addie Abrams	cameras

Puzzle #33

January	Wade	CR-260	solar storms
February	Mercedes	TV-412	radiation
March	Rose	GX-13	plant enzymes
April	Francis	ZF-15	ant colonies
May	Katherine	WB-664	gamma rays

Puzzle #34

1683	Vlietmolen	Smit	Den Bommel
1706	Oostmolen	De Vries	Moerkapelle
1729	Grosmolen	Visser	Aarlanderveen
1752	Doesmolen	Bakker	Schiedam
1775	Zemelmolen	Van Den Berg	Leiderdorp

Puzzle #35

$5.50	basswood	Midge Mintz	Unity
$6.50	clover	Heddy Heath	Fowler
$7.50	lemon blossom	Linda Lynn	Kellerton
$8.50	sage	Jim Joyner	Troy
$9.50	alfalfa	Nick Norris	Nevada

Puzzle #36

$24.99	Calculus	Tara Tyne	2010
$29.99	Pre-Calculus	Steve Spark	2008
$34.99	Algebra	Velma Vintz	2005
$39.99	Trigonometry	Mina Morton	2015
$44.99	Set Theory	Pat Peterson	2007

Logic Puzzles (continued)

Puzzle #37

March 3	*Zamora* v. *Pibb*	2–7	Quinn
March 10	*Watts* v. *Yang*	3–6	Olson
March 17	*Carson* v. *Dunn*	4–5	Hatfield
March 24	*Ayers* v. *Byrd*	7–2	Larson
March 31	*Short* v. *Metz*	5–4	Caldwell

Puzzle #38

first	Wendy	swimming	4443
second	Kendra	leadership	3094
third	Ollie	ceramics	4781
fourth	Gayle	dance	4031
fifth	Dolores	theater	5025

Puzzle #39

9:30 am	Hatha	Sandra	12
10:30 am	Bikram	Leah	6
11:30 am	Ashtanga	Marilyn	14
12:30 pm	Prenatal	Opal	9
1:30 pm	Vinyasa	Teresa	5

Puzzle #40

25-liter	Freddie	Bistric	silver
30-liter	Gene	Grennel	gray
35-liter	Salvador	Lugmor	orange
40-liter	Betty	Pinkster	blue
45-liter	Myrna	Adironda	purple

Mathdoku

Puzzle #1

8	−	2	−	5	=	1
−		×		+		
3	÷	1	+	7	=	10
+		+		+		
9	×	4	−	6	=	30
=		=		=		
14		6		18		

Puzzle #2

8	×	4	+	1	=	33
×		×		−		
9	×	3	+	2	=	29
−		+		+		
5	+	6	−	7	=	4
=		=		=		
67		18		6		

Puzzle #3

1	×	8	−	6	=	2
×		×		÷		
7	+	9	−	3	=	13
−		+		−		
5	+	4	−	2	=	7
=		=		=		
2		76		0		

Puzzle #4

7	×	6	+	3	=	45
−		÷		×		
8	−	2	−	4	=	2
+		+		−		
5	×	9	−	1	=	44
=		=		=		
4		12		11		

Puzzle #5

8	÷	1	+	2	=	10
×		×		+		
5	+	4	+	3	=	12
+		+		+		
7	×	6	+	9	=	51
=		=		=		
47		10		14		

Puzzle #6

2	+	9	−	4	=	7
×		×		+		
3	÷	1	+	5	=	8
−		−				
6	+	8	+	7	=	21
=		=		=		
0		1		2		

Puzzle #7

6	−	7	+	9	=	8
÷		×		×		
3	×	4	−	8	=	4
+		+		+		
5	×	1	−	2	=	3
=		=		=		
7		29		74		

Puzzle #8

8	−	4	+	1	=	5
+		+		×		
2	+	7	−	5	=	4
−		−		+		
6	×	9	−	3	=	51
=		=		=		
4		2		8		

Puzzle #9

3	+	7	+	1	=	11
−		×		+		
4	×	2	+	6	=	14
+		−		+		
5	×	8	+	9	=	49
=		=		=		
4		6		16		

Mathdoku (continued)

Puzzle #10

7	×	8	−	6	=	50
−		×		+		
4	×	5	+	2	=	22
−		−		−		
1	+	9	+	3	=	13
=		=		=		
2		31		5		

Puzzle #11

2	×	6	−	8	=	4
+		×		+		
9	+	5	+	3	=	17
+		−		+		
7	÷	1	−	4	=	3
=		=		=		
18		29		15		

Puzzle #12

3	+	8	−	9	=	2
+		−		−		
4	−	1	+	7	=	10
+				+		
5	+	2	+	6	=	13
=		=		=		
12		5		8		

Puzzle #13

3	×	7	+	1	=	22
+		×		×		
9	−	2	−	6	=	1
+		+		−		
4	×	8	+	5	=	37
=		=		=		
16		22		1		

Puzzle #14

2	+	3	+	8	=	13
×		×		−		
9	−	4	−	5	=	0
−		+		+		
1	+	6	−	7	=	0
=		=		=		
17		18		10		

Puzzle #15

9	×	1	−	6	=	3
+		×		−		
5	+	7	+	3	=	15
+		−		−		
8	−	4	−	2	=	2
=		=		=		
22		3		1		

Puzzle #16

2	×	6	−	8	=	4
+		×		+		
3	+	1	+	4	=	8
+		+		−		
7	−	5	+	9	=	11
=		=		=		
12		11		3		

Puzzle #17

3	×	6	−	7	=	11
+		+		×		
8	−	9	+	2	=	1
−		−				
5	×	4	+	1	=	21
=		=		=		
6		11		13		

Puzzle #18

3	×	2	+	9	=	15
+		×		×		
1	+	5	−	4	=	2
+		−		+		
8	+	6	−	7	=	7
=		=		=		
12		4		43		

Mathdoku (continued)

Puzzle #19

6	×	7	+	1	=	43
+		+		×		
9	+	3	+	5	=	17
−		−		+		
2	+	4	+	8	=	14
=		=		=		
13		6		13		

Puzzle #20

4	+	8	+	3	=	15
+		+		+		
9	×	2	+	7	=	25
−		+		+		
6	÷	1	+	5	=	11
=		=		=		
7		11		15		

More or Less

(4X4)

Puzzle #1

2	4	1	3
1	3 > 2	4
3	2	4	1
4	1	3	2

Puzzle #2

2 > 1	4	3
4	3	1 < 2
1	2	3 < 4
3	4 > 2	1

(5X5)

Puzzle #3

3	4	1	2	5
1	3	2	5 > 4
4	2	5	1	3
2	5 > 3	4	1
5	1	4	3 > 2

Puzzle #4

2 < 5	1	3	4
1	4	2	5	3
4	3	5	1	2
5	2 < 3	4	1
3	1	4 > 2	5

More or Less (continued)

(6X6)

Puzzle #5

```
6    4    1 < 2 < 3    5
2    6    5 > 4    1    3
5    1    2    3    4    6
     ^    ^    ^
1    2 < 3    5    6    4
          ^    ^
3    5    4    6    2 > 1
^    v              ^
4    3    6    1 < 5    2
```

Puzzle #6

```
3    6    5    4    1 < 2
          v
4    1    3 > 2    5 < 6
     ^
2    3    1    5    6    4
     ^              v
6 > 5    2 < 3 < 4    1
     v         v
5    4    6    1    2 < 3
          v
1 < 2    4    6    3    5
```

Puzzle #7

```
3    1    2    6    5    4
v         v         v
2    6    1    3    4    5
          ^    ^
1    2    5    4    6    3
               v         v
4    5    6    2    3    1
5    3    4    1 < 2    6
     ^
6 > 4    3    5    1 < 2
```

Puzzle #8

```
2    6    1    4    5    3
5    3    6    2    4    1
4 > 2    3 > 1    6 > 5
                        v
3 > 1    5 < 6    2    4
^                   v
6 > 5    4    3    1    2
     v                   ^
1 < 4    2    5    3    6
```

(7X7)

Puzzle #9

```
3   7   2 > 1   4 < 5 < 6
            ^
6   2   4   5   1   7   3
            v
2   3   1   7   6   4   5
v       ^       v
1   5   6   4 > 3   2   7
    ^   v
7   6   3   2   5   1 < 4

5   4   7   3 > 2 < 6   1

4   1 < 5 < 6 < 7   3 > 2
```

Puzzle #10

```
4 > 3   1   6   5   2   7
    v       v
7   2   4   5 > 1   6 > 3
            v
2   7   3   4   6   5 > 1
v           v
1   4   6   3 > 2   7   5
    ^
5   6 < 7   1 < 3 < 4 > 2

6   1   5   2   7   3 < 4
                        ^
3   5 > 2   7 > 4 > 1   6
```

Puzzle #11

```
3   5   6   7 > 2 < 4   1
            v
6   7   4   2   1   5   3
v       ^
4   1 < 5   6 > 3   2   7
v
2   6 < 7   1   5   3   4
    v
7   3 > 2   5 > 4   1   6
            v
1   2 < 3 < 4   7   6   5

5 > 4   1 < 3   6 < 7   2
```

Puzzle #12

```
4   7   1 < 2 < 5   3   6
                        v
2   3   5   1   6 < 7   4
            v           v
3   5   4   7   1   6   2

7   1   3   6   4   2   5
            v   v
1   2   6   4   3   5   7
        ^
5   6   7   3   2   4   1
        v
6   4   2 < 5 < 7   1 < 3
```

Neighbors

(4X4)

Puzzle #1

3	4	1	2
4	2	3	1
2	1	4	3
1	3	2	4

Puzzle #2

4	2	1	3
3	1	2	4
1	3	4	2
2	4	3	1

(5X5)

Puzzle #3

5	1	3	4	2
2	5	4	3	1
1	3	5	2	4
3	4	2	1	5
4	2	1	5	3

Puzzle #4

2	1	5	4	3
3	2	4	5	1
1	5	2	3	4
4	3	1	2	5
5	4	3	1	2

Neighbors (continued)

(6X6)

Puzzle #5

6	4	2	3	5	1
4	2	3	1	6	5
2	1	5	6	3	4
3	5	6	4	1	2
1	3	4	5	2	6
5	6	1	2	4	3

Puzzle #6

3	2	4	6	5	1
5	3	2	1	4	6
2	4	6	5	1	3
6	5	1	3	2	4
1	6	5	4	3	2
4	1	3	2	6	5

Puzzle #7

5	1	6	3	2	4
6	2	5	4	3	1
1	4	3	6	5	2
3	6	1	2	4	5
2	5	4	1	6	3
4	3	2	5	1	6

Puzzle #8

1	5	4	2	3	6
4	2	3	6	1	5
5	4	2	3	6	1
3	6	1	5	4	2
6	1	5	4	2	3
2	3	6	1	5	4

Neighbors (continued)

(7X7)

Puzzle #9

6	4	3	1	7	2	5
2	5	6	4	3	1	7
5	3	1	2	6	7	4
4	2	7	6	5	3	1
3	7	4	5	1	6	2
7	1	2	3	4	5	6
1	6	5	7	2	4	3

Puzzle #10

3	5	6	1	7	2	4
7	2	1	4	6	5	3
5	6	3	7	4	1	2
6	1	5	2	3	4	7
2	3	4	6	1	7	5
4	7	2	3	5	6	1
1	4	7	5	2	3	6

Puzzle #11

2	7	6	4	1	5	3
3	6	1	7	4	2	5
5	4	3	2	7	1	6
7	1	2	5	3	6	4
4	2	5	1	6	3	7
1	3	7	6	5	4	2
6	5	4	3	2	7	1

Puzzle #12

3	2	6	4	1	5	7
6	4	1	5	7	2	3
2	1	7	6	4	3	5
7	5	2	1	3	6	4
4	3	5	2	6	7	1
5	7	4	3	2	1	6
1	6	3	7	5	4	2

(7X7)

Puzzle #13

4	2	1	6	3	7	5
1	5	4	2	7	3	6
3	1	2	4	6	5	7
7	4	6	1	5	2	3
6	3	7	5	4	1	2
2	7	5	3	1	6	4
5	6	3	7	2	4	1

(9X9)

Puzzle #14

8	7	6	1	9	4	2	3	5
6	3	4	8	5	2	7	9	1
3	9	8	5	1	6	4	2	7
7	2	1	4	8	5	9	6	3
5	4	9	7	6	3	1	8	2
9	5	2	3	7	8	6	1	4
2	1	7	6	3	9	5	4	8
1	6	3	2	4	7	8	5	9
4	8	5	9	2	1	3	7	6

Puzzle #15

5	7	8	2	9	1	4	6	3
8	6	2	7	1	4	9	3	5
2	8	3	4	7	5	1	9	6
4	3	1	6	5	9	2	7	8
6	9	5	1	3	8	7	2	4
1	2	9	5	4	6	3	8	7
3	4	7	9	8	2	6	5	1
9	5	4	3	6	7	8	1	2
7	1	6	8	2	3	5	4	9

Neighbors (continued)

(9X9)

Puzzle #16

7	5	9	8	1	6	2	4	3
9	4	3	1	7	8	5	2	6
4	9	1	6	5	2	3	8	7
6	1	2	3	9	4	8	7	5
2	8	4	5	6	7	1	3	9
1	3	6	4	8	9	7	5	2
3	7	5	9	2	1	4	6	8
8	6	7	2	3	5	9	1	4
5	2	8	7	4	3	6	9	1

Puzzle #17

1	8	3	2	4	5	7	9	6
4	6	2	7	9	1	8	3	5
9	5	7	6	8	3	2	4	1
8	1	6	4	2	7	9	5	3
5	2	4	3	7	8	1	6	9
6	4	9	1	5	2	3	7	8
2	3	5	9	1	6	4	8	7
7	9	8	5	3	4	6	1	2
3	7	1	8	6	9	5	2	4

Puzzle #18

1	2	4	5	6	8	7	9	3
5	9	8	4	7	3	6	2	1
9	6	1	8	2	4	5	3	7
3	5	7	9	8	2	4	1	6
2	8	6	7	4	1	3	5	9
8	4	3	2	9	7	1	6	5
7	1	9	3	5	6	2	8	4
4	3	2	6	1	5	9	7	8
6	7	5	1	3	9	8	4	2

Reverse Word Searches

Puzzle #1

I	M	P	O	S	E	S	M	B	T
K	B			U	T	K	A	I	B
		C	B	R	O	A	R	T	L	U
	S	A	A	I	G	O	T	L	O
F	D	C	B	R	I	W	E	S	D
S	L	H	W	A	T	H	E	F	T
D	R	U	O	G	S	C	R	L	A
E	O	G	R	E	A	T	I	O	I
H	W	S	C	R	C	A	E	P	N
S	E	N	E	G	Y	P	R	S	T

Puzzle #2

A	D	V	I	S	E	D	T	E	
D	I	T	C	H	O	R	S	E	S
O	K	A	Y	S	W	E	A	R	S
B	R	E	A	T	H	L	E	S	S
E	U	E		T	O	E	L		E
S	F	O	O	R	P	E	R	I	F
E	L	U	Y	P	P	O	L	F	
C	I	N	O	S	E	D	I	R	B
I	E	C	T	O	R	N	A	D	O
D	R	E	I	D	A	E	B		

Puzzle #3

D	E	H	S	A	L	A	B	I	R	T
	L	S	P	Y	F	O	R	G	E	S
F	B	E	I	G	H	T		N	G	B
A	A	T	R	O	O	S	T	E	R	S
C	G	I	I	L	N	S	P	A	E	R
I	N	L	T	O	N	V	V	D	M	E
A	I	E	U	H	Y	E	I	E	X	G
L	M	T	A	C	L	X	G	C		G
G	A	I	L	Y	O	E	U	U		U
	T	N	L	S	N	S	S	A	O	M
	U	Y	P	E	R	E	S	I	R

Puzzle #4

W	Y	L	C	P	L	S	B		V	
R	A	L	O	P	A	A	N		I	B
	P	I	N	L	C	N	E	W	R	L
A	E	F	V	K	I	S	T	U	A	T
G	R	E	E	E	X	W	T	S	L	Y
E	N	R	Y	N	O	E	E	I	O	D
C	S	I	A		D	R	N		N	E
N	A	M	N	Y	A	E	U		G	G
U	E	P	C	N	R	D	R	A	U	G
D	L	D	E	C	A	Y	B	A		U
	F		S	R	P	B	E	E	C	H

Reverse Word Searches (continued)

Puzzle #5

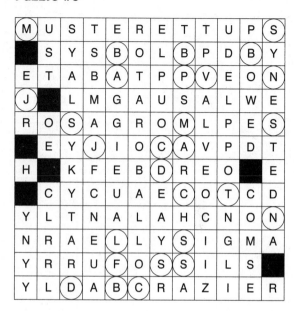

	H	T	Y	P	E	D	B	E	R	E	T
C	G	B	L	U	R	T	S	R	I	F	A
A	I	D	E	T	A	C	A	L	P		K
C	H	U	G	S	T	E	P	P	E	D	E
H	T		R	R	L	O	A	N	E	D	N
E	L	B	A	C	I	L	P	X	E	N	I
S	D	D	L	B	R	O	I	L	I	N	G
R	I	E	O	G	N	I	Y	R	R	U	H
O	C	S	P	U	O	B	I	N	D	S	T
D	I	S	T	I	N	C	T	I	O	N	S
N	N	A	I	D	E	S	V	E	R	B	S
E	G	G	C	E	S	Y	G	R	E	N	E

Puzzle #6

M	U	S	T	E	R	E	T	T	U	P	S
	S	Y	S	B	O	L	B	P	D	B	Y
E	T	A	B	A	T	P	P	V	E	O	N
J		L	M	G	A	U	S	A	L	W	E
R	O	S	A	G	R	O	M	L	P	E	S
	E	Y	J	I	O	C	A	V	P	D	T
H		K	F	E	B	D	R	E	O		E
	C	Y	C	U	A	E	C	O	T	C	D
Y	L	T	N	A	L	A	H	C	N	O	N
N	R	A	E	L	L	Y	S	I	G	M	A
Y	R	R	U	F	O	S	S	I	L	S	
Y	L	D	A	B	C	R	A	Z	I	E	R

Puzzle #7

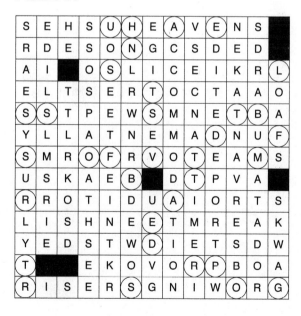

S	E	H	S	U	H	E	A	V	E	N	S	
R	D	E	S	O	N	G	C	S	D	E	D	
A	I		O	S	L	I	C	E	I	K	R	L
E	L	T	S	E	R	T	O	C	T	A	A	O
S	S	T	P	E	W	S	M	N	E	T	B	A
Y	L	L	A	T	N	E	M	A	D	N	U	F
S	M	R	O	F	R	V	O	T	E	A	M	S
U	S	K	A	E	B		D	T	P	V	A	
R	R	O	T	I	D	U	A	I	O	R	T	S
L	I	S	H	N	E	E	T	M	R	E	A	K
Y	E	D	S	T	W	D	I	E	T	S	D	W
T			E	K	O	V	O	R	P	B	O	A
R	I	S	E	R	S	G	N	I	W	O	R	G

Puzzle #8

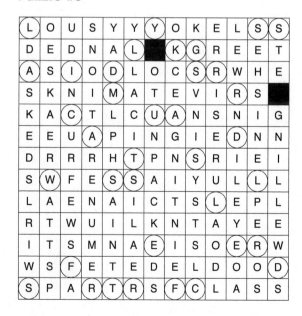

L	O	U	S	Y	Y	Y	O	K	E	L	S	S
D	E	D	N	A	L		K	G	R	E	E	T
A	S	I	O	D	L	O	C	S	R	W	H	E
S	K	N	I	M	A	T	E	V	I	R	S	
K	A	C	T	L	C	U	A	N	S	N	I	G
E	E	U	A	P	I	N	G	I	E	D	N	N
D	R	R	R	H	T	P	N	S	R	I	E	I
S	W	F	E	S	S	A	I	Y	U	L	L	L
L	A	E	N	A	I	C	T	S	L	E	P	L
R	T	W	U	I	L	K	N	T	A	Y	E	E
I	T	S	M	N	A	E	I	S	O	E	R	W
W	S	F	E	T	E	D	E	L	D	O	O	D
S	P	A	R	T	R	S	F	C	L	A	S	S

Reverse Word Searches (continued)

Puzzle #9

Puzzle #10

Puzzle #11

Puzzle #12

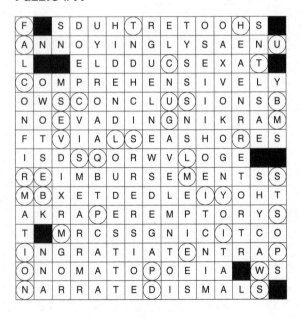

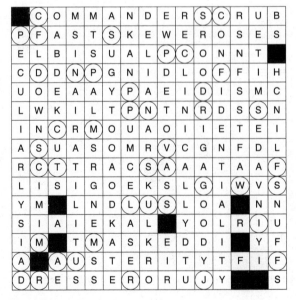

Reverse Word Searches (continued)

Puzzle #13

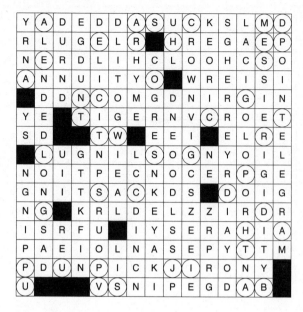

Puzzle #14

Puzzle #15

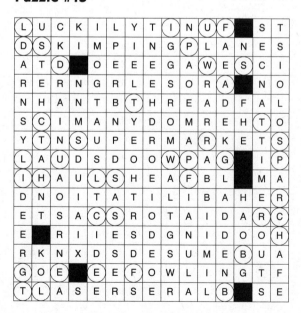

Puzzle #16

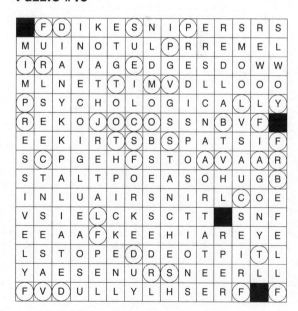

Reverse Word Searches (continued)

Puzzle #17

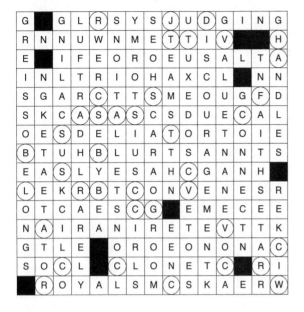

Puzzle #18

Puzzle #19

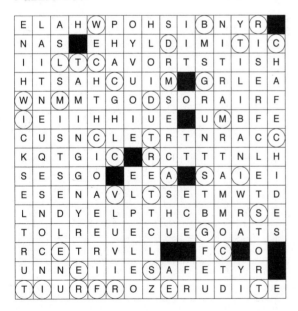

Puzzle #20

Sudoku

Puzzle #1

8	5	6	7	1	9	2	3	4
3	1	2	4	5	6	7	8	9
4	7	9	2	8	3	5	6	1
7	6	3	5	9	2	4	1	8
1	8	4	3	6	7	9	2	5
9	2	5	8	4	1	3	7	6
2	4	8	6	3	5	1	9	7
5	3	1	9	7	8	6	4	2
6	9	7	1	2	4	8	5	3

Puzzle #2

7	8	5	9	6	2	1	3	4
9	1	4	3	5	7	2	6	8
3	6	2	8	4	1	5	7	9
6	4	3	2	9	5	8	1	7
5	7	8	4	1	3	6	9	2
2	9	1	6	7	8	3	4	5
8	3	6	7	2	9	4	5	1
4	5	7	1	8	6	9	2	3
1	2	9	5	3	4	7	8	6

Puzzle #3

5	7	8	9	6	4	1	2	3
2	1	6	8	3	5	4	7	9
3	9	4	7	1	2	5	8	6
4	3	7	1	8	9	6	5	2
6	5	1	4	2	3	7	9	8
8	2	9	5	7	6	3	1	4
7	4	5	6	9	8	2	3	1
9	6	2	3	5	1	8	4	7
1	8	3	2	4	7	9	6	5

Puzzle #4

2	8	3	9	4	7	6	1	5
9	1	4	3	5	6	7	8	2
7	5	6	8	1	2	4	9	3
1	2	9	6	7	3	5	4	8
6	3	5	1	8	4	9	2	7
8	4	7	2	9	5	1	3	6
3	7	2	4	6	1	8	5	9
4	6	8	5	2	9	3	7	1
5	9	1	7	3	8	2	6	4

Puzzle #5

6	1	8	9	5	7	2	3	4
3	9	2	6	1	4	5	7	8
7	4	5	2	8	3	6	9	1
2	6	9	4	7	1	8	5	3
8	5	7	3	9	2	1	4	6
1	3	4	5	6	8	7	2	9
9	7	1	8	4	5	3	6	2
4	8	3	7	2	6	9	1	5
5	2	6	1	3	9	4	8	7

Puzzle #6

4	5	1	6	3	7	8	9	2
3	7	6	8	9	2	1	4	5
8	9	2	4	5	1	7	6	3
7	3	4	2	1	5	9	8	6
6	8	9	7	4	3	2	5	1
1	2	5	9	8	6	3	7	4
2	4	7	1	6	8	5	3	9
5	6	8	3	2	9	4	1	7
9	1	3	5	7	4	6	2	8

Puzzle #7

9	1	7	2	6	3	4	5	8
2	3	8	4	5	1	6	7	9
4	5	6	7	8	9	2	1	3
6	7	4	9	1	8	3	2	5
5	2	9	6	3	4	7	8	1
3	8	1	5	7	2	9	4	6
1	6	2	8	9	7	5	3	4
7	9	3	1	4	5	8	6	2
8	4	5	3	2	6	1	9	7

Puzzle #8

6	3	2	4	5	8	7	9	1
4	9	7	6	1	2	8	3	5
5	8	1	3	7	9	2	4	6
3	4	6	2	9	7	1	5	8
1	7	5	8	4	6	9	2	3
9	2	8	1	3	5	4	6	7
8	5	9	7	2	3	6	1	4
2	6	4	5	8	1	3	7	9
7	1	3	9	6	4	5	8	2

Puzzle #9

4	8	5	6	1	7	9	3	2
6	7	1	9	2	3	4	8	5
9	2	3	8	4	5	1	6	7
7	4	8	1	5	2	3	9	6
3	1	9	7	6	4	2	5	8
2	5	6	3	8	9	7	1	4
8	6	4	2	9	1	5	7	3
1	3	2	5	7	6	8	4	9
5	9	7	4	3	8	6	2	1

Sudoku (continued)

Puzzle #10

4	7	3	6	5	8	9	1	2
5	8	1	7	9	2	3	6	4
2	9	6	3	1	4	8	5	7
3	4	8	9	2	6	1	7	5
1	5	2	4	7	3	6	8	9
7	6	9	1	8	5	2	4	3
6	1	4	2	3	7	5	9	8
9	2	5	8	4	1	7	3	6
8	3	7	5	6	9	4	2	1

Puzzle #11

6	7	4	8	5	9	2	1	3
8	1	9	2	3	6	7	4	5
5	2	3	4	7	1	6	8	9
1	9	2	3	6	8	5	7	4
7	6	5	9	4	2	8	3	1
3	4	8	5	1	7	9	6	2
9	8	1	7	2	3	4	5	6
2	5	6	1	8	4	3	9	7
4	3	7	6	9	5	1	2	8

Puzzle #12

7	5	9	8	2	6	1	3	4
2	3	6	9	1	4	5	7	8
4	8	1	5	3	7	6	2	9
5	7	2	6	4	3	8	9	1
8	9	3	7	5	1	4	6	2
1	6	4	2	8	9	3	5	7
3	2	8	1	9	5	7	4	6
6	1	5	4	7	2	9	8	3
9	4	7	3	6	8	2	1	5

Puzzle #13

6	4	8	9	2	5	7	1	3
1	5	2	3	7	8	6	4	9
7	3	9	4	6	1	8	2	5
3	8	5	1	4	6	9	7	2
2	1	7	8	3	9	4	5	6
4	9	6	7	5	2	1	3	8
5	7	1	6	8	3	2	9	4
9	6	3	2	1	4	5	8	7
8	2	4	5	9	7	3	6	1

Puzzle #14

7	8	1	3	4	5	9	2	6
9	6	2	7	8	1	3	4	5
3	4	5	6	9	2	8	7	1
4	9	3	5	1	6	7	8	2
8	5	6	4	2	7	1	9	3
1	2	7	8	3	9	5	6	4
2	7	4	9	5	3	6	1	8
5	1	9	2	6	8	4	3	7
6	3	8	1	7	4	2	5	9

Puzzle #15

6	2	8	3	7	9	4	5	1
9	1	4	5	8	6	7	2	3
5	7	3	1	2	4	6	9	8
7	4	5	2	9	1	8	3	6
1	8	9	6	3	7	5	4	2
2	3	6	4	5	8	1	7	9
3	5	1	8	4	2	9	6	7
4	6	7	9	1	3	2	8	5
8	9	2	7	6	5	3	1	4

Puzzle #16

1	3	4	7	2	8	5	6	9
8	5	9	1	3	6	2	4	7
6	7	2	4	5	9	3	8	1
2	4	8	9	6	1	7	5	3
7	6	1	3	4	5	8	9	2
3	9	5	8	7	2	6	1	4
9	1	6	2	8	3	4	7	5
4	8	3	5	9	7	1	2	6
5	2	7	6	1	4	9	3	8

Puzzle #17

3	1	9	7	5	6	8	2	4
7	5	6	8	4	2	3	1	9
8	2	4	3	9	1	5	6	7
4	3	7	6	1	5	2	9	8
5	6	2	9	7	8	4	3	1
9	8	1	2	3	4	6	7	5
2	7	5	4	6	9	1	8	3
1	9	8	5	2	3	7	4	6
6	4	3	1	8	7	9	5	2

Puzzle #18

3	4	9	5	6	7	8	1	2
5	6	7	8	1	2	3	9	4
8	1	2	4	9	3	5	6	7
2	5	4	1	7	6	9	8	3
6	3	1	9	8	4	7	2	5
9	7	8	2	3	5	1	4	6
7	9	6	3	2	8	4	5	1
1	2	5	7	4	9	6	3	8
4	8	3	6	5	1	2	7	9

Sudoku (continued)

Puzzle #19

3	2	8	5	1	4	6	7	9
9	4	6	3	7	2	5	8	1
7	1	5	6	8	9	2	3	4
4	3	7	8	2	6	9	1	5
6	5	9	7	3	1	4	2	8
2	8	1	4	9	5	7	6	3
8	6	3	9	4	7	1	5	2
1	7	4	2	5	8	3	9	6
5	9	2	1	6	3	8	4	7

Puzzle #20

7	4	6	1	2	8	9	3	5
8	2	3	9	7	5	4	6	1
1	5	9	3	4	6	2	7	8
2	1	4	5	6	7	3	8	9
9	3	8	4	1	2	6	5	7
6	7	5	8	9	3	1	2	4
5	9	2	6	8	1	7	4	3
3	6	1	7	5	4	8	9	2
4	8	7	2	3	9	5	1	6

Word Search

Puzzle #1

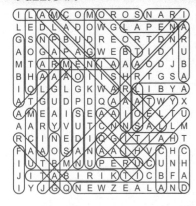

Puzzle #2

Puzzle #3

Puzzle #4

Puzzle #5

Puzzle #6

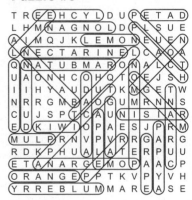

Puzzle #7

Puzzle #8

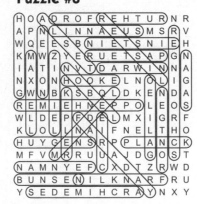

Puzzle #9

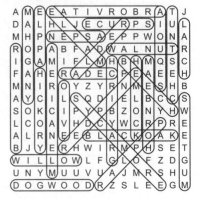

Word Search (continued)

Puzzle #10

Puzzle #11
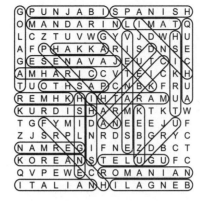

Puzzle #12
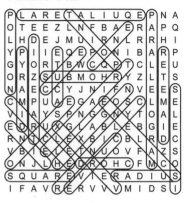

Puzzle #13
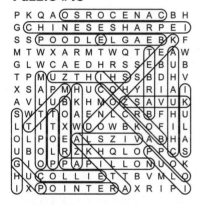

Puzzle #14
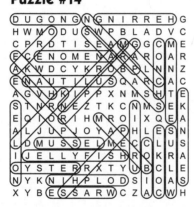

Puzzle #15
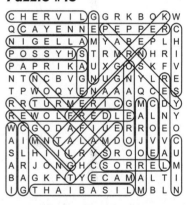

Puzzle #16
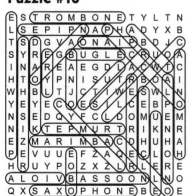

Puzzle #17
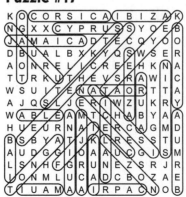

Puzzle #18
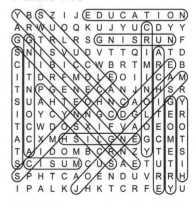

Word Search (continued)

Puzzle #19

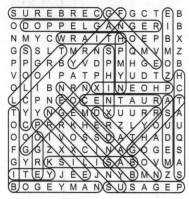

Puzzle #20

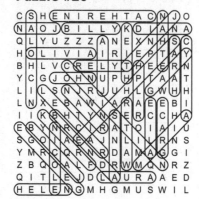